Terrorist Financing, Money Laundering, and Tax Evasion

Examining the Performance of Financial Intelligence Units

Terrorist Financing, Money Laundering, and Tax Evasion

Examining the Performance of Financial Intelligence Units

Jayesh D'Souza

CRC Press
Taylor & Francis Group
Boca Raton London New York

CRC Press is an imprint of the
Taylor & Francis Group, an **informa** business

CRC Press
Taylor & Francis Group
6000 Broken Sound Parkway NW, Suite 300
Boca Raton, FL 33487-2742

© 2012 by Taylor and Francis Group, LLC
CRC Press is an imprint of Taylor & Francis Group, an Informa business

No claim to original U.S. Government works

Printed in the United States of America on acid-free paper
10 9 8 7 6 5 4 3 2 1

International Standard Book Number: 978-1-4398-2850-2 (Paperback)

Library of Congress Cataloging-in-Publication Data

D'Souza, Jayesh.
    Terrorist financing, money laundering, and tax evasion : examining the performance of financial intelligence units / Author, Jayesh D'Souza.
        p. cm.
    Includes bibliographical references and index.
    ISBN 978-1-4398-2850-2
        1. Commercial crimes--Investigation. 2. Intelligence service. 3. Terrorism--Finance.
    4. Money laundering. 5. Tax evasion. I. Title.

    HV6768.D76 2011
    363.25'968--dc22   2011004904

Visit the Taylor & Francis Web site at
http://www.taylorandfrancis.com

and the CRC Press Web site at
http://www.crcpress.com

Table of Contents

Acknowledgments

I wish to thank Philip, Roberta, Sean, Susan, and Valerie for their assistance in some way, shape, or form during the writing process. I would also like to thank Florida International University's Graduate Students Association, Jack D. Gordon Institute for Public Policy and Citizenship Studies, and the Miami-Florida European Union Center of Excellence at Florida International University for partially funding this research.

Introduction

As terrorist attacks become more prevalent, countries have become increasingly vigilant about the means by which terrorists raise funds to finance their draconian acts against human life and property. Among the many counterterrorism agencies in operation, governments have set up financial intelligence units (FIUs) within their borders to track terrorists' funds. By investigating reported suspicious transactions, FIUs attempt to weed out financial criminals who use these illegal funds to finance terrorist activity.

Structure of Financial Intelligence Units

FIUs differ from one another in structure and reporting authority. Accordingly, there are three types:

Administrative-Type FIUs

These are usually part of a regulatory body or ministerial department and serve as a link between reporting entities and law enforcement. They have the advantage of being independent of law enforcement and judicial influence, but they lack the authority enjoyed by these entities in obtaining evidence and taking immediate action such as freezing assets or arresting suspects. Examples of countries that have this type of FIU include Andorra, Aruba, Australia, Belgium, Bolivia, Bulgaria, Canada, Colombia, Croatia, the Czech Republic, France, Israel, the Republic of Korea, Liechtenstein, Malta, Monaco, Panama, Poland, Romania, Russia, Slovenia, Spain, Ukraine, the United States, and Venezuela (Schott 2002).

Law-Enforcement-Type FIUs

These are attached to police units. They have certain law enforcement powers and work with other law enforcement agencies, reaping the benefits of their expertise and sources of information in solving financial crime. However, reporting entities may hold back when making financial disclosures if they feel their clients may be investigated for other crimes besides terrorist financing and money laundering. Examples include Austria, Estonia, Germany,

Guernsey, Hungary, Iceland, Ireland, Jersey, Slovakia, Sweden, and the United Kingdom (Schott 2002).

Judicial- or Prosecutorial-Type FIUs

These fall under a country's judiciary. They are suited to jurisdictions where strong bank secrecy laws make it necessary to seek the assistance of judicial or prosecutorial authorities to secure the cooperation of financial institutions. According to Schott (2002), "Such an arrangement is typically found in countries with a continental law tradition, where the public prosecutors are part of the judicial system and have authority over the investigatory bodies." Examples are Cyprus and Luxembourg.

Hybrid FIUs

Hybrid FIUs encompass elements of two or more of the previously described FIUs in an effort to gain the advantages of these disparate approaches. Countries with hybrid FIUs include Denmark, Jersey, Guernsey, and Norway (Schott 2002).

Functions of Financial Intelligence Units

While the span of authority of an FIU depends on its type, all FIUs essentially perform the same functions. The Egmont Group views an FIU as a "central, national agency" that serves as a point of exchange for information for other FIUs within the group and performs three core functions: receiving, analyzing, and disseminating "to the competent authorities, disclosures of financial information" (Egmont Group 2004a, 2004b). Recommendation 26 of the Financial Action Task Force's (FATF) 40 Recommendations states: "Countries should establish a FIU that serves as a national center for the receiving (and, as permitted, requesting), analysis and dissemination of suspicious transaction report (STR) and other information regarding potential money laundering or terrorist financing." (Financial Action Task Force 2006).

Receiving Information

FIUs receive information from reporting entities, other FIUs, and domestic agencies. Reporting entities vary with the means used by criminals to carry out their illegal activities and generally include financial institutions, insurance and securities firms, casinos, dealers in precious metals and precious stones, real estate agents, lawyers, notaries, and accountants. The kind of information reported to FIUs varies with the jurisdiction. In most juris-dictions, entities are required to report suspicious *transactions* to their FIU. However, in jurisdictions like the United States, entities are required to report suspicious *activities* (Reuter and Truman 2004, 106). A suspicious transac-tion report (STR) is defined as "a report that financial institutions must file to a country's FIU if a transaction is suspected to be linked to criminal activ-ity or to terrorism" (Reuter and Truman 2004, 207). Suspicious activities are broader in scope than suspicious transactions, and failure to file either of these with the concerned FIU can result in the noncompliant entity being fined and, in some cases, losing its authorization to operate or even facing criminal charges (Gottselig and Underwood 2004, 43, 56). In the Netherlands, entities report "unusual" transactions (Gottselig and Underwood 2004, 46), which will be discussed later in the book.

Do STR reports forwarded by FIUs to law enforcement help build cases for prosecution? This varies by country. In the United States, this is a gray area. For example, a study conducted by the U.S. Government Accountability Office (GAO) in 2002

> that examined all SARs [suspicious activity reports] involving credit cards during a two-year period from October 1, 1999, to September 30, 2001, found 499 such filings, of which 70 were referred to law enforcement agencies (39 federal, 31 state or local). But the GAO noted that FINCEN [Financial Crime Enforcement Network] was unable to report whether any of these referrals resulted in criminal prosecutions (Reuter and Truman 2004, 108).

With respect to the anti-money laundering (AML) regime of the United Kingdom, according to a government-funded KPMG study (Reuter and Truman 2004, 114),

> at least 6 percent of a sample of SARs disseminated by the (former) UK National Crime Intelligence Service resulted in "a positive law enforcement outcome" (i.e., prosecution, confiscation, cash seizure, etc.), while another 5 percent were still being used in an active investigation. The study also noted, however, that there was little feedback from law enforcement agencies to the filing institutions. In England and Wales, there were only 357 prosecutions for violation of money-laundering statutes in the 12 years from 1987–98.

The volume of information received by FIUs from reporting entities is immense. Hence, an FIU must have the capacity to store and analyze reported information (Gottselig and Underwood 2004, 46).

Analyzing Information

Once data is received from reporting entities, the FIU must analyze it to detect financial transactions related to crime. According to Schott (2002), "distinguishing truly suspect transactions from those that are only benignly unusual requires informed analysis" (Schott 2002). There are three kinds of analyses performed by FIUs:

Tactical Analysis

This is the starting point in determining whether suspicious activity constitutes financial crime and collecting data to build a case thereafter (Schott 2002). In other words, the FIU attempts to establish a link between received information and information from the FIU's own data or data that is publicly available (Schott 2002). This is a preliminary step to future action by the FIU.

Operational Analysis

If tactical analysis leads the FIU to believe that an individual, group of individuals, or organization has engaged in suspicious activity, it undertakes operational analysis whereby it uses the information available at its disposal to create a criminal profile and identifies patterns, targets, and accomplices that help identify future criminal behavior (Schott 2002). That is, the FIU produces operational intelligence through which law enforcement can take action. One method used in this process is financial profiling, which involves identifying the source of discrepancy between a suspect's income and cash outflow. According to Schott (2002), "The tracing of a person's assets may also provide leads linking the subject with predicate offenses." Once the FIU completes this process, it is in the hands of law enforcement to pursue the case further.

Strategic Analysis

This is "the process of developing knowledge (strategic intelligence) to be used in shaping the work of the FIU in the future" (Gottselig and Underwood 2004, 60). It documents new issues and trends from recently completed cases and incorporates them into current procedures for future intelligence operations and analysis. For example, recent evidence might suggest the emergence of criminal patterns or a number of suspicious transactions within a particular industry or region. This might cause the FIU to impose new requirements on reporting entities or expand the types of entities that report to it. Strategic analysis has broader AML/CTF (anti-money laundering/counterterrorist financing) implications than operational or tactical analyses (Gottselig and Underwood 2004, 60–61).

Disseminating Information

After the FIU has received and analyzed data, it must disseminate or distribute it to the appropriate agency, domestic or international. There are three kinds of exchanges for the purpose of dissemination. The first involves "the duty of the FIU to transmit information to the competent authorities for further investigation or prosecution whenever its analysis reveals money laundering or other criminal activity" (Gottselig and Underwood 2004, 61). An important responsibility of FIUs is to exchange information with other FIUs and other domestic agencies. The Egmont Group's "Principles for Information Exchange" (June 2001) and "Best Practices for the Exchange of Information" (November 2004) serve as guides to the international exchange of information (Egmont Group 2004a, 2004b). Domestically, FIUs exchange information on a number of levels: with reporting entities, regulators, police, prosecutors, tax authorities, anticorruption agencies, customs and excise agencies, and intelligence agencies (Schott 2002).

Besides receiving, analyzing, and disseminating information, FIUs monitor reporting entity compliance with AML/CTF requirements, block transactions when appropriate, train the staff of reporting entities (REs) on reporting and other AML/CTF obligations to increase compliance, conduct research in the areas of activities that enhance its core functions, and enhance public awareness of AML/CFT issues (Gottselig and Underwood 2004, 71, 81).

The prominent role played by FIUs means that their performance is always under the spotlight. This book reports the results of a study conducted by interviewing and surveying experts to determine their perceptions of FIU performance. The target group of experts included personnel from financial institutions, civilian agents, law enforcement personnel, academicians, and consultants. Questions for the interviews and surveys were based on the Kaplan and Norton's Balanced Scorecard (BSC) methodology. While FIUs in this study generally measure performance through outputs such as the number of suspicious transaction reports (STRs) investigated, experts call for a focus on outcomes and an integrated approach to performance measurement. Some of the highly rated performance measures included the quality and timeliness of intelligence and the number of financial criminals interdicted.

References

Egmont Group. 2004a. "Information paper on Financial Intelligence Units and the Egmont Group," September. http://www.egmontgroup.org/info_paper_final_oct_2004.pdf.

Egmont Group. 2004b. "Interpretive note concerning the Egmont definition of a Financial Intelligence Unit." November 15. http://www.egmontgroup.org/egmont_final_interpretive.pdf.

FATF. 2006. "The forty recommendations." http://www.fatf-gafi.org/document/28/0,
2340,en_32250379_32236930_33658140_1_1_1_1,00.html#40recs.

Gottselig, Glenn, and Sarah Underwood. 2004. *Financial Intelligence Units: An over-view.* Washington, DC: International Monetary Fund, World Bank Group.

Reuter, Peter, and Edwin Truman. 2004. *Chasing dirty money: The fight against money laundering.* Washington, DC: Institute for International Economics.

Schott, Paul Allan. 2002. *Reference guide to anti-money laundering and combating the financing of terrorism: A manual for countries to establish and improve their institutional framework.* Washington, DC: World Bank: VII-9.

Author

Jayesh D'Souza is a doctoral graduate from Florida International University's Public Administration Program. Mr. D'Souza is a specialist in public policy, finance, and economics and has a number of publications and presentations in governmental financial performance, counterterrorism, economic development, energy and the environment, education, and health care. His past employers include the Government of Ontario and T. D. Waterhouse.

List of Abbreviations

AIC: Australian Intelligence Community
AML: Anti-Money Laundering
APG: Asia/Pacific Group on Money Laundering
ASIO: Australian Security Intelligence Organization
AUC: United Self-Defense Forces of Colombia or Autodefensas Unidas de Colombia
AUSTRAC: Australian Transaction Reports and Analysis Centre
BLOM: Office of Operational Support of the National Public Prosecutor or Bureau voor politiële ondersteuning van de Landelijke officier van justitie voor de Wet Melding ongebruikelijke transacties
BMPE: Colombian Black Market Peso
BSA: Bank Secrecy Act
CFATF: Caribbean Financial Action Task Force
CIA: Central Intelligence Agency
CSIS: Canadian Security Intelligence Service
CTF: Counter-Terrorist Financing
DHS: Department of Homeland Security
ESAAMLG: Eastern and Southern Africa Anti-Money Laundering Group
EU: European Union
FARC: Revolutionary Armed Forces of Colombia or Fuerzas Armadas Revolucionarias de Colombia
FATF: Financial Action Task Force
FBI: Federal Bureau of Investigation
FINCEN: Financial Crime Enforcement Network
FINTRAC: The Financial Transactions and Reports Analysis Centre of Canada
FIU: Financial Intelligence Unit
FIU-India: Financial Intelligence Unit-India
FIU-NL: Financial Intelligence Unit – Netherlands
FSA: Financial Services Authority
FTZ: Free Trade Zone
GAFISUD: Financial Action Task Force on Money Laundering in South America or Grupo de Acción Financiera
GAO: U.S. Government Accountability Office
GCHQ: Government Communications Headquarters

IFT: Informal Fund Transfer
IRA: Irish Republican Army
IRS-CI: Internal Revenue Service – Criminal Investigation Division
ISI: Inter-Services Intelligence Directorate
JMLSG: Joint Money Laundering Steering Group
JTTF: Joint Terrorism Task Forces
KLPD: National Police Services Agency or Korps landelijke politiediensten
KYC: Know Your Client
LAC: Latin America and the Caribbean
MENA: The Middle East and North Africa
MONEYVAL: Committee of Experts on the Evaluation of Anti-Money Laundering Measures and the Financing of Terrorism – Council of Europe
MOT: Office for the Disclosure of Unusual Transactions or Meldpunt Ongebruikelijke Transacties
MSB: Money Services Business
MSBs: Money Service Businesses
NPO: Non-Profit Organization
ODNI: Office of the Director of National Intelligence
OECD: Organization for Economic Cooperation and Development
OFC: Offshore Financial Center
ORT: Organized Retail Theft
PLO: Palestinian Liberation Organization
PSEPC: Department of Public Safety and Emergency Preparedness Canada
SAR: Suspicious Activity Report
SEPBLAC: Executive Service or Servicio Ejecutivo de la Comisión de Prevención de Blanqueo de Capitales e Infracciones Monetarias
STR: Suspicious Transaction Report
UKFIU: U.K. Financial Intelligence Unit
UN: United Nations
USA Patriot Act: Uniting and Strengthening America by Providing Appropriate Tools Required to Intercept and Obstruct Terrorism Act of 2001
9/11 Commission: National Commission on Terrorist Attacks Upon the United States

The Organization of Terrorism and the Reorganization of Intelligence

1

The president of the Islamic Republic of Kamistan, Omar Hassan, is about to sign an agreement with the United States to dismantle its nuclear weapons program. But he faces opposition in his own country by those who are disappointed with his concessions on disarmament. Hassan becomes a target of terrorists, a key member of which is his head of security, Tarin Faroush. Once the authorities associate Faroush with the conspirators, they initiate a manhunt for him and trace him to a hotel in Manhattan. A tactical team from the U.S. Counterterrorism Unit (CTU) is sent to the hotel to capture Faroush. The local police force, NYPD, gets there first. Both authorities agree that the NYPD will form a perimeter around the hotel and only make a move once CTU's tactical team gets to the hotel. This is a scene from the television series *24*. Although fictional, it is an example of counterterrorism units at different levels of government working together in perfect harmony. Sadly, this is not the case in real life, as you will find out as this book unfolds. Let us start at the very beginning.

The Roots of Religion-Based Terrorism

The essence of terrorism has changed over the years and has varied with the social and historical context with which it has been associated. From the actions of the French government during the French revolution to those of labor organizations, anarchists, nationalist groups revolting against foreign powers, and ultranationalist political organizations—all have constituted terrorism at some point in history or another. The causes of these have been conflict, political power, repression, crime, religion, etc.

Issues pertaining to modern terrorism have created new challenges for government administrators after the terrorist attacks of September 11, 2001, when four commercial jets were hijacked and three of them were crashed into significant landmarks in the United States (CNN 2001). The sense of insecurity around the world was heightened after civilian-targeted bombings in Bali on October 12, 2002, in Madrid on March 11, 2004, and London on July 7, 2005. In 2003, then Australian prime minister John Howard announced that al-Qaeda had explored targets for destruction in Australia as far back as 2000 or 2001 (*USA Today* 2003). At the other end of the globe, the Canadian

Table 1.1   International Terrorism in the United Kingdom

The United Kingdom is a prominent target for international terrorist groups. There have been bomb and gun attacks on British citizens and interests in a number of countries over the last few years, as well as targets in the United Kingdom itself:

- November 2003: Al-Qaeda attacked the British consulate and HSBC building in Istanbul, killing 27 people including three British citizens.
- September 2004: A British national residing in Saudi Arabia was killed in a Riyadh shopping center by al-Qaeda gunmen.
- October 2004: British engineer Kenneth Bigley was murdered in Iraq by the al-Qaeda in Iraq group.
- March 2005: A British teacher was killed in a car bomb explosion in Doha, Qatar.
- July 2005: Four suicide bombers attacked the London transport system, killing themselves and 52 other passengers. A subsequent attempted attack failed, with no casualties caused.

British and foreign nationals linked to or sympathetic with al-Qaeda are known to be present within the United Kingdom. They are supporting the activities of terrorist groups in a range of ways:

- Providing resources for terrorist networks engaged in conflicts overseas
- Fund-raising for terrorist networks overseas and in the United Kingdom
- Acquiring and disseminating false documents for use by terrorists in the United Kingdom and overseas
- Facilitating training in the United Kingdom and overseas in extremist ideology and terrorist techniques.

In some cases they have also been engaged in directly planning or attempting to carry out terrorist attacks. Some of the terrorists have received military and other specialist training in camps overseas. Relationships forged in these training camps have formed the basis of loose networks of terrorists who can operate outside structured organization.

Source: "The Financial Challenge to Crime and Terrorism," HM Treasury, United Kingdom, February 2007.

Broadcasting Corporation (CBC) cited a Canadian Security Intelligence Service (CSIS) report declaring that al-Qaeda recruits were being trained in Canada (CBC 2005). A year later, in 2006, the Royal Canadian Mounted Police arrested 17 men who were allegedly planning bomb attacks on targets around Southern Ontario (CTV 2006). Besides the United Kingdom and Spain, other parts of Europe have not been spared either. Police have arrested suspects for terrorism-related offences in a number of countries across the continent including Belgium (*The Australian* 2008), Holland (BBC News 2005), Germany (*The Guardian* 2008), Italy (Europol 2010), and Norway and Sweden (*The Local* 2008). These incidents are identified with what is known as Islamic terrorism—a problem with no borders and with potentially cataclysmic results. Islamic terrorism, as the name suggests, has its origins in religion.

Table 1.1 shows the mark that terrorism has left on the United Kingdom during the past decade and demonstrates the scourge of terrorism in modern day society. Religious conflict is not confined to Islam but exists in all the corners of the world, as is discussed next.

The Middle East

The main conflict in the Middle East is a struggle between Jewish fundamentalists wanting to safeguard Israel and Islamic militants seeking a Palestinian state. Jewish fundamentalists such as Kach, Kahane Chai, and Gush Emunim seek to establish the Greater Israel of biblical times. Their purpose is to keep Israel's traditional covenant with God and prepare Israel for the coming of the messiah. To do so, they use violent means against non-Jews and those Jews who betray their mission of creating an all-Jewish Israel. The Islamic militia in the Middle East advances the cause of a Palestinian state and hope to rid it of all Jews.

One of the most significant events that led to instability in the Middle East was the recognition of Israel as a nation-state in 1948. Since then, Jewish-Islamic relationships in the region have grown increasingly volatile, with terrorism often being used as a means of settling conflict. One of the groups associated with terrorism is the Palestinian Liberation Organization (PLO), whose members were displaced when Israel was established. In 1993, the PLO renounced terrorism, a decision that in some ways created more tension. Some Arab groups were critical of this decision while others were in favor of it. Political parties surrounding the issue in Israel adopted the same mentality, with some all for the peace process while others were war-ready. In summary, the "Middle Eastern peace is a very fragile process, and terrorism is a wild card. It can upset delicate negotiations at any time, even after a peace treaty has been signed and implemented" (White 2002, 96).

The United States of America

Historically, religious conflict in the United States has come from the Christian right. Some of it stemmed from the concept of white supremacy. These supremacists are an anti-Semitic group that believes that people of the white race are the direct descendants of God, while Jews are the descendants of the devil and the first white woman. They also believe that those of non-white races are subhuman, as they were spawned from animals. Terrorism in the United States has also been a product of the abortion debate. While the 1980s saw bombings of abortion clinics, the 1990s witnessed attacks on abortion workers.

Islamic militancy has also swept ashore the United States, whose association with Israel has prompted attacks not only on American soil, but also on Americans throughout the world. The seeds of this conflict were sown during the Soviet Union's occupation of Afghanistan. The United States supported the mujahideen or freedom fighters of Afghanistan with arms and financial support. Once the Soviets withdrew their forces, the mujahideen and its Muslim supporters turned their attention to the United States and Israel. One of these supporters was Osama bin Laden, who formed his own group of guerrilla fighters known as al-Qaeda. The entry of U.S. forces into his homeland of Saudi Arabia during Operation Desert Shield incensed bin Laden. His network of terrorists set off a series of attacks on American interests, both in the United States and abroad, the most notorious being the attacks of September 11, 2001. Al-Qaeda's modus operandi was reminiscent of Islamic Jihad, a political movement within a transnational organization called the Muslim Brotherhood, which later became associated with terrorism. Jihadis had three characteristics: They were part of an organizational network; they got their message across via suicide bombings; and they engaged in hijackings and hostage taking and, later, kidnappings (White 2002, 156, 298).

The Indian Subcontinent

The religious divide between Hindus and Muslims is seen as the main contributing factor for the conflict in India. With the partition of the country into Hindu-majority India and Muslim-majority Pakistan in 1947, the two countries have been at war over Pakistan's claim to the only Muslim-majority state in India, Kashmir. Terrorist groups in Pakistan, backed by the establishment, joined the fight for the "freedom" of Kashmir from India (White 2002, 57). Reports suggest that the country's Inter-Services Intelligence (ISI) directorate provides support to militant groups in the region with money, weapons, and training. One of these groups is the Lashkar-e-Taiba, which the Indian government claims carried out the terrorist attacks in Mumbai on November 26, 2008, under the direction of the ISI (Gul 2009, 163).

Northern Ireland

The division in Northern Ireland is more along political lines, with those wanting to rid the country of British rule (the republicans) generally being the country's Catholic community, and those wanting to see Northern Ireland remain part of the United Kingdom (the unionists) generally being the country's Protestants. While both sides of this divide have used terrorism to settle politics, religion is subordinate to the political issue at hand. The seeds of this conflict were sown in the early 1800s when the Act of Union was passed by the British government to incorporate Ireland into the United Kingdom. This was supported by unionists who dominated the north, while the republicans, who controlled southern Ireland and were in favor of an independent Ireland, protested the passage of the act. The relationship between the two soon turned antagonistic, with the unionists drawing the support of the British military and police and the republicans developing their own militant arm, the Irish Republican Army (IRA) (White 2002, 81, 82).

South America

According to one author, Latin America is becoming an alternative base for Islamic terrorists attacking the United States. This assessment is based on reports that the triple borders of Paraguay, Brazil, and Argentina have become a hideout for terrorists who dwell among the growing Islamic population in that area. The lack of police forces there makes it a conducive environment for terrorists to organize themselves. In 2002, the U.S. State Department reported that the Hezbollah and other terrorist groups, including Hamas and possibly al-Qaeda, were raising finances in the region for terrorism. Their activities included smuggling in the tri-border area and the production of counterfeit U.S. currency. It is from this region that terrorists involved in the bombings of the Israeli embassy and a Jewish cultural center in Buenos Aires, Argentina, have sprung. Other incidents involve a Lebanese national allegedly planning to bomb the U.S. embassy in Asuncion, Paraguay. A few years later, he was arrested for funding the Hezbollah and recruiting members for them, and convicted for tax evasion. In 1999, an al-Qaeda operative was arrested for establishing terror cells in the region. A number of similar arrests were also made post-9/11. Operatives in the region have been connected with terrorist attacks on three continents, and Arab entrepreneurs here have been accused of financially backing Islamic radicals.

The activities of Islamic radicals in South America are not confined to the tri-border area. In 2003, 16 Bangladeshi Muslims were arrested in Bolivia for plotting to hijack a plane they planned to use to attack American targets. Islamic terrorists have also set up base in Mexico to make it easier for them to cross the border. Reports suggest that nationals of Iran, Syria, Pakistan, Afghanistan, and Iraq have been sneaking across the U.S.-Mexican border. This was confirmed with the arrest of five Pakistanis in the United States with fake Venezuelan passports. These terrorists also work out business deals with Mexican drug cartels that help smuggle them across the border. The United States is apprehensive that, if this continues, it will have to deal with the prospect of nuclear or biological weapons being smuggled into its territory (Gabriel 2008, 27).

The United States has made an attempt, with mixed results, to win over allies in the Americas in order to fight Islamic militants with a common front. One of these coalitions—the Organization of American States, established by the Inter-American Convention against Terrorism—lacked the strong backing of the Brazilian government. The Brazilian president did not seem keen on damaging his intention to build economic ties with the Arab countries and losing their support for a permanent seat on the U.N. Security Council (Gabriel 2008, 33).

The main focus of this book is terrorism driven by Islamic radicalism—terrorist acts committed for the purpose of "killing God's enemies or the enemies of Islam" (White 2002, 6, 7). The book also strongly focuses on how these terrorists can be stopped, which brings us to the next section.

Recent Developments in Counterterrorism

In a report published by the European Union (EU), counterterrorism measures are either proactive or defensive. Proactive measures are those that target terrorists with the purpose of weakening their ability to mount future attacks. Such an attack was carried out by the United States and its allies against the Taliban in Afghanistan. Defensive measures are those that reduce the risk to potential targets through protective action. The creation of the Department of Homeland Security (DHS) after the 9/11 attacks is an example. The mission of DHS is to identify and protect key targets that could possibly be subject to terrorist attack, improve emergency preparedness when disaster strikes, and secure the borders against potential terrorists (Zegart 2007, 173). DHS has also been reorganized to include a domestic intelligence agency within the department (Posner 2007, 218). Counterterrorism measures aim to thwart terrorism by minimizing the number of terrorist attacks and the damage of individual attacks (European Union 2007). An effective counterterrorism policy is one that is able to identify terrorists and possible terrorist attacks with the least number of false positives or false negatives while at the same time upholding the concept of social justice (Borgesen and Valeri 2009, 111). The effectiveness of counterterrorism measures also depends on the efficient allocation of resources. For example, DHS allocates funds to cities to help protect them against terrorist attacks. For many years, big cities such as New York City and Washington that are considered prime targets for terrorism received a major share of these funds. A few years into the program, DHS decided to provide a greater share of its allocation to cities that were considered to be minor targets to enhance their capacity to respond to terrorist attacks (Posner 2007, 219).

Counterterrorism measures can be in the form of legislation, surveillance, law enforcement, and intelligence gathering. The United States was among the most active in implementing these measures after the 9/11 attacks. The following sections provide a list and explain more commonly used counterterrorism measures.

Legislation and Surveillance

Arguably some of the most sweeping changes in recent history were brought about with the passage of the Uniting and Strengthening America by Providing Appropriate Tools Required to Intercept and Obstruct Terrorism Act of 2001 (USA PATRIOT Act). Passed by the U.S. Congress only six weeks after the 9/11 attacks, the law expanded the country's surveillance powers over its own citizens. As stated by Lynch (2003):

> The Patriot Act was designed to reduce privacy and increase security. It has succeeded in at least reducing privacy. Financial privacy is essentially gone. The feds have turned banks, brokerage houses, insurers and other financial institutions into state informers. Those firms must notify the Treasury Department about 'suspicious' transactions, and the government can subpoena your checking-account records even if there is no evidence of wrongdoing.

The U.S. Department of Justice claims criticisms of The USA PATRIOT Act are unfounded. However, a lawsuit against the Justice Department by a convert to Islam, whose home the Federal Bureau of Investigation (FBI) admitted to searching in his absence with the help of a special court order, is one example that seems to prove the critics right. The expansion of the government's authority to use national security letters, a type of subpoena that U.S. intelligence can use to seize financial, communication, and other records without judicial approval, is seen as a violation of the First and Fourth Amendments of the U.S. Constitution (National Public Radio 2005).

Law Enforcement

Immediately after the events of September 11, 2001, there was a focus on developing law enforcement's counterterrorism function. While it continues to focus on specific types of crime such as organized crime, gangs, or white-collar crime, it seeks to strike a balance between routine criminal intelligence and intelligence related to terrorist threats (Law enforcement expert 2009). A study published in 2004 by the RAND Corporation, a policy think tank, to assess how well domestic law enforcement agencies in the United States were prepared to counter incidents of terrorism found the response machinery among state and local law enforcement agencies lacking. Among the problems listed in the study were poor communication with officials at the federal and state levels, substandard training in terrorism preparedness, and subpar intelligence and threat assessment capability. This could be partly attributed to the lack of experience of local law enforcement agencies, before the events of September 11, 2001, in responding to and investigating incidents of terrorism. Also, these agencies considered terrorism in their respective jurisdictions as a low-level threat, and preparing themselves for terrorism-related incidents was seen to be a low priority. Not surprisingly, the attendance of these local law enforcement agencies in federally sponsored training programs was modest.

Although the study did not find that the perception of risk was related to the size of the jurisdiction, state law enforcement agencies and those agencies in bigger counties generally had higher levels of preparedness. The study also did not find the size of the jurisdiction related to the risk of terrorism. If a jurisdiction had critical infrastructure, regardless of whether it was a smaller community or a rural area, law enforcement was more proactive about improving its level of preparedness. Other reasons for poor preparedness among agencies included inadequate funding to meet the response requirements of first responders, outdated communication systems, and differences in resource priorities among agencies. The study found that agencies that perceived their risk to a terrorist threat as high received a higher level of external funding for preparedness. This was probably due to their aggressive pursuit of antiterror funds (Davis et al. 2004).

Another study, published in 2005, shed more light on this issue. The first finding was in regard to intelligence administration. The amount of intelligence received by state and local law enforcement agencies rose tremendously after 9/11 due to an increase in information sharing. Also, the amount of intelligence gathering increased through intercepted communications such as wiretaps. The study found that local law enforcement agencies had criminal intelligence units but none devoted specifically to counterterrorism. While a few departments had adopted their own guidelines for handling intelligence information, they generally followed federal guidelines. The second finding pertained to the commitment of resources. If local police committed more personnel to counterterrorism efforts, it was usually at the expense of other areas of responsibility. They used federal grants for equipment and consequence management but not for training. However, these federal grants could not be used for hiring, which negatively affected their capacity for intelligence analysis. They used the reallocation of internal financial resources to the best possible extent to accomplish this. The study questioned how long local law enforcement would be able to sustain these financial pressures without compromising the quality of service. The report also called for an improvement in training practices, succinct mission statements, and consistently high standards for data collection and file maintenance (Riley et al. 2005).

A third study published in 2006 detailed other problems that first-response units face in counterterrorism efforts. Interagency communication is one of these. The study documents a communications block between the FBI and state and local law enforcement. In 2003, for example, only half of the law enforcement agencies in the country had received guidance from the FBI regarding intelligence gathering. Bureaucratic impediments such as the hassle of getting security clearances for local law enforcement officers contributed to only one-third of law enforcement agencies collaborating with the FBI's joint terrorism task forces (JTTFs). On the positive side, local response organizations had updated their mutual-aid agreements for emergencies and response plans for weapons of mass destruction. These efforts do not tell us much, as the study points out: "Although state and local organizations undertook a range of activities following the 9/11 attacks to improve their response capabilities, it is difficult to quantify the preparedness of those organizations without standardized measures of organizational and community preparedness" (Davis et al. 2007). Possible measures include the extent of law enforcement present at ports, the level of interagency coordination, and the number of terrorist plots foiled. It is also useful to measure the indirect impact of a change in the focus of law enforcement and the diversion of resources to counterterrorism from other areas of policing, such as a change in the rate of routine crime (Law enforcement expert 2009).

Research suggests that measuring performance in counterterrorism is difficult and not easily quantifiable. The Gilmore Commission, a congressional advisory panel in the United States, conducted a study to assess response capabilities of domestic agencies to counterterrorism. In its report, it explained the difficulty in measuring performance:

> It is extremely difficult to assess the magnitude and character of the current threat, much less do a genuinely useful, specific, or actionable threat projection. This clearly will hamper any efforts to develop even crude metrics or measures of performance that reflect whether the threat is being reduced to a strategically meaningful degree. Fortunately, we have had to this point few attacks against which to measure certain performance. It is likely that future attacks will provide the only meaningful measure of certain aspects of our preparedness. It can be argued, however, that the absence of attacks is one appropriate measure of how well we are doing in deterring and preventing attacks (Gilmore Commission 2003).

The counterterrorism function of law enforcement is evolutionary. Until only recently, resources were being expended on preventing bioterror attacks; now it is suicide bombing. In fact, the responsibilities of law enforcement have expanded in scope. For example, one of the tasks of the Los Angeles police department is the development of overseas relationships. Besides strategic planning and function, first-response units also changed their approach in implementing their counterterrorism strategies (Law enforcement expert 2009). This now involves the use of fusion centers, terrorism working groups, and the National Incident Management System (NIMS) to better coordinate carrying out counterterrorism plans. These are explained as follows:

Fusion Centers: These have typically been created by states and larger cities for the purpose of intelligence sharing with each other and the federal government. DHS assists in staffing these with personnel with relevant expertise (DHS n.d.).

Terrorism Working Group (TWG): This consists of first responders from different fields of service that address issues such as first-responder safety and public health consequences of bioterrorism. A subcommittee of this group, the Terrorism Early Warning Group (TEWG), is responsible for intelligence gathering and analysis and conducting threat assessments (Carona n.d.).

National Incident Management System (NIMS): The function of NIMS involves establishing incident-management best practices and standardizing processes, protocols, and procedures for first responders' counterterrorism operations. The purpose is to enable them to respond more effectively and cohesively when terror strikes (DHS 2004). It also helps sort out which agency takes the lead for what type of incident (Law enforcement expert 2009).

It has been suggested that law enforcement incorporates risk management and assessment to provide more effective counterterrorism services. The Gilmore Commission report outlines three methods for reducing risk associated with terrorism

In an environment where you cannot do it all, where will the nation get the greatest return on investment? ... a) Threat reduction through direct action to destroy or dismantle terrorist groups and deny such groups chemical, biological, radiological and nuclear weapons and other instruments of terror; b) Vulnerability reduction through a wide variety of pre-attack terrorism-specific actions that would be effectively independent of near-term strategic or tactical warning; and c) Vulnerability reduction through terrorism-specific actions that would be implemented upon tactical warning of an imminent attack or that an attack is on the way but has not yet arrived (Gilmore Commission 2003).

Figure 1.1 presents the risk management model outlined in the Gilmore Commission report.

Law enforcement can manage risk better by making the public and its associated city council part of its counterterrorism effort. The public is a valuable source in providing information on certain suspects. City council funds law enforcement and, therefore, holds it accountable for the outcomes

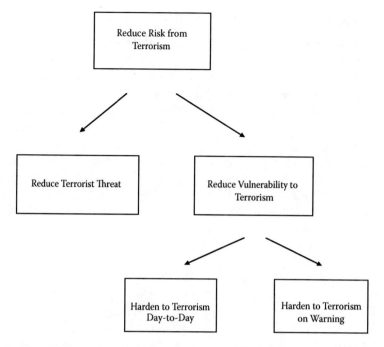

Figure 1.1 Risk reduction components. (The Fifth Annual Report to the President and the Congress of the Advisory Panel to Assess Domestic Response Capabilities for Terrorism Involving Weapons of Mass Destruction, Gilmore Commission, USA, December 15, 2003.)

it produces. If law enforcement is to produce desired outcomes, it is important to train its personnel in areas such as how to report information and to whom to report it. This takes time and investment and the acceptance of potentially high training costs. This is because counterterrorism training is specialized and therefore intensive. For example, training for NIMS takes place over three years. While officers attend training, their units have to pay for temporary replacements to take their place. So, how should law enforcement measure return on investment? It should set a desired skill level for its officers and then establish a metric for the number of officers who reach that level. The evaluation of processes equates with outcome evaluation. Outcome production can be measured in terms of cost of human life. For example, DHS offers a number of grants for counterterrorism preparedness under its state, local, and tribal grants programs like the Urban Areas Security Initiative (UASI). If these grants funded the hiring of police offers, then for every officer out on the street, law enforcement should measure how much crime is prevented (Law enforcement expert 2009).

Intelligence Reform

Intelligence services are vital to the survival of nations. Effective intelligence services help nations anticipate and prevent attacks, thereby protecting themselves from forces that are detrimental to the security and stability of a country. The inability of governments to keep intelligence agencies in check, on the other hand, puts national interests and civil liberties at risk. In many democracies, legislative oversight and accountability standards did not apply to the intelligence services. They were autonomous in operation, and administrative reform was undertaken internally by the service. All this changed in the mid-20th century. The United States was the first country to legislate its intelligence services through the National Security Act of 1947 and the Central Intelligence Agency (CIA) Act of 1949, which defined the boundaries of its intelligence agencies. The Senate and House Committees on Intelligence were also established, in 1976 and 1977, respectively, to curb misuse of power by the intelligence service. These reform efforts were gradually adopted by some countries in Europe (Watts 2003).

After September 11, 2001, the focus shifted from control of the powers of the intelligence service to the improvement of their operations and functional coordination. Communication, cooperation, and information sharing among agencies are now viewed as key to addressing the threat of international terrorism and its associated evils of drug trafficking, money laundering, and organized crime. What follows next is a review of intelligence reform in countries at the forefront of the war on terror.

United States of America

The U.S. intelligence services do not come cheap. They currently drain American coffers of approximately $44 billion in tax revenue. The total military expenditures of most countries don't even compare to this staggering figure. The 16 intelligence agencies that comprise the U.S. intelligence community employ about 100,000 personnel. In spite of this investment and manpower, the U.S. intelligence community failed miserably on two occasions in the last decade. First was its failure to effectively detect and warn against the terrorist threat that led to the attacks of September 11, 2001. Secondly, it wrongly assessed that the then-Iraqi regime under Saddam Hussein was in possession of weapons of mass destruction (Russell 2007). These failures have led to initiatives to reorganize the intelligence community.

The attacks of September 11, 2001, evoked a sharp reaction from the U.S. government in the form of the passage of the USA PATRIOT Act, the creation of the Department of Homeland Security, and the launch of the Joint Inquiry of 9/11 by the Congressional Intelligence Committees (Zegart 2007, 170). In its recommendations of July 22, 2004, the National Commission on Terrorist Attacks upon the United States (9/11 Commission) made a couple of key recommendations pertaining to the organization of the intelligence community. The first was the formation of the National Counter-Terrorism Center (NCTC) and the Office of the Director of National Intelligence (ODNI). The former was assigned the responsibility of joint operational planning, while the latter was put in charge of overseeing constituent intelligence agencies (Best 2004). It has been suggested that the 9/11 Commission report was quickly written and its recommendations accepted by the U.S. Congress without serious reflection of its merits or the insight of experienced professionals in the field. Its recommendation to create an intelligence czar would only add to the layers of bureaucracy while providing it with limited administrative or budgetary clout to manage the intelligence agencies (*Washington Post* 2008). As it turns out, the ODNI has been accused of micromanaging agencies and being engaged in a turf war with the CIA (Bruno 2009).

Another of these agencies, the FBI, has borne the brunt of the blame for the intelligence failure that led to the 9/11 attacks. The Congressional Joint Inquiry into the Terrorist Attacks called out the FBI for its lack of focus on domestic terror and its inadequate efforts to gather, analyze, and disseminate intelligence. These deficiencies have led to reform efforts within the FBI in the hope that these will enable the bureau to prevent terrorism rather than react to it. Some of these efforts include centralizing its operations and improving its IT systems. There is a newly created position of executive assistant director for intelligence and an office of intelligence to oversee the FBI's field office operations. Like all reform efforts, this has had its share of critics. Some say the reforms are limited and difficult to implement. Others base their skepticism on the widely varied cultures of law enforcement and intelligence (Cumming and Masse 2004). They call for the creation of a separate domestic agency in the United States modeled after the Canadian Security Intelligence Service (CSIS) and staffed with newly hired personnel while the FBI continues in a law enforcement capacity with its existing personnel (Posner 2005). Others are more positive about the post-9/11 reforms, stating that the FBI, with its law enforcement capabilities and improved intelligence program, can overcome its shortcomings in countering future threats (Cumming and Masse 2004).

Other changes in the U.S. intelligence apparatus took place in the form of legislation, namely the Intelligence Reform and Terrorism Prevention Act of 2004. Central to this legislation was the development of an information-sharing protocol for the intelligence community, the details of which were published in a report by the ODNI in 2008. It was built around the tenets of governance, policy, technology, culture, and economics. Figure 1.2 presents the details.

ODNI acknowledges that its implementation is a long-term process and will show results over time. While the American public waits in hope for the possible success of the new reform initiatives, lapses continue to take place.

	Description	Key Questions
Governance The "environment" influencing sharing	Oversight and leadership that help govern information sharing. How managers drive initiatives within organization and across agencies. Standards and guidelines to ensure a consistent approach.	• Is there a clear value proposition for sharing among partners, i.e., quid pro qeo or negotiated trade-offs? Are MOUs or service-level agreements required? • Do people understand how to abide by the law and policies? • How are information sharing disputes resolved? • Who are the key stakeholders?
Policy The "rules" for sharing	National policies, internal policies, rules of engagement, standards, and role of players internal and external to the organization.	• Are laws, regulations, policies , and procedures in place that authorize, mandate and/or enable the organization to share? Is the organization complying with these mandates? • Do laws/regulations/policies/procedures impede or constrain the organization/people from sharing? • Are privacy and civil liberties sufficiently protected?
Technology The "capability" to enable sharing	The technology, systems, and protocols that provide the platform for enabling the sharing of information and that address security and privacy issues.	• Are there common data standards and systems for organizing, identifying, and searching? • Can participants push and pull data across networks? • How is information protected; is the system auditable? • Are tools/mechanisms available to manage identities; authorize, authenticate, and audit users; and ensure confidentiality?
Culture The "will" to share	The organizational approach and philosophy around sharing information and its ability to realign and adapt as circumstances change.	• How do we motivate people and create incentives to collaborate and share information across organizations? • Does the organization communicate across all levels? • How does the organization adapt to change, and how responsive is it to stresses and opportunities? • How are decisions and conclusions reached?
Economics The "value" of sharing	Ability to obtain and provide resources for information sharing initiatives, and external pressures (e.g., budget) that influence how resources are allocated and managed.	• Has sufficient funding been appropriated to support the initiative? • Have incentive structures been developed? • Is the funding reaching the appropriate level within the enterprise to fully implement the sharing program? • How do we measure performance?

Figure 1.2 Building blocks and key questions. ("United States Intelligence Community Information Sharing Strategy," Office of the Director of National Intelligence, February 22, 2008.)

In 2009, there was a botched attempt to detonate explosives aboard an airliner over Detroit. This was considered to be a failure of the intelligence agencies to connect the dots, as they had the necessary information to thwart the perpetrator (Yahoo News 2010). With the problems of the past, such as lack of leadership and coordination, some feel it best for the U.S. government to build on the existing foundation of the country's intelligence services rather than overhauling the intelligence structure to prevent potential tragedies such as these (Bruno 2009). This leads one to question what really defines the success of an intelligence agency.

For one, the success of an intelligence agency depends on its level of organization or, more specifically, its structure, culture, and incentives. Structure provides order to the organization in terms of task assignment, delegation of authority, and the role of the intelligence agency within the system. Culture determines the agency's approach in tackling problems. Incentives influence how an agency prioritizes the issues in front of it. While the organization of the agency is important, it is not the only determinant of policy outcomes; it also has to be backed by strong leadership. In the final assessment,

> Yes, tremendous effort has been expended, individuals have made extraordinary sacrifices, and improvements have been made. But some perspective is in order. Effort often does not translate into performance. And progress is not the same as success. The question is not whether the CIA and FBI are better equipped than they were on September 10, 2001—certainly a low standard. Nor is it whether the CIA and FBI have smart and dedicated officials; they always have. The question is whether these two agencies, and the rest of the U.S. Intelligence Community, have adapted to the point where they now stand a reasonable chance of preventing the next catastrophe. The evidence is not encouraging (Zegart 2007, 195–196).

United Kingdom

The British intelligence service consists of MI5 (Military Intelligence, Section 5; officially known as the Security Service), MI6 (officially known as the Secret Intelligence Service), and the Government Communications Headquarters (GCHQ) (U.K. Intelligence and Security Committee 2008). This intelligence mechanism in the United Kingdom failed to prevent the terrorist attacks in London on July 7, 2007, as those involved in the attacks were not identified as potential threats by counterterrorism forces. While the U.K. agencies had no intelligence of the July 7 plot, they had previously placed a couple of those involved in the attacks under surveillance for their association with a terrorist cell. However, other suspects in the investigation were considered to be of higher risk, and no further intelligence was gathered on the July 7 perpetrators. In analyzing these developments, there are number of factors that could be attributed to the failure of U.K. intelligence to prevent the attacks of July 7. The first is that it had a narrow investigative focus. MI5 has limited financial and human resources, which affects its ability to effectively use investigative techniques such as directed surveillance operations and the bugging of private property, which are expensive and labor intensive. It, therefore, spends these resources on what it determines are high-risk targets and leaves routine criminal activity to the local police. The police, on the other hand, focus their resources on community policing and not on investigating probable terrorist suspects. Peripheral operatives, such as those who commit fraud to raise funds for terrorist activities, fall on the list of low-level intelligence monitoring. At least one of the July 7 terrorists fell into this category (Field 2009).

Some have questioned why more economical means of intelligence were not used to trace the suspect. "Desk" intelligence and "community" intelligence could have revealed that he was traveling to Pakistan to attend terrorist training camps and liaising with individuals associated with planning terrorist attacks. Besides lack of suitable techniques, some of the intelligence gathered on the July 7 terrorists was problematic. The information on them, shared between intelligence officials and the police, was poor in content and inadequate in detail. When intelligence of this nature lacks a broader context, it is difficult to assess the risk of the individuals mentioned in it. Some of the intelligence was also considered not important enough and therefore was not shared. Finally, British intelligences agencies are constrained by the law, as described in Table 1.2.

While communication problems are not uncommon in a multiagency working environment, they are augmented when intelligence agencies have different databases and procedures for information sharing. Untraceable intelligence, misspelled names, and the inability to put things together also contributed to the intelligence failure (Field 2009).

In an effort to counter this failure and better deal with the threat of terrorism, the British government brought about a number of changes that it hoped would address the intelligence failures of July 7. To improve coordination within the counterterrorism network in the country, the government focused on setting up a regional network by creating a number of counterterrorism hubs and five regional MI5s across the country. Reform efforts also saw the creation of fusion centers such as the Joint Terrorism Analysis Centre (JTAC), which comprises intelligence officials, police, and other concerned government representatives. The government has also encouraged cross training, as seen by the increase in GCHQ staff engaged in temporary assignments at other agencies (Field 2009). Structural changes were also instituted. The two counterterrorism branches of the metropolitan police—the special and antiterrorism branches—were merged so that intelligence and law enforcement could work better with one another. This new branch came to be known as the counterterrorism command. Finally, funding poured into the

Table 1.2   The Power of the MI5 and Individual Rights

Commentary
There are strict limitations on what MI5 is allowed to do when investigating an individual. There are laws (covering MI5 and others) that ensure that an individual's right to privacy cannot be overridden without very good cause. In addition, MI5 has its own Act of Parliament that demands it only obtain information in order to carry out its lawful work—in particular, the protection of national security.
MI5 can use what it calls "intrusive techniques" against an investigative target if there is sufficient justification on national security grounds. These techniques might include intercepting telephone communications, interfering with property (for example, planting eavesdropping devices in a person's house or car), "intrusive surveillance" (watching and eavesdropping on private homes or vehicles), or carrying out "directed surveillance" (following and photographing targets and recording where they go, who they meet, and so on).
There must be good justification for using these techniques. In order to intercept telephone communications, interfere with property, or conduct "intrusive surveillance," a warrant must be obtained that authorizes precisely what action will be taken. Such warrants are issued by the secretary of state and remain valid until the operation is complete, or for up to six months (whichever is the shorter). The authorizations are reviewed by independent commissioners to ensure that they comply with the law.
In urgent cases, warrants may be signed by a senior official within the Home Office, but only where the secretary of state has given express permission to the official. These warrants last for between only two and five days (depending on the type of action) unless they are confirmed by the secretary of state.
"Directed surveillance" is deemed less intrusive (a person being watched in public is a lesser invasion of privacy), and this kind of action can be authorized by officers within MI5. Nevertheless, such authorizations are still subject to independent review by the commissioners.
The warrant and authorization system, together with the independent review process, is a legal safeguard to ensure that MI5 does not use any intrusive techniques without very good reason.

Source: "Could 7/7 Have Been Prevented? Review of the Intelligence on the London Terrorist Attacks on 7 July 2005," Intelligence and Security Committee, United Kingdom, May 2009.

British intelligence services. In 2004, for example, the government provided funding to MI5 to increase its personnel from 1,900 to 3,500 over four years (Foley 2009).

Australia

Changes to the Australian intelligence system after the terrorist attacks of September 11, 2001, came in the form of funding as well as organizational and legislative changes to the six national agencies of the Australian Intelligence Community (AIC). However, it is first important to understand the structure of Australia's intelligence agencies. Table 1.3 explains the role played by each of its agencies.

Table 1.3 Australian Intelligence Structure

Office of National Assessments (ONA): An all-source intelligence assessment agency reporting directly to the prime minister and senior cabinet ministers. ONA was established in 1977 by an act of Parliament. The director-general of ONA is the nominal head of the Australian Intelligence Community (AIC).

Australian Secret Intelligence Service (ASIS): Modeled on the British SIS or MI6, ASIS is a foreign human intelligence (humint) collection agency based in the Department of Foreign Affairs and Trade.

Australian Security Intelligence Organisation (ASIO): Created by the Chifley government after World War II, ASIO is responsible for the security of Australians and Australian interests, including protecting the country from terrorism and acts of foreign interference and espionage.

Defence Signals Directorate (DSD): Australia's signals intelligence agency responsible for the interception of foreign communications and for providing advice on Australia's information security.

Defence Intelligence Organisation (DIO): Provides high-level analysis and advice to the defense minister and cabinet on military capabilities and support for deployed forces.

Defence Imagery and Geospatial Organisation (DIGO): Working closely with intelligence partners overseas, DIGO provides a wide range of geospatial services, including mapping and photography, to support military operations.

Source: Carl Ungerer, "The Intelligence Reform Agenda: What Next?" Australian Strategic Policy Institute, February 27, 2008.

The Australian government began its intelligence reform effort two years before the attacks of September 11, 2001, in preparation for the Sydney Olympic Games in 2000. The country's main antiterrorism intelligence agency, the ASIO, which is responsible for gathering foreign intelligence within the country, received an increase in funding of 12 percent from 1998 to 2001. The additional funding was used to enhance its analytical capacity in the form of new hires, new equipment, and an increase in the number of threat assessments. Cooperation with international partners became an essential element with respect to sharing information on terrorists and related matters. Additionally, the law was amended so that the ASIO could use tracking devices (under warrant) for assistance and to intercept telecommunications (Grono 2007).

After September 11, 2001, intelligence agency funding increased even further, totaling AUD 96 million over four years. The beneficiaries were the ASIO, the ASIS, the ONA, and the defense intelligence agencies. The increase in funding is presented in Table 1.4.

It has been reported that this rate of increase is higher than that in the United States and that intelligence spending accounts for $1.3 billion annually. Much of this has been allocated for the hiring of intelligence officers and analysts who have a sound understanding of the Australian security environment and foreign language skills (Ungerer 2008).

Besides increasing funding for intelligences agencies, the Australian government also addressed organizational issues. Among the structural changes

Table 1.4 Intelligence Funding by Agency, 2001–2008

	Funding ($ million)		
	2001–02	2007–08	Percent Increase
ASIO	69	441	539
ASIS	54	161	198
ONA	7	36	414
Defense Intelligence Group (DSD, DIO, DIGO)	311	431	38.6

Source: Carl Ungerer, "The Intelligence Reform Agenda: What Next?" Australian Strategic Policy Institute, February 27, 2008.

instituted post-9/11 was the establishment of the National Threat Assessment Center (NTAC), which is on-call for 24 hours a day; the Joint Counter-Terrorism Intelligence Coordination Unit, which analyzes collected intelligence; the Counter-Terrorism Information Oversight Committee (CTIOC), which is responsible for identifying gaps in intelligence practices; the Terrorist Threat Coordination Group (TTCG), which engages in discussion on current threats and the intelligence requirements to meet them; and the Travel Advisory Threat Assessment meeting to exchange views on travel advisory issues (Australian Department of the Prime Minister and Cabinet 2004). The backbone of these changes was the introduction of new legislation such as the passage of the Intelligence Services Act, which generally sharpened the role, function, and oversight of intelligence. There was also the ASIO Legislation Amendment (Terrorism) Bill that gave intelligence agencies stronger powers to deal with detainees in terrorism cases (Grono 2007). The government-commissioned inquiry into Australian intelligence agencies, the Flood review, also recommended that Australian intelligence go through external review every five to seven years (Ungerer 2008).

In a review of Australian intelligence reform post-9/11, it was pointed out that problems continue to exist despite the recent pouring of resources into the Australian intelligence system. The AIC's constituent agencies were set up during the Cold War to deal with a different threat; they have not adapted structurally and functionally to deal with the modern day threat of terrorism. The foreign and domestic intelligence systems in Australia also appear inharmonious in countering national security threats. The review concludes:

One of the principal dangers is that the new funding and resources given to the AIC have created an expectation that there are intelligence solutions to the full range of national security problems confronting Australia, from the proliferation of nuclear, biological and chemicals weapons to home-grown terrorism. As several former officials have noted, such expectations are not valid. But with an investment of over $1 billion per annum and growing, the public will want to know that they are getting good value for money (Ungerer 2008).

Canada

In Canada, national security was the responsibility of the federal Royal Canadian Mounted Police (RCMP) until 1983. However, a series of investigations into the abuse of power by the Security Service of the RCMP resulted in an inquiry by the McDonald Commission and the passage of the Canadian Security Intelligence Service Act in 1984 (CSIS Act). This was followed by the establishment of the CSIS, which targets illegal activities ranging from espionage to the overthrow of the Canadian government using violence. In the context of counterterrorism, its functions are traditional, i.e., it collects and analyzes intelligence on threats to the security of Canada (Hannah, O'Brien, and Rathmell 2005).

Similar to the other countries discussed earlier, Canadian reform initiatives in the intelligence arena came in the form of legislation, restructuring, and increased funding after the terrorist attacks in 2001. These were designed to increase the protection and security of Canadians without violating any of their rights. Legislative changes were in the forms of bills C-36 and C-7. The former, known as the Anti-Terrorism Act, gave increasing powers to the Communications Security Establishment (CSE), Canada's signal intelligence agency to collect foreign intelligence by monitoring communications to and from Canada pending the authorization of the minister of national defense. The CSE commissioner, responsible for oversight, assured the Canadian public that the CSE would carry out its new responsibilities without violating the Canadian Charter of Rights and Freedoms. The Public Safety Act of 2002 (C-7), on the other hand, addressed airport and aviation security, the containment of weapons of mass destruction, and the improvement of interagency coordination (Shore 2006).

As a result of heightened vigilance after the terrorist attacks of September 11, 2001, a new Department of Public Safety and Emergency Preparedness Canada (PSEPC) was created in 2004, which subsumed the CSIS, the Office of the Inspector-General, the Security Intelligence Review Committee (SIRC), the RCMP, and the Solicitor General of Canada, all of which are responsible for countering terrorism (Hannah, O'Brien, and Rathmell 2005). The purpose of having all of these agencies under one roof was to enhance interagency cooperation and accountability. The centralized structure also enables the PSEPC to provide policy direction to its constituent agencies (Shore 2006). Other organizational changes involved the creation of the position of national security advisor to the prime minister and the National Security Advisory Council, which is made up of experts from outside the government. The government also established the Integrated Threat Assessment Center (ITAC), which comprises members of different agencies such as the CSIS and the CSE (Shore 2006).

Post-9/11 reforms also saw a huge increase in funding to intelligence agencies. The CSIS received $47 million, the RCMP $54 million, and the CSE $37 million to increase operational capacity for intelligence gathering and counterterrorism purposes (Shore 2006).

Other Countries

Countries like Spain and India that were victimized by terrorist attacks have also attempted to revamp their intelligence systems. Spain increased the lines of communication between security and intelligence counterterrorism units and hired Arabic-speaking intelligence and judiciary personnel (Rolfe 2005). The Lisbon Treaty, the European Union's new legal framework, allows for enhanced cooperation and information sharing among member nations in tackling terrorism. The powers of Europe's police force (Europol) were also increased under the Spanish EU presidency, and its investigations cover terrorism in the form of chemical, biological, and nuclear weapons; cybercrime; and Islamist extremism on the Web (EUObserver.com 2010).

The Mumbai terrorist attacks of November 26, 2008, in India were also blamed on the lack of coordination among intelligence agencies (Raghavan n.d.). In response to these attacks, India has begun to shore up the intelligence-gathering and -sharing capability of its domestic agency, the Intelligence Bureau (IB). The bureau's Multi-Agency Centre (MAC) has been reorganized so that it can operate around the clock. An executive order was issued directing the MAC to share intelligence with other agencies, including those at the state level and vice versa. The flow of funds and technical know-how has been increased to promote the effectiveness of state agencies and the interconnectivity among all agencies within the Indian system (*India Post* 2009). Nevertheless, as reported by BBC News (2008), some critics have objected to the Indian government's plans to bolster security:

Interior Minister P. Chidambaram has announced a raft of measures to boost security—setting up a federal investigation agency, strengthening coastal security, training more commandos, beefing up anti-terror laws, and filling vacancies in depleted intelligence agencies. What he did not mention is the lack of instructors, police officers, infrastructure, laws and money which, experts say, will definitely hinder the government's well-meaning plans to make India safer.

The Next Steps in Intelligence Reform

In some quarters, Europe is seen as the most vulnerable target of terrorists, and it is the main location where terrorist support groups have established bases. This has coincided with the growth of the local Muslim population and subsequent increased tensions with the locals. Islamic radicals have taken advantage of the freedom conferred by European countries to organize in local mosques and cultural organizations, and many Muslims have been indoctrinated by the radical ideology espoused by visiting religious dignitaries. These Muslim immigrants complain that they have been marginalized by Western society, which they accuse of creating barriers to their full integration as citizens. There are also immigrants who were not interested in integration, as they wanted to preserve their religious and ethnic identities and resented the call of secularism. First-generation immigrants generally focus on making ends meet while living peacefully, but they do not have control over the actions of their off-spring, who can end up being drawn into religious fanaticism. The number of radicals appears small as judged by the 13 percent of the British Muslim population that has declared its support for terrorist attacks. However, this figure does not take into account those who held back their views, and it represents a substantial number who might support future terrorist threats. Nevertheless, radicalism is subjective. For example, the Turkish Muslims who dominate the Muslim population of Germany have shown a smaller propensity for extremism than those countries where Muslim society is dominated by Arab and North African immigrants (Laqueur 2004). Accordingly, counterterrorism approaches have to be adapted to the circumstances.

Balancing Counterterrorism Action with Civil Liberties

The response to Islamic radicalism has varied. There have been instances where controls were tightened and arrests made post-9/11, but security services have generally been pegged back by legal and political impediments that limit the effectiveness of counterterrorism measures. National and international laws have generally fallen short of dealing with terrorists or suspected terrorists, and in many instances, those who have been detained have not been convicted due to the supporting evidence against them being declared inadmissible or the reluctance of authorities to disclose their sources of information. Consequently, it has sometimes been difficult to arrest those linked to terrorist activity or, indeed, to hold those who have been arrested or placed in custody. Advocates argue for their release on the basis of human rights violations, that they are being wrongfully held, or being held without a trial. There is also some concern that counterterrorism measures that are perceived as unfair could antagonize and alienate moderate Muslims. For example, there have been complaints from Muslim organizations in Britain that Pakistani or Arab youth are 10 times more likely to be questioned by the police than the youth of other segments of the population. This has compelled some people to question if the war on terror is the real threat to society. With the constant threat of weapons of mass destruction, antiterrorism authorities have to draw a balance between rigorous law enforcement and civil liberties (Laqueur 2004).

Cross-Training Intelligence Personnel to Enhance Coordination

To counter threats such as terrorism, the ascendance of rogue states, and proliferation of weapons of mass destruction, intelligence agencies must develop very specific capabilities. It has been suggested that agencies should look beyond mere reorganization and rearranging their organizational charts. However, the road to reform for the intelligence community is strewn with barriers. Intelligence agencies operate under a shroud of secrecy that prohibits sharing information with other agencies. They adopt policies to protect information rather than standardize procedures and protocols. Analysts, case officers, and technical specialists are impeded from cooperating with their counterparts by a strict set of security procedures. Lack of coordination is a result of organizational policies created by individual agencies. These barriers must be broken down in the same way that the Goldwater-Nichols Act of 1986 did for the U.S. military by compelling the army, navy and air force to work together. It reformed the U.S. Defense Department, where communication and weapon systems were designed according to a common standard and where personnel were required to serve outside their own service in order to gain different perspectives (Cline 2009).

Providing Incentives for Cooperation and Disincentives for Failure

Some have suggested using incentives to encourage intelligence agencies to work together. This involves creating an environment that rewards interagency cooperation, interagency exchanges of personnel for at least a year, and establishing liaison teams that enhance communication between their home agency and others. This, along with a sound strategy, is the recipe for success. As one study puts it:

> Perhaps the first and most critical point involving interagency coordination improvements is that the best interagency processes in the world will not make bad policies and strategies succeed. Focusing exclusively on the process rather than broader strategic issues is a recipe for overall failure. Conversely, major blockages in interagency processes can create failure of even well-crafted strategies (Cline 2009).

If this doesn't work, ineffective agencies must be weeded out in favor of new ones that can tackle the threats of these times:

[Intelligence agencies] must be transformed into durable institutions that can carry out specialized missions over time. That process will require us to restructure the organizations we have, eliminate those that cannot execute their expected missions efficiently, or create new organizations and build them into the high-capacity institutions needed (Shemella 2009).

References

The Australian. 2008. "Terror suspects arrested in Belgium," December 13. http://www.theaustralian.com.au/news/terror-suspects-arrested-in-belgium/story-e6frg6to-1111118302362.

Australian Department of the Prime Minister and Cabinet. 2004. "Report of the inquiry into Australian intelligence agencies," July 20.

Australian Strategic Policy Institute. 2008. "The Intelligence Reform Agenda: What Next?" February 27.

BBC News. 2005. "London bomber called accomplices," August 24. http://news.bbc.co.uk/2/hi/uk_news/4181454.stm.

BBC News. 2008. "Will India's security overhaul work?" December 11. http://news.bbc.co.uk/2/hi/south_asia/7777185.stm.

Best, Richard A., Jr. 2004. "Proposals for intelligence reorganization, 1949–2004," CRS Report for Congress 32500, updated on September 24.

Borgeson, K., and R. Valeri. 2009. *Terrorism in America.* Sudbury, MA: Jones and Bartlett.

Bruno, Greg. 2009. "Getting smart on foreign relations," Council on Foreign Relations, January 14. http://www.cfr.org/publication/18217/getting_smart_on_intelligence_reform.html.

Carona, Michael S. n.d. "Orange County's response to terrorism." http://www.adl.org/learn/columns/Carona.asp.

CBC. 2005. "Al-Qaeda's Canadian recruits 'highly prized': Report," May. http://www.cbc.ca/story/canada/national/2005/05/14/alqaeda-canada050514.html.

Cline, Lawrence E. 2009. "The interagency process and U.S. support of other governments." Paper presented at the ISSS/ISAC conference, Monterey, California, October 15–17.

CNN. 2001. "Terror attacks hit U.S.," September 11. http://archives.cnn.com/2001/US/09/11/worldtrade.crash/index.html.

CTV. 2006. "RCMP arrests 17, foiling alleged Ontario bomb plot," June 3. http://www.ctv.ca/servlet/ArticleNews/story/CTVNews/20060603/toronto_arrests_060603/20060603/.

Cumming, Alfred, and Todd Masse. 2004. "FBI intelligence reform since September 11, 2001: Issues and options for Congress," CRS Report for Congress 32336, April 6.

Davis, L. M., Louis T. Mariano, Jennifer E. Pace, Sarah K. Cotton, and Paul Steinberg. 2007. "Combating terrorism: How prepared are state and local response organizations?" RAND National Defense Research Institute.

Davis, L. M., Jack Riley, Greg Ridgeway, Jennifer Pace, Sarah K. Cotton, Paul S. Steinberg, Kelly Damphouse, and Brent L. Smith. 2004. "When terrorism hits home: How prepared are state and local law enforcement?" RAND Corporation Research Brief.

Department of Homeland Security. 2004. "Fact sheet: National Incident Management System (NIMS)," March 1. http://www.dhs.gov/xnews/releases/press_release_0363.shtm.

Department of Homeland Security. n.d. "State and local fusion centers." http://www.dhs.gov/files/programs/gc_1156877184684.shtm.

EUObserver.com. 2010. "Madrid set to boost EU counter-terrorism activities," January 4. http://euobserver.com/9/29211.

European Union. 2007. "Theoretical treatise on counter-terrorism approaches," October 19. http://www.transnationalterrorism.eu/tekst/publications/WP6%20Del%2010.pdf.

Europol. 2010. "TE-SAT 2010: EU terrorism situation and trend report." http://www.consilium.europa.eu/uedocs/cmsUpload/TE-SAT%202010.pdf.

Field, Antony. 2009. "Tracking terrorist networks: Problems of intelligence sharing within the UK intelligence community." Review of International Studies.

Foley, Frank. 2009. "The expansion of intelligence agency mandates: British counter-terrorism in comparative perspective." Review of International Studies.

Gabriel, Brigitte. 2008. They must be stopped: Why we must defeat radical Islam and how we can do it. New York: St. Martin's Press.

Gilmore Commission. 2003. "The fifth annual report to the president and the Congress of the advisory panel to assess domestic response capabilities for terrorism involving weapons of mass destruction," December 15.

Grono, Nicholas. 2007. "Australia's response to terrorism: Strengthening the global intelligence network," Central Intelligence Agency, April 14. https://www.cia.gov/library/center-for-the-study-of-intelligence/csi-publications/csi-studies/studies/vol48no1/article03.html.

The Guardian. 2008. "Terror suspects arrested at Cologne airport," September 26. http://www.guardian.co.uk/world/2008/sep/26/germany.terrorism1.

Gul, Imtiaz. 2009. The al Qaeda connection. Penguin Books India, 163.

Hannah, G., Kevin A. O'Brien, and Andrew Rathmell. 2005. "Intelligence and security legislation for security sector reform," RAND Europe technical report.

HM Treasury. 2007. "The Financial Challenge to Crime and Terrorism." United Kingdom.

India Post. 2009. "Security strengthened to meet challenges post 26/11," November 29. http://www.theindiapost.com/2009/11/29/security-strengthened-to-meet-challenges-post-2611/.

Interview with law enforcement expert, October 19, 2009.

Laqueur, Walter. 2004. "The terrorism to come." Hoover Institution Policy Review (August/September). http://www.hoover.org/publications/policyreview/3437231.html.

The Local. 2008. "Terror suspects arrested in Sweden," February 28. http://www.thelocal.se/10152/20080228/.

Lynch, Timothy. 2003. "More surveillance equals less liberty: Patriot Act reduces privacy, undercuts judicial review," September 10. http://www.cato.org/research/articles/lynch-030910.html.

National Public Radio. 2005. "The Patriot Act: Alleged abuses of the law," July 20. http://www.npr.org/templates/story/story.php?storyId=4756403.

Office of the Director of National Intelligence. 2008. "United States Intelligence Community Information Sharing Strategy." February 22.

Posner, Richard. 2007. *Countering terrorism: Blurred focus, halting steps.* Lanham, MD: Rowman & Littlefield.

Posner, Richard A. 2005. "Remaking domestic intelligence," June 16. http://media.hoover.org/documents/oped_2821821.pdf.

Raghavan, Srinath. n.d. "Intelligence failures and reforms." http://www.india-seminar.com/2009/599/599_srinath_raghavan.htm.

Riley, K. J., Gregory F. Treverton, Jeremy M. Wilson, and Lois M. Davis. 2005. "State and local intelligence in the war on terrorism," RAND Corporation Infrastructure, Safety and Environment.

Rolfe, Pamela. 2005. "A year after Madrid attacks, Europe stalled in terror fight." *Washington Post*, March 11, A.012.

Russell, Richard. 2007. *Sharpening strategic intelligence: Why the CIA gets it wrong and what needs to be done to get it right.* Cambridge, UK: Cambridge University Press, 1–2.

Shemella, P. 2009. "Yours, mine and ours: Building the institutional capacity to fight terrorism." Paper presented at the ISSS/ISAC conference, Monterey, California, October 15–17.

Shore, Jacques J. M. 2006. "Intelligence review and oversight in post-9/11 Canada." *International Journal of Intelligence and CounterIntelligence*, 3.

U.K. Intelligence and Security Committee. 2008. "Review of the intelligence on the London terrorist attacks on 7 July 2005," July 8.

U.K. Intelligence and Security Committee. 2009. "Could 7/7 Have Been Prevented?: Review of the Intelligence on the London Terrorist Attacks on 7 July 2005."May.

Ungerer, Carl. 2008. "The intelligence reform agenda: What next?" Australian Strategic Policy Institute, February 27. http://www.aspi.org.au/publications/publication_details.aspx?ContentID=155&pubtype=9.

USA Today. 2003. "Al-Qaeda plotted strikes in Australia before 9/11," June 3. http://www.usatoday.com/news/world/2003-05-29-australia-alqaeda_x.htm.

Washington Post. 2008. "An intelligence reform reality check," February 18. http://www.washingtonpost.com/wp-dyn/content/article/2008/02/17/AR2008021701733.html.

Watts, Larry L. 2003. "Intelligence reform in Europe's emerging democracies." *Studies in Intelligence* 48, 1.

White, Jonathan R. 2002. *Terrorism: An introduction, 2002 Update.* Belmont, CA: Wadsworth Thomson Learning.

Yahoo News. 2010. "Grim Obama says terror attack 'dots' not connected," January 6. http://news.yahoo.com/s/ap/20100105/ap_on_go_pr_wh/us_obama_airline_security.

Zegart, Amy. 2007. *Spying blind: The CIA, the FBI, and the origins of 9/11.* Princeton, NJ: Princeton University Press.

How Financial Crime Is Committed
The Source of Funds

2

The previous chapter provided an introduction to the proliferation of terrorism and the need to stop its spread. There is consensus that the heart of terrorism is its financing, and stopping the flow of funds to terrorist groups is like sticking a dagger into the heart of the problem. This is easier said than done, given how widespread terrorist networks have grown. The international nature of financial crime is evident from the activities of al-Qaeda, as revealed in a report by HM Treasury (2007):

> In recent years, Al-Qaida and the groups that they have inspired have attacked over 25 countries and killed thousands of people. The financing of this activity is equally international with funds very often being raised in one country, used for training in a second, for procurement in a third and for terrorist acts in a fourth—and the outcomes broadcast in propaganda across the world.

In this book, terrorist financing and its composite activities—money laundering and tax evasion/fraud—are referred to as financial crime. Financial crime has traditionally been defined as "activities involving: 1) transactions to avoid government-imposed impediments to the efficient conduct of business and to avoid taxation; and 2) criminal transactions involving drugs, robbery, contract murder, prostitution, racketeering, and the like—basically economically motivated criminal activities" (Walter 1990). Given the expansive nature of financial crime, the global network of financial criminals, and the vitality of international cooperation to counter it, a deeper understanding of the problem is compulsory.

Terrorist Financing

In simplistic terms, terrorist financing is "the act of knowingly providing something of value to persons and groups engaged in terrorist activity" (Breinholt 2004). Terrorist networks raise funds for the purpose of purchasing arms, covering operational expenses, recruitment and training, and providing salaries and compensation (Kiser 2005). The cost of carrying out an attack depends on the scale of the attack. The September 11 attacks cost (excluding training) $400,000 to $500,000 according to the findings of the

Table 2.1   Direct Costs of Recent Terrorist Attacks

Attack	Date	Estimated Cost
London transport system	7 July 2005	GBP 8,000
Madrid train bombings	11 March 2004	USD 10,000
Istanbul truck bomb attacks	15 and 20 November 2003	USD 40,000
Jakarta JW Marriot Hotel bombing	5 August 2003	USD 30,000
Bali bombings	12 October 2002	USD 50,000
USS *Cole* attack	12 October 2000	USD 10,000

Source: Financial Action Task Force (FATF), "Terrorist Financing," February 29, 2008.

9/11 Commission. A United Nations (UN) sanctions-monitoring committee revealed that subsequent attacks by al-Qaeda cost less than $50,000 per attack, and it no longer had to pay an estimated $10 million to $20 million a year owed to its Taliban hosts in Afghanistan via cross-border transfers (*New York Times* 2004). Table 2.1 lists the direct costs (vehicles, improvised bomb-making components, maps, surveillance material, etc.) of the major terrorist attacks that took place before and after the September 11 attacks.

Besides these, there are other costs associated with maintaining terrorist networks. A government report interestingly notes,

> In relation to terrorism, while individual attacks can yield great damage at low financial cost, a significant financial infrastructure is required to sustain international terrorist networks and promote their goals. Funds are required to promote a militant ideology, pay operatives and their families, arrange for travel, train new members, forge documents, pay bribes, acquire weapons, and stage attacks. Often, a variety of higher cost services, including propaganda and ostensibly legitimate "social" activities are needed to provide a veil of legitimacy for organizations that promote their objectives through terrorism. For example, according to the United States Commission into 9/11, Al-Qaida was assessed to have spent some $30 million per year prior to 9/11 on funding operations, maintaining its training and military apparatus, contributing to the Taliban and their high-level officials, and sporadically contributing to related terrorist organizations (HM Treasury 2007).

Apart from training costs, terrorist networks also pay compensation and salaries to their members. A report in an Indian newspaper stated that Pakistani authorities pay terrorists trained in their country a monthly salary to carry out attacks in India. These terrorists have recently had their salary doubled from Rs (rupees) 5,000 to 10,000 each month to provide a growth spurt in terrorist attacks in Kashmir (*Times of India* 2010).

What keeps these global terrorist networks running are funds from a variety of sources. The Financial Action Task Force (FATF) has identified the major sources of terrorist funds, which include drug trafficking, extortion and kidnapping, robbery, fraud, gambling, smuggling and trafficking in counterfeit goods, sponsorship from certain governments, contributions and donations, sale of publications (legal and illegal), and funds derived from legitimate businesses (Anonymous 2003A).

State Sponsors

According to a U.S. Department of State release in April 2001, Iran, Iraq, Syria, Libya, Cuba, North Korea, and Sudan were designated state sponsors of international terrorism by the U.S. Secretary of State (U.S. Department of State 2001). A later update (2004) suggested that while Libya and Sudan were cooperating in the global war on terrorism and the terrorist-supporting regime in Iraq had been expelled from power, the rest of the countries were still associated with state-sponsored terrorism (CNN 2002).

Individual/Corporate Contributors

The most notorious individual contributor of terrorist funding is Osama bin Laden. According to U.S. prosecutors, bin Laden is not only the mastermind behind a number of strikes on U.S. targets, but also used an estimated $250 million in personal wealth to fund his causes (CNN 2001). His personal businesses, including a bakery, a furniture company, and a cattle-breeding operation, were used to funnel money for the purpose of financing and committing terrorist acts (Brooks, Riley, and Thomas 2005).

Nonprofit Organizations

According to Interpol, a nonprofit organization that supports a terrorist's cause could fund the terrorist's activity through a charitable donation to that terrorist's network. Because these funds are cash-based, it is difficult to verify either the origin or final destination of the funds (Interpol 2003). Also, charitable donations form one of the five pillars of Islam, and it is a religious duty for Muslims to provide charity to poorer Muslims. Terrorist networks use this opportunity to set up charities for humanitarian purposes within their community to increase support for their causes. Governments in Islamic countries where these donations end up are reluctant to take action against these networks and their charities because they fear the dissent of the public (Childs 2005). However, there has been some government action in this regard: In December 2001, shortly after the attacks of 9/11, the U.S. Treasury Department took action against two charitable organizations, Global Relief Foundation and Benevolence International Foundation, for providing funds in support of terrorist activity (CNN 2002). In mid-2004, the Holy Land

Foundation for Relief and Development was indicted by a federal grand jury in Dallas for providing more than $12.4 million in support of the Palestinian terrorist group, Hamas (Mintz 2004).

Government Programs

The Oil-for-Food program in Iraq was a humanitarian program introduced by the UN Security Council to help Iraqis cope with the consequences of the sanctions imposed after the 1991 Gulf War (Congressional Research Service 2005). According to the program, Iraq could sell a limited amount of crude oil and use the proceeds to purchase essentials such as food and medicine. Also, Iraq could determine to whom to sell oil and from whom to buy essentials. However, the Iraq dictator Saddam Hussein cheated the program of billions of dollars by engaging in operations outside the scheme and accepting kickbacks for these (Anonymous 2004). Furthermore, an opinion published in the *Wall Street Journal* suggested that some of this money may have been used to finance terrorism: "In a world beset right now by terrorist threats—which depend on terrorist financing—it's time to acknowledge that the U.N.'s Oil-for-Food program was worse than simply a case of grand larceny. Given Saddam's proclivities for deceit and violence, Oil-for-Food was also a menace to security" (Rosett 2004).

Illegal Sources

Sources of funding for terrorist activity through illegal means can take the form of any one or a combination of methods such as the sale of drugs, theft, kidnappings, extortion and revolutionary taxes, protection money, etc.

Drugs and Extortion

Drug money used to finance terrorism ranges from the sale of traditional drugs like heroin, hashish, and marijuana, and newer drugs such as pseudoephedrine and methamphetamines to counterfeit pharmaceuticals. The case study in Box 2.1 is an example of how terrorist organizations raise money through drug trafficking.

In Colombia, people are also known to be forced to grow coca and charged a "tax" on the proceeds (Brooks, Riley, and Thomas 2005).

The Islamic radical group, Abu Sayyaf, in the Southern Philippines uses extortion to raise funds to buy arms. It kidnaps Western tourists, Christian missionaries, and local businessmen and has raised an estimated $5.5 million from ransoms (Paz 2000).

BOX 2.1   FINANCIAL CRIME COMMITTED THROUGH DRUG TRAFFICKING

Case Study

Paramilitary organization F currently supplies more than 50 percent of the world's cocaine and more than 60 percent of the cocaine that enters the United States. Organization F initially taxed other narcotics traffickers involved in the manufacture and distribution of cocaine in areas it controlled. Recognizing the increased profits available from the 1990s up to the present, Organization F moved to become directly involved in the production and distribution of cocaine. Methods included, among other criminal activities, setting the prices to be paid to farmers across Colombia for cocaine paste, the raw material used to produce cocaine, and transporting cocaine paste to jungle laboratories under its control where it was converted into ton quantities of finished cocaine and then shipped out of Colombia to the United States and other countries.

Organization F leaders allegedly ordered the murder of Colombian farmers who sold cocaine paste to external buyers or otherwise violated its strict cocaine policies. Colombian farmers who violated rules were allegedly shot, stabbed, or dismembered alive, and the bodies of murdered farmers were cut open, filled with rocks, and sunk in nearby rivers. Organization F Leadership also allegedly ordered members to kidnap and murder U.S. citizens to discourage the U.S. government from disrupting its cocaine-trafficking activities. In July 2007, a senior leader was convicted of conspiring to commit hostage taking. Organization F leaders allegedly authorized their members to shoot down U.S. fumigation planes and plotted to retaliate against U.S. law enforcement officers who were conducting the investigation into the organization's narcotics activities.

Recognizing that cocaine was the lifeblood of Organization F, its leaders allegedly collected millions of dollars in cocaine proceeds and used the money to purchase weapons for terrorist activities against the government and people of Colombia.

Source: "Terrorist Financing," Financial Action Task Force (FATF), February 29, 2008.

Organized Retail Theft

According to testimony presented to the U.S. Congress, organized retail theft (ORT) is one of the means by which financial criminals raise funds. The loss to the supermarket industry via ORT is approximately $15 billion annually, while the effect on all retail operations is an estimated loss of $34 billion.

There are two groups involved in ORT in the United States. The first group usually consists of immigrants from Central American countries. They steal consumer merchandise from retail outlets such as supermarkets, chain drug stores, independent pharmacies, mass merchandisers, convenience stores, and discount businesses. The second group usually consists of immigrants from Middle Eastern and East Asian countries. They purchase and resell this merchandise through their own businesses, which typically include convenience stores, grocery stores, etc. (Emerson 2005). Box 2.2 illustrates how ORT takes place.

Another similar scheme involved drug addicts and indigents stealing baby formula on behalf of shoplifting gangs in exchange for $1 per can. These gangs repackaged the formula in counterfeit boxes and shipped them to retailers across the United States. One ring was reported to have made $44 million in 18 months from this scheme. In another case, a rental truck pulled over by police in Texas was found to be carrying a whole load of infant formula. The resulting investigation found that the driver was linked to a terrorist group and a theft ring that forwarded these criminal proceeds to the Middle East (Olson 2007). Box 2.3 presents other examples of financial crime committed through theft.

Other forms of theft used by financial criminals include automobile and intellectual property theft (piracy). Investigations of stolen vehicles have revealed links between members of organized crime and terrorist financing (Emerson 2005). In other cases, the purchase and resale of bootleg copies of software at a marked up price presents a big payout and low-risk operation for terrorist financers. Besides theft, financial criminals also indulge in fraud: credit card, welfare, social security, insurance, food stamps, and coupon fraud through identity theft or other means (Olson 2007). Box 2.4 explains coupon redemption fraud with the help of an example.

A former New York City police detective found a link between one such scheme and terrorists involved in the World Trade Center bombing in 1993 (ABCNews.com 2004).

Credit/Debit Card and Check Fraud

Credit card fraudsters either steal credit card information or use fraudulent credit card accounts. The techniques used to do so involve:

- Hacking into computer systems of credit card processing companies to steal credit card information (PCMag.com 2010)
- Cloning or skimming, where employees with access to customer credit cards use an electronic device to copy credit card details stored in its magnetic strip and then copy it onto a bogus credit card or overwrite a stolen credit card (Creditnet n.d.)

BOX 2.2 FINANCIAL CRIME COMMITTED THROUGH ORGANIZED RETAIL TRADE

CASE STUDY

In February 2005, Mohammed Khalil Ghali was sentenced to 14 years imprisonment following his conviction in April 2004 on 15 counts of a superseding indictment charging him and seven other individuals with various federal felony violations linked to organized retail theft in North Texas. According to the indictment, Ghali was the organizer and leader of a Palestinian gang known as the Ghali organization, which ran one of the nation's most notorious retail theft rings from Fort Worth, Texas. At the direction of Mohammed Ghali, members of his organization purchased stolen property that was being held at various metroplex convenience stores by store owners/operators who served as fences for the Ghali organization. Stolen property, including infant formula, pharmaceuticals, cigarettes, health and beauty aids, medicinal products, glucose test strips, nicotine gum and transdermal patches, and razors and razor blades were then delivered to warehouses where price tags and antitheft devices were removed and the merchandise repackaged and shipped to customers throughout the United States.

Despite incarceration of its top leaders, the Ghali crime family continues to operate its illegal business from behind bars with the aid of unjailed associates. Testimony at the sentencing hearing accused Ghali of making inquiries as to how much it would cost to have the Texas prosecutor and a federal agent killed by gang members. According to court transcripts, jailed family leader Mohammed Ghali attempted to hire Crip gang members to arrange the hits for $500. Members of the Ghali family also made attempts to bribe U.S. Immigration and Customs Enforcement (ICE) supervisors to get the charges against Ghali dismissed. More recently, federal authorities unraveled a plot targeting Fort Worth Police Detective Scott Campbell, his family, and ICE agent Scott Springer. It has been reported that profits generated from the sale of goods were wired to banks in the Middle East.

Source: Steven Emerson, "Money Laundering and Terror Financing Issues in the Middle East," testimony of Steven Emerson before the U.S. Senate Committee on Banking, Housing, and Urban Affairs, July 13, 2005.

BOX 2.3   FINANCIAL CRIME
COMMITTED THROUGH THEFT

CASE STUDY

A wholesaler in infant formula, the Tempe-based company owned and operated by Samih Fadl Jamal, was the center of a fencing operation for stolen or fraudulently obtained infant formula that generated more than $11 million dollars in profits. Stolen infant formula was repackaged at a JTC warehouse and distributed and sold to various retail and wholesale businesses. Most of the defendants indicted in the case were from Iraq, Jordan, or Lebanon. Of the 27 defendants indicted, 22 were located and arrested, 17 have pleaded guilty, and 4 have been sentenced and deported. Jamal, a naturalized U.S. citizen born in Lebanon, was convicted in April 2005 on 20 counts of conspiracy to traffic in stolen infant formula, money laundering, and other related charges. All counts carried a fine of $250,000.

Similarly, a June 8, 2005, indictment charged Carlos Javier Medina-Castellanos, Mahmoud Bassar, and Jose Francisco of organized theft of baby formula, over-the-counter medicines, and other items related to personal health and hygiene. According to the indictment, the stolen items would be collected from different locations in North Carolina and Georgia and delivered to various depositories that included private residences or temporary storage facilities. The stolen merchandise would then be transported by passenger vehicles and rented trucks to commercial trucking firms, where it was loaded onto larger trucks. The merchandise would then be shipped to various destinations across the country. The retail value of particular shipments of the stolen merchandise shipments in some instances exceeded $50,000.

Source: **Steven Emerson, "Money Laundering and Terror Financing Issues in the Middle East," testimony of Steven Emerson before the U.S. Senate Committee on Banking, Housing, and Urban Affairs, July 13, 2005.**

- Phishing schemes, which involve sending out fraudulent official-looking e-mails to a business's clients and requesting personal information like social security and credit card account numbers (CreditCards.com 2008a)

While there are no statistics available to determine how much of credit card fraud is tied to terrorist financing, anecdotal evidence suggests that

BOX 2.4   FINANCIAL CRIME COMMITTED THROUGH COUPON REDEMPTION FRAUD

CASE STUDY

In New York and Florida, hundreds of thousands of coupon inserts were obtained from newspapers and sent to cutters who clipped the specific coupons and sent them to a clearinghouse run by International Data and located in El Paso, Texas, in the name of the recruited businesses. The clearinghouse would redeem the value of the coupons from the manufacturers and checks would be issued to the businesses, some of which were fronts that existed only to further the scheme. In order to perpetuate the scheme, Robert W. MacDonald, an executive at International Data, in Memphis, received kickbacks for accepting falsified questionnaires filled out by the scheme's leader, Abdel Rahim Jebara of Miami. MacDonald would take these questionnaires and accept them as valid even though no purchases of the products were made.

Once the checks were cut to the companies, they were collected by individuals including Jebara's son, Medre A. Medre, who would give the store owners their cut and then cash the checks in Yonkers, New York. After the checks were cashed, the money was sent to Medre's parents, Shahira Hamideh Jebara and Abdel Rahim Jebara, in Miami. Jebara, in turn, wired the money to Ramallah, where he claimed to have a million-dollar house.

In all, the scheme involved over 350 stores in 15 states including Alabama, Connecticut, Florida, Illinois, Louisiana, Massachusetts, Mississippi, New Jersey, New York, Ohio, Pennsylvania, Tennessee, Texas, Rhode Island, and Wisconsin. On March 4, 2003, 15 people were indicted by a federal grand jury with offenses including mail fraud, wire fraud, money laundering, interstate transportation of stolen property, and receiving stolen property that crossed state lines. The FBI is still investigating the overseas financial transactions and other aspects of the scheme.

Source: "Progress since 9/11: The Effectiveness of U.S. Anti-Terrorist Financing Efforts," testimony of Steven Emerson before the U.S. House Committee on Financial Services Subcommittee on Oversight and Investigations, March 11, 2003.

BOX 2.5   FINANCIAL CRIME COMMITTED THROUGH CREDIT CARD FRAUD (A)

CASE STUDY

Person A frequented criminal Internet sites that specifically bought and sold credit card information (including shadowcrew.com, investigated by the U.S. Secret Service in 2003). Stolen credit card numbers were passed to Associate B, and then on to C, a computer expert specializing in facilitating the creation and management of Web sites that provided forums for extremists and downloads of highly violent material intended to incite attacks. The associates were later found to be linked, via telephone and e-mail records, to a terrorist cell in Bosnia and were arrested on the brink of launching an attack.

COMMENTARY

The case illustrates how terrorists' needs for funds can go far beyond those required to launch specific attacks. In this case, terrorist facilitators fully exploited the opportunities of new technology to acquire funds illicitly and anonymously, extending the distance between their identity and their actions. The case also highlighted how sophisticated forensic skills can be needed to recover financial data.

Source: **"Terrorist Financing," Financial Action Task Force (FATF), February 29, 2008.**

there is a relation. A case of homegrown terrorism in Australia that was preemptively foiled by authorities revealed that the conspirators bought credit card information from taxi drivers for $10. The stolen credit card data was used to cover the operating costs of a plot that involved attempting to blow up the Melbourne Cricket Grounds during the 2005 Australian Football League Grand Final (CreditCards.com 2008b). Box 2.5 and Box 2.6 provide other illustrations of this type of financial crime.

Like credit card fraud, check fraud takes place when organized criminals set up a fraudulent checking account and use checks drawn from this account to make purchases simultaneously at different locations (FATF 2008). The purchases are returned for cash before the checks can bounce (*Sunday Times* 2004). Box 2.7 presents an example.

Financial criminals also commit credit card fraud in combination with other methods to finance terrorism. This is discussed in Box 2.8 with the help of an example.

BOX 2.6 FINANCIAL CRIME COMMITTED THROUGH CREDIT CARD FRAUD (B)

CASE STUDY

A North African terrorist funding group accumulated details of nearly 200 stolen cards and raised more than GBP 200,000 to fund the al-Qaeda terrorist network through international credit card fraud. The names and credit card details of almost 200 different bank accounts were collected by 20–30 "runners" from contacts working in service industries such as restaurants. These details were not used in their country of origin (the United Kingdom) but sent on to associates in Spain and the Netherlands. These associates used the cards to fraudulently collect more than GBP 200,000 for al-Qaeda cells around Europe.

COMMENTARY

This case illustrates that the high returns achievable from credit card fraud are not lost on terrorists and that sophisticated arrangements can be put in place to operate a fraud ring linked to terrorism.

Source: "Terrorist Financing," Financial Action Task Force (FATF), February 29, 2008.

BOX 2.7 FINANCIAL CRIME COMMITTED THROUGH BANK FRAUD

CASE STUDY

A network of North African terrorists used organized, low-level bank fraud against a number of U.K. banks to raise funds in support of terrorist activity. Using in excess of 50 individuals, the group raised at least GBP 550,000 within 12 months. Once raised, this money was used to support terrorist training, procurement, travel, and subsistence costs incurred by terrorists and extremists across Europe.

Source: "Terrorist Financing," Financial Action Task Force (FATF), February 29, 2008

BOX 2.8   FINANCIAL CRIME COMMITTED THROUGH A COMBINATION OF METHODS

CASE STUDY

A terrorist financier was a member of an enterprise that created a complex cigarette smuggling scheme in the United States. This financier would purchase low-taxed cigarettes from one U.S. state, apply forged tax stamps to the goods, and then smuggle the untaxed cigarettes into Michigan (where state cigarette taxes are considerably higher) for resale.

In parallel with this exercise, the organization defrauded retail and wholesale merchants with counterfeit credit cards. The cash garnered from these unlawful activities would then be laundered by members of the enterprise by purchasing businesses, buying additional cigarettes, and obtaining additional fraudulent credit cards.

The enterprise also committed acts of arson and attempted to engage in insurance fraud by burning down a cigarette shop that it owned on an Indian reservation in New York, and then attempted to recover on their fire insurance policy.

The terrorist financier used the profits from these activities to provide material support to a designated terrorist organization.

COMMENTARY

This case demonstrates the wide range of fraudulent activities that terrorist supporters will engage in, such as trading in illegal contraband, and tax, credit card and insurance fraud, to generate funds to support terrorist groups.

Source: **"Terrorist Financing," Financial Action Task Force (FATF), February 29, 2008.**

As with credit card fraud, financial criminals commit debit card fraud by installing miniature cameras and bank card readers on ATM machines. While the reader captures customers' bank account information, the camera helps the criminals take note of their PINs. The criminals then use a card-writer to duplicate these debit cards and steal money from the accounts (CTV News 2005).

Money Laundering

Defined generally, money laundering is "the process of concealing the existence, illegal source, or application of income derived from criminal activity, and the subsequent disguising of the source of that income to make it appear legitimate" (Moneylaundering.com n.d.). Such criminal activity includes illegal arms sales, smuggling, drug trafficking, prostitution rings, embezzlement, insider trading, bribery, and computer fraud schemes. Money laundering not only affects the integrity of business and financial services, but also the economic development of countries where it occurs (OECD 1999). It adversely influences public confidence in banks and financial markets, especially in emerging economies (Norgren 2004). Money launderers work with "dirty money," which is not always the case for terrorist financers, who sometimes raise funds by legal means. The amounts they launder also tend to be bigger than those used for terrorist financing. In the case of money laundering, criminal activity takes place prior to funds being laundered, unlike in the case of terrorist financing. In other words, "Money laundering cleans dirty money; terrorist financing dirties clean money" (Waszak 2004).

Money laundering is generally carried out in three steps. The first step in the money-laundering process is placement. This is when dirty money first enters the financial system, for example when drugs are sold illegally for cash and then deposited at a financial institution (UNODC n.d.). Another example is using this dirty money to purchase money orders. The next step is layering, which perhaps represents the most complex stage of the process. Here the launderer, through a series of financial transactions, attempts to conceal the original source of the funds (Molander, Mussington, and Wilson 1998). This may involve transferring the dirty money from one bank to many banks after breaking it down into smaller amounts (UNODC n.d.). This is followed by the last step, integration, which occurs when the illicit funds are assimilated with the commercial economy through legal commercial transactions. Together, these constitute money laundering, one of the most notorious forms of criminal financial crime, which provides a means for criminals such as drug dealers, terrorist organizations, arms dealers, and other criminals to make illegally earned funds appear legitimate (Canadian Institute of Chartered Accountants 2004). Box 2.9 provides a case in point.

The proceeds of crime from money laundering are generally high and make it an attractive source of income for financial criminals. The estimated amount of money laundered internationally is difficult to estimate; some reports place this figure as high as $3 trillion each year (Sinason, Pacini, and Hillson 2003; Rettig and Robbins 2005), while others estimate it to be between $500 billion to $1 trillion (George and Lacey 2003). KPMG's "Global Anti-Money Laundering Survey 2004: How Banks Are Facing up to the Challenge" exposes the institutional impact of money laundering. The study revealed:

BOX 2.9   FINANCIAL CRIME COMMITTED
THROUGH MONEY LAUNDERING

CASE STUDY

The financial intelligence unit (FIU) in Country L received a suspicious transaction report from a bank regarding an account held by an offshore investment company. The bank's suspicions arose after the company's manager made several large cash deposits in different foreign currencies. According to the customer, these funds were intended to finance companies in the media sector. The FIU requested information from several financial institutions. Through these inquiries, it learned that the managers of the offshore investment company were residing in Country L and a bordering country. They had opened accounts at various banks in Country L under the names of media companies and a nonprofit organization involved in the promotion of cultural activities.

According to the analysis by the FIU, the managers of the offshore investment company and several other clients had made cash deposits to the accounts. These funds were ostensibly intended for the financing of media-based projects. The analysis further revealed that the account held by the nonprofit organization was receiving almost daily deposits in small amounts by third parties. The manager of this organization stated that the money deposited in this account was coming from its members for the funding of cultural activities.

Police information obtained by the FIU revealed that the managers of the offshore investment company were known to have been involved in money laundering and that an investigation was already underway into their activities. The managers appeared to be members of a terrorist group that was financed by extortion and narcotics trafficking. Funds were collected through the nonprofit organization from the different suspects involved in this case. This case is currently under investigation.

Source: **"Guidance for Financial Institutions in Detecting Terrorist Financing," Financial Action Task Force, April 24, 2002.**

Of the 209 financial institutions interviewed, 67 percent of banks reported an increase in the volume of suspicious activities that they report to law enforcement officials, 83 percent stated they are investing an average of 61 percent more to combat money laundering and most banks agreed that they foresee this spending to continue to increase upwards of 40 percent over the next three years (KPMG 2004).

In 2003, Canada's Financial Intelligence Unit (FIU) investigated 197 cases involving $700 million (Canadian) in suspicious financial transactions, up from $460 million (Canadian) the previous year. While 90 percent of these were suspected money-laundering cases, $70 million (Canadian) was suspected to be linked to financing terrorism (CBC 2004).

There are those who feel that even crime that does not involve money laundering is being "sold" as money laundering by those trying to advance anti-money-laundering legislation, "Money laundering legislation is being applied to situations unrelated to any traditional notion of organized crime and in situations where illicit proceeds are deposited or otherwise used but where there is no 'cleansing' involved" (Beare 2002).

Closely related to money laundering is illegal capital flight, which is the term used to describe the movement of private and commercial capital from one country to another. Box 2.10 presents a discussion of its impact on society.

Legal capital flight should not be mistaken for illegal flight. It involves moving after-tax money for which there is proper documentation and a bookkeeping record. Illegal capital flight involves just the opposite: mispriced or falsified transactions to facilitate the movement of money from one country to another, improper documentation, and no record in the country of origin (Baker 2009).

Tax Evasion/Fraud

Tax evasion is related to terrorist financing under the simple assumption that terrorists do not pay taxes on income they use to finance their activities.

A perception of tax evasion is expected to generate a Suspicious Activities Report (SAR) in U.S. banks. Yet, when an exact percentage of proceeds from an international trade transaction is taken out of the domestic party's account and deposited into the foreign party's account within the walls of the same bank, even transaction after transaction, no SAR is filed, although from long experience the bankers and business people involved know full well that tax evasion is a result of these kickbacks (Baker 1999).

Also, money launderers are involved in tax evasion schemes, as they often attempt to make laundered funds appear to stem from nontaxable sources. The case study in Box 2.11 illustrates how terrorist networks are supported by tax fraud.

The government and the courts have attempted to clamp down on tax schemes used to support terrorist networks. Information reported to FIUs has been instrumental in exposing tax evaders and fraudsters as it has with other forms of financial crime. An Australian government audit

BOX 2.10   THE BENEFITS AND COSTS OF CAPITAL FLIGHT

COMMENTARY

The costs and benefits of this illegal capital flight merit clear analysis. The benefit is that it spreads several hundred billion dollars annually across Europe and North America in bank accounts, markets and properties. The cost can be seen in the impact on both domestic and foreign interests.

Illegal capital flight provides the cover that is necessary for laundering of criminal money. These two flows, which are dealt with differently within most countries' laws, move along precisely the same paths, constituting two rails on the same tracks through the international financial system. Treasury Department officials in the United States recently estimated that 99.9 percent of the criminal money that is presented for deposit gets into secure accounts, and German and Swiss bankers and officials reported higher percentages for their countries. The fact is, money laundering is almost universally successful. The easiest thing for criminals to do is to make their criminal money look like it is merely corrupt or commercial tax-evading money, and when they do, it passes readily into foreign economies. Indeed, with European and North American banks and corporations aggressively competing to service illegal capital flight, the perception is widespread elsewhere that the West is not serious about its anti-money-laundering programs, preferring instead to take advantage of ambiguities available in legal systems and profit from the combined flows. Thus, the domestic cost of illegal capital flight for wealthy countries is apparent: It removes anti-money-laundering efforts as an effective instrument in the fight against drugs, crime, and terrorism, thereby weakening the ability to prevail in facing some of the more perilous threats to our societies.

Illegal capital flight similarly undermines key foreign policy interests of western nations. Russia, of strategic importance, has suffered the greatest illicit diversion of resources out of any country in a short period of time, an estimated $200–$500 billion in a decade. Yet what has happened in Russia, so much in the news of late, is no different than what has been happening in many other parts of the world for years. Nigeria has been impoverished, with 70 percent of its population living on the equivalent of $0.20 a day. Fraud and capital flight contributed to the overthrow of democracy in Pakistan, a new nuclear state in a volatile subcontinent. From Mexico, the only developing country that has a border with a major industrialized democracy, comes a surge of drugs and economically depressed aliens, presenting a difficult foreign policy challenge for the United States. China, with estimated illicit outflows already reported to be running upwards of $10 billion annually, is beginning to show domestic strains that are likely to become more severe. Thus, the foreign cost of illegal capital flight is that it erodes our strategic objectives in transitional economies and undermines economic progress in developing countries, draining hard currency reserves, heightening inflation, reducing tax collection, worsening income gaps, canceling investment, hurting competition, and undermining free trade, all contributing to political instability. Furthermore, for every dollar allocated in foreign aid, two or three dollars at a minimum are taken back in ill-gotten gains belonging to foreign citizens in aid-recipient countries, offsetting development assistance flows with practices condoned by donor governments.

Source: **Baker, Raymond W. 2000. "Illegal Flight Capital Dangers for Global Stability,"** *International Politik*, **no. 6 (original in German).**

report, released in the year 2000, disclosed that over the preceding five years, $160 million (Australian) had been collected, through tax assessments, with the help of data from the Australian Transaction Reports and Analysis Centre (AUSTRAC). This use of this data also contributed to the Australian Tax Office's (ATO) overall revenue collection ($47 million Australian in 1998–99) and made a valuable contribution to tax administration. It is considered an important intelligence source that aids compliance activities. Awareness of the ATO/AUSTRAC relationship also increased the level of voluntary tax compliance and deterred potential tax evaders (Australian Taxation Office 2000).

In the United States, a number of branches of the Internal Revenue Service (IRS) are assigned to counter tax evasion related to terrorist financing and money laundering. One of these is the Criminal Investigation Division (IRS-CI) that conducts fraud investigations. The IRS-CI is a recipient of $3 million in annual funding to staff its task forces in High Risk Money Laundering and Related Financial Crimes Areas. Also part of the IRS's responsibilities is ensuring compliance in relation to the maintenance of offshore accounts through the Report of Foreign Bank and Financial Accounts (FBARs) (Rettig and Robbins 2005).

A recent court ruling in the United States has tied money laundering to tax evasion. A case was filed against the owners of a supermarket in the U.S. Virgin Islands who transmitted $60 million of business income

BOX 2.11   FINANCIAL CRIME COMMITTED THROUGH TAX FRAUD

CASE STUDY

A familiar pattern among fundraisers for terrorism is their sophisticated use of tax laws to maximize funds for terrorist operations. In addition to using 501(c)(3) corporations to solicit tax free contributions, Palestinian Islamic Jihad (PIJ) laundered money through wealthy U.S. citizens to create fraudulent tax deductions.

As captured by FBI wiretaps on March 6, 1994, Sami Al-Arian engaged in a telephone conversation with unindicted coconspirator 1 (who has been identified as Fawaz Damra) in which Sami Al-Arian described returning from Chicago after raising $53,000, $25,000 of which was collected in cash. Sami Al-Arian and Damra discussed a scheme in which Sami Al-Arian would send a portion of the donations collected in Chicago to Damra, who would arrange for the donations to be redonated by a private individual, who would then take the donation as a tax deduction of 40 percent. Later, the private individual would contribute a portion of the fraudulent tax deduction to Sami Al-Arian, thereby increasing the overall amount of the donations. Damra and Sami Al-Arian discussed how the private individuals who would participate in the scheme all made over $200,000 per year and were in the 40 percent tax bracket.

On February 20, 2003, the U.S. Department of Justice indicted Sami Al-Arian and seven coconspirators for their role in directing the activities of the PIJ from the United States. The indictment provides a rare and detailed look into the inner workings of an international terrorist organization operating from the safety and sanctuary of Tampa, Florida.

The PIJ is a U.S. government-designated foreign terrorist organization, committed to suicide bombings and violent jihad activities. This organization is responsible for the murder of over 100 innocent people in Israel, the West Bank, and Gaza, including at least two young Americans, Alisa Flatow, age 20, and Shoshana Ben-Yishai, age 16.

Source: **"Progress since 9/11: The Effectiveness of U.S. Anti-Terrorist Financing Efforts," testimony of Steven Emerson before the U.S. House Committee on Financial Services Subcommittee on Oversight and Investigations, March 11, 2003.**

to bank accounts in Jordan and did not report it to the tax authorities. The judge ruled against the defendants on more serious charges of tax evasion that constitute a predicate crime for money laundering. The court also considered the owners' reporting of false tax returns as mail fraud and ruled in favor of the prosecutor's case that "unpaid taxes were profits of the mail fraud that had been laundered by the defendants" (Moneylaundering.com 2008).

Stopping Terrorist Funding: Laws, Directives, and Multilateral Agreements

As terrorist financing has increasingly been put under the spotlight, so have government efforts to counter it. While governments around the world have enacted and strengthened anti-money-laundering (AML) and counterterrorism financing (CTF) legislation in their respective countries, they have also entered into multilateral agreements with each other (Foreign Affairs Canada 2002).

The United States has led the way in combating terrorist financing through what is described as an "aggressive, multifaceted approach" that was initiated by the executive order signed by the president on September 24, 2001. This included freezing the assets of terrorist financers and their terrorist networks and publicly labeling more than 400 individuals and entities as designated terrorists and organizations, including Hezbollah, Hamas, Palestinian Islamic Jihad, and al-Qaeda and its affiliates. The Justice Department has actively prosecuted individuals and entities for terrorist financing under the "material support" statute (Jacobson 2007b). The USA PATRIOT Act espoused the new financial regulations that were introduced post-9/11 (Wolosky and Heifetz 2002).

Other countries have followed suit. In the United Kingdom, a special unit called the Terrorist Asset Freezing Unit was established within Her Majesty's Treasury (HMT), and special powers were granted to HMT to use classified information to freeze assets in certain cases (Jacobson 2007b). While financial institutions in several countries including the United States and the United Kingdom have the legal duty to report transactions that meet a certain criterion of suspicion of financial crime, in many countries, they do not. This calls for multilateral action, as

intervention is needed on the part of the Organisation for Economic Cooperation and Development (OECD), Financial Action Task Force (FATF), the United Nations (UN), the International Monetary Fund (IMF), the World Bank, the Organization of American States (OAS) and Transparency International (TI) to halt business corruption by pressuring financial institutions in all jurisdictions to lift the veil of secrecy and engage in the exchange of information with the home countries of foreign investors (George and Lacey 2003).

Of these bodies, the FATF and the UN arguably have the biggest impact on the universal adoption and advancement of AML/CTF initiatives.

The FATF was established at the G7 summit in Paris in 1989 with the responsibilities of reviewing AML actions taken in the past, recommending new measures to combat financial crime, and analyzing trends and techniques in financial crime. It is an intergovernmental body whose objective is to develop policy guidelines that will bring about regulatory and legislative change in combating financial crime. In 1990, the FATF released the Forty Recommendations, a blueprint outlining the steps necessary to tackle money laundering (Anonymous 2003B). In 2001, the FATF issued eight special Recommendations on Terrorist Financing to supplement its recommendations on money laundering (Australian Department of Foreign Affairs and Trade 2002). In 2004, it issued Special Recommendation IX, which addressed financial crime committed through cross-border movements of cash and the importance of information sharing in countering it (Deloitte n.d.). The FATF conducts periodic evaluations, known as mutual evaluations, which assess the effectiveness of countries in implementing FATF standards (FATF, 2005). Countries are evaluated based on adequacy and implementation of laws and regulations and effective compliance with FATF recommendations. Assessors assign one of four ratings—compliant, largely compliant, partially compliant, noncompliant—based on the level of compliance with each recommendation (FATF 2004). In 2000, FATF announced a "name and shame" policy whereby it would disclose the names of those countries that did not comply with international standards and improve their weak anti-money-laundering regimes. They would face the possibility of countermeasures that would go as far as banning transactions with noncooperative countries (OECD 2000).

Besides the FATF, the UN, IMF, and World Bank are prominent players in the coordination and enforcement of global AML/CTF initiatives. The United Nations Convention against Illicit Traffic in Narcotic Drugs and Psychotropic Substances in 1988 resulted in signatories criminalizing money laundering and removing barriers to criminal investigation such as bank secrecy. The UN also provides member nations with assistance in developing the tools to combat money laundering (Zagaris 2002). The Global Program against Money Laundering run by the UN Office on Drug Control and Crime Protection (ODCCP) in conjunction with the FATF, Council of Europe, Interpol, and Organization of American States (OAS) administers training to those exposed to financial crime such as business, law enforcement, and judicial professionals, assists in the development of legal and institutional frameworks, and raises awareness of international AML efforts (George and Lacey 2003). The UN quickly rose to the occasion after the 9/11 attacks by maintaining a terrorist blacklist and taking incisive action against financial crime that was criminalized under UN Security Council Resolutions 1267, 1333, and 1390. These also required countries to detect, deter, and freeze terrorist funds (Aufhauser 2003). The UN's other key multilateral initiatives include the 1999 International Convention for the Suppression of the Financing of Terrorism (New York) and the establishment of the United Nations Counter Terrorism Committee (CTC) under Security Council Resolution 1373 (Australian Department of Foreign Affairs and Trade 2002). Despite all of these measures, the UN has had its critics, "The organization has seen its role greatly diminished over the past several years. Since early 2004, the independent group responsible for monitoring compliance was replaced by a team with far less autonomy; the pace of terrorist designations has slowed; and countries have tired of the UN's reporting requirements" (Jacobson 2007a).

The IMF and World Bank conduct their own independent assessments of counterterrorism regimes and provide technical assistance when necessary (Aufhauser 2003). Both organizations tightened their approach in countering financial crime after conducting a joint 12-month pilot program that assessed the AML/CTF programs of 41 countries, at different stages of development, against international standards. During this assessment, more than 100 countries requested help with their programs, prompting the IMF and World Bank to declare their intention to conduct 10 assessments each year as part of their Bank/Fund Financial Sector Assessment Program (FSAP) (America.gov 2004) and carry out a technical assistance delivery plan (IMF and World Bank 2003). The two organizations also proposed developing a methodology document that could be used to evaluate AML systems. This document would be periodically updated based on the organizations' experience through assessments and feedback from industry supervisors and other bodies like the FATF (IMF and World Bank 2001). Initiatives of the World Bank, IMF, and FATF are supplemented by measures imposed by regional governments like the European Union (EU); regional bodies like the Council of Europe (with its initiative - Committee of Experts on the Evaluation of Anti-Money Laundering Measures and the Financing of Terrorism - MONEYVAL) (George and Lacey 2003), the Eurasian group on combating money laundering and financing of terrorism (EAG) and the Inter Governmental Action Group against Money Laundering in West Africa (GIABA) (the World Bank n.d.); regional task forces like the Caribbean FATF, the Asia Pacific Group on Money Laundering, the Latin American group GAFISUD, the Middle East & North Africa Financial Action Task Force, and the Eastern and Southern Africa Anti-Money-Laundering Group; and regional development banks such as the Inter-American Development

Bank, the European Bank for Reconstruction and Development (EBRD), and the Asian Development Bank (ABD) (Morais 2002). There are also anticorruption organizations such as Transparency International (TI) whose representatives helped draft anti-money-laundering guidelines for private banks (Wolfsberg Group n.d.). This will be discussed in the next chapter.

The use of these various means of financing terrorism, some of them legitimate, has posed a problem in detecting them. According to the 9/11 Commission Report, the U.S. government had been unable to trace the source of funds used to finance the terrorist attacks of September 11, 2001. Banks and other business entities file suspicious-activity reports (SARs) with the FIU, which opens its SAR database to all U.S. attorneys and 59 law-enforcement agencies. In spite of this, "none of them saw the $100,000 received by Mohamed Atta weeks before September 11th, even though that transaction was in the database and Atta's name was on the FBI's list of 'most wanted' terrorists" (Latimer 2004). The scale of misuse of funds for financing terrorism calls for greater investment in resources and large-scale cooperation. However, it would still be difficult to measure the success of these antiterrorism tactics because a decline in terrorists' use of one source of terrorist financing could mean an increase in the use of other sources that are not familiar to intelligence agencies and law enforcement (Passas 2003).

References

ABCNews.com. 2004. "Terrorists collect millions from coupon schemes," September 30. http://abcnews.go.com/GMA/story?id=126419&page=1.

America.gov. 2004. "World Bank, IMF focus on money laundering, terrorist financing," April 5. http://www.america.gov/st/washfile-english/2004/April/20040405 132300MBzemoG0.4624903.html.

Anonymous. 2003a. "The law in context; Sub-group 2: Impact of the initiatives against terrorist property on banks and financial institutions." *Journal of Money Laundering Control* 6: 233.

Anonymous. 2003b. "The law: An overview; Sub-group 2: Impact of the initiatives against terrorist property on banks and financial institutions." *Journal of Money Laundering Control* (Winter).

Anonymous. 2004. "The biggest scandal ever? The UN's oil-for-food row." *The Economist* 371 (May 1): 58.

Aufhauser, David D. 2003. "Terrorist financing: Foxes run to ground." *Journal of Money Laundering Control* (Spring).

Australian Department of Foreign Affairs and Trade. 2002. "Co-chairs' report," Conference on Combating Money Laundering and Terrorist Financing, December, Introduction.

Australian Taxation Office. 2000. "The Australian taxation office's use of AUSTRAC data." http://www.anao.gov.au/WebSite.nsf/Publications/4A256AE90015F69B4 A2569510020CC9D#Recommendation.

Baker, Raymond. 1999. "Money laundering and capital flight: The impact on private banking," Brookings Institution, November 10.

Baker, Raymond W. 2000. "Illegal flight capital dangers for global stability." *International Politik* (June).

Beare, Margaret E. 2002. "Searching for wayward dollars: Money laundering or tax evasion—which dollars are we really after?" *Journal of Financial Crime* (February).

Breinholt, Jeff. 2004. "Reaching the white collar terrorist: Operational challenges," IMF Seminar Program, September, 3.

Brooks, Richard, Richard A. Riley, Jr., and Jason Thomas. 2005. "Detecting and preventing the financing of terrorist activities: A role for government accountants." *The Journal of Government Financial Management* 54: 12.

Canadian Institute of Chartered Accountants. 2004. "Canada's anti-money laundering and anti-terrorist financing requirements," February.

CBC News. 2004. "More money laundering reported in Canada," November 4. http://www.cbc.ca/story/canada/national/2004/11/04/money_launder_041104.html.

Childs, David. 2005. "Combating terrorist financing: A key aspect of the war on terrorism," May 20. http://www.cdi.org/friendlyversion/printversion.cfm?documentID=3024.

CNN. 2001. "Bin Laden, millionaire with a dangerous grudge," September 27. http://archives.cnn.com/2001/US/09/12/binladen.profile/.

CNN. 2002. "Islamic charity fights asset freeze," January 28. http://archives.cnn.com/2002/LAW/01/28/inv.charilty.lawsuit/.

Congressional Research Service. 2001. "Iraq: Oil-for-food program, illicit trade, and investigations," September 27. http://www.opencrs.com/document/RL30472/.

CreditCards.com. 2008a. "Credit card 'phishing': What it means, how to prevent it," June 20. http://www.creditcards.com/credit-card-news/phishing-credit-card-scam-fraud-1282.php.

CreditCards.com. 2008b. "The credit card terrorism connection," May 15. http://www.creditcards.com/credit-card-news/credit-cards-terrorism-1282.php.

Creditnet. n.d. "How do credit cards get cloned?" http://consumers.creditnet.com/Library/Credit_Card_FAQ/How_do_credit_cards_get_cloned.ccfaq_019.php.

CTVNews. 2005. "Debit card fraud," January 8. http://www.ctv.ca/servlet/ArticleNews/story/CTVNews/1105142446966_16/?hub=WFive.

Deloitte. n.d. "What's new." http://www.dttgfsi.com/aml/news.html.

Emerson, S. 2003. "Progress since 9/11: The Effectiveness of U.S. Anti-Terrorist Financing Efforts." U.S. House Committee on Financial Services Subcommittee on Oversight and Investigations, March 11.

Emerson, S. 2005. "Money laundering and terrorist financing issues in the Middle East." U.S. Senate Committee of Banking, Housing and Urban Affairs, July 13.

FATF. 2002. "Guidance for Financial Institutions in Detecting Terrorist Financing," Financial Action Task Force, April 24.

FATF. 2004. "Methodology for assessing compliance with the FATF 40 recommendations and the FATF 9 special recommendations," February 27. http://www.fatf-gafi.org/dataoecd/16/54/40339628.pdf.

FATF. 2005. "FATF standards: Third round of mutual evaluations." In *2004–2005 FATF Annual Report*. http://www1.oecd.org/fatf/TerFinance_en.htm.

FATF. 2008. "Terrorist financing," February 29. http://www.fatf-gafi.org/dataoecd/28/43/40285899.pdf.

Foreign Affairs Canada. 2002. "Terrorist financing," July 4. http://www.dfait-maeci. gc.ca/internationalcrime/financing_terrorism-en.asp.

George, Barbara C., and Kathleen A. Lacey. 2003. "Crackdown on money launder- ing: A comparative analysis of the feasibility and effectiveness of domestic and multilateral policy reforms." *Northwestern Journal of International Law and Business.*

HM Treasury. 2007. "The financial challenge to crime and terrorism," February.

IMF and World Bank. 2001. "Enhancing contributions to combating money launder- ing," April 26.

IMF and World Bank. 2003. "Twelve month pilot program of anti-money laundering and combating the financing of terrorism (AML/CTF) assessments and deliv- ery of AML/CTF technical assistance," March 31.

Interpol. 2003. "The links between intellectual property crime and terrorist financ- ing," July 16. http://www.interpol.com/Public/ICPO/speeches/SG20030716.asp.

Jacobson, Michael. 2007a. "Combating terrorism financing in Europe: Gradual prog- ress," The Washington Institute for Near East Policy, *PolicyWatch*, 1213 (March 26).

Jacobson, Michael. 2007b. "Grading U.S. performance against terrorism financing," The Washington Institute for Near East Policy, *PolicyWatch*, 1280 (September 5).

Kiser, Steve. 2005. "Financing terror: An analysis and simulation for affecting al-Qae- da's financial infrastructure," RAND Corporation.

KPMG. 2004. "Canada remains attractive haven for money laundering/terrorist activities," September 20. http://www.kpmg.ca/en/news/pr20040920.html.

Latimer, Paul. 2004. "Bank secrecy in Australia: Terrorism legislation as the new exception to the Tournier rule." *Journal of Money Laundering Control* 8: 56–65.

Mintz, John. 2004. "Muslim charity, officials indicted; Funding groups with Hamas ties at issue." *Washington Post*, July 28.

Molander, Roger C., David A. Mussington, and Peter A. Wilson. 1998. *Cyberpayments and money laundering: Problems and promise.* Santa Monica, CA: RAND.

Moneylaundering.com. n.d. "Money laundering." http://www.moneylaundering. com/freeresources/mldefinition.aspx.

Moneylaundering.com. 2008. "Court ruling may more closely tie tax evasion and money laundering charges," July 9.

Morais, Herbert. 2002. "The war against money laundering, terrorism and the financ- ing of terrorism." *Lawasia*, 25.

New York Times. 2004. "UN seeks tighter sanctions as Qaeda skirts money controls," August 31, A7.

Norgren, Claes. 2004. "The control of risks associated with crime, terror and subver- sion." *Journal of Money Laundering Control* 7: 201–206.

OECD. 1999. "Money laundering." *OECD Policy Brief*, 3.

OECD. 2000. "Name and shame can work for money laundering." *OECD Observer* (October). http://www.oecdobserver.org/news/fullstory.php/ aid/358/%93Name_and_shame%94_can_work_for_money_laundering.html.

Olson, Dean T. 2007. "Financing terror." *FBI Law Enforcement Bulletin*, February. http://www.au.af.mil/au/awc/awcgate/fbi/financing_terror.pdf.

Passas, Nikos. 2003. "Informal value transfer systems, terrorism and money launder- ing," November. http://www.ncjrs.gov/pdffiles1/nij/grants/208301.pdf.

Paz, R. 2000. "Targeting terrorist financing in the Middle East." Paper presented at the International Conference on Countering Terrorism through Enhanced International Cooperation, Courmayeur Mont Blanc, Italy, September 22–24.

PCMag.com. 2010. "Hacker hit with 20-year prison sentence," March 26. http://www.pcmag.com/article2/0,2817,2361854,00.asp.

Rettig, Charles, and Edward Robbins, Jr. 2005. "Structuring transactions and currency violations: The 'tax crime' of the future." *Tax Practice and Procedure* 7, 1 (February/March).

Rosett, Claudia. 2004. "Oil-for-terror." *Wall Street Journal*, April 28, A.16; *Washington Post*, July 28, A.01.

Sinason, David, Carl Pacini, and William Hillson. 2003. "The internal auditor's role in fighting terrorist financing." *Internal Auditing* 18, 2: 11–19.

Sunday Times. 2004. "High street fraud raises millions for terrorism," November 25.

Times of India. 2010. "Kashmir terrorists get pay hike," May 17.

UNODC. n.d. "The money laundering cycle." http://www.unodc.org/unodc/en/money_laundering_cycle.html.

U.S. Department of State. 2001. "Patterns of global terrorism—2000," April 30. http://www.state.gov/s/ct/rls/pgtrpt/2000/2441.htm.

U.S. Department of State. 2004. "Patterns of global terrorism—2003," April 29. http://www.state.gov/s/ct/rls/pgtrpt/2003/31644.htm.

Walter, Ingo. 1990. *The secret money market: Inside the dark world of tax evasion, financial fraud, insider trading, money laundering, and capital flight.* New York: Harper & Row, Ballinger Division.

Waszak, John. 2004. "The obstacles to suppressing radical Islamic terrorist financing." *Case Western Review Journal of International Law* 36 (2/3): 673–710.

Wolfsberg Group. n.d. "Global banks: global standards." http://www.wolfsberg-principles.com/.

Wolosky, L., and Stephen Heifetz. 2002. "Regulating terrorism." *Law and Policy in International Business* (Fall).

World Bank n.d. Available online: http://web.worldbank.org/WBSITE/EXTERNAL/TOPICS/EXTFINANCIALSECTOR/0,,contentMDK:21996325~menuPK:6115645~pagePK:210058~piPK:210062~theSitePK:282885,00.html

Zagaris, Bruce. 2002. "The merging of the counter-terrorism and anti-money laundering regimes." *Law and Policy in International Business* 34, 1 (Fall): 45.

How Financial Crime Is Committed
The Transfer of Funds

3

It is notable how terrorism and its financing have been linked to capitalism and the opening of markets around the world.

> Privatization, deregulation, openness, the free movement of labor and capital, technological advances—all hailed as key ingredients of economic success in the last 20 years—have been exploited by and adapted into the terror economy in a macabre form of geo-political ju-jitsu: the very strengths of legitimate economies have been turned into double-edged swords. The irony is that the new economy of terror is a product of globalization, particularly of the globalization that emerged after the fall of the Berlin Wall. Globalization allowed non-state entities to promote a variety of liberal causes, social changes and economic advancement but has also facilitated the networking of terrorist movements such as al-Qaida and the growing sophistication of the "terror economy" (Napoleoni 2003).

The size of this economy is estimated at $500 billion, with a sizeable contribution from legitimate sources as described in the previous chapter.

> A further irony is that many of the states the terror economy seeks to displace are themselves the source, directly or indirectly, of arms, logistics, refuge and finance for terror groups. The U.S. dollar, the world's reserve currency, is the new economy of terror's main currency. Western and, more recently, Islamic banks are the vehicles through which this currency is transacted. Small, informal, legitimate businesses are often the agents (Napoleoni 2003).

Funds used for terrorism-related activity are sometimes moved through the banking system (and savings and investment houses such as brokerage houses, insurance companies, mutual funds, and other investment companies that operate along similar lines) or wire. There are also alternative means for transfer of funds such as informal value-transfer systems, charities, commodities, international trade, prepaid cards, the Internet, digital currency, cash couriers, and real estate. This chapter unravels all of these methods with the help of case studies.

Financial Institutions

Financial criminals use banks to transfer funds through legitimate accounts, dormant accounts, telegraphic transfers, and money service businesses. Table 3.1 provides a detailed explanation of how financial criminals use these accounts.

While it is difficult to estimate the amount of money moved through the banking system to finance terrorism, evidence suggests the need to strengthen regulatory and procedural guidelines to deal with the problem. In light of this, both the public and private sectors have attempted to enforce measures that will result in banks being more vigilant in detecting and reporting suspicious activity. The thrust for banking reform to counter the financing of terrorism has come from three main endeavors: the Basel Committee, the Wolfsberg Group, and individual government efforts. Established in 1974, the Basel Committee is a group of representatives from central banks and banking authorities from these countries: Argentina, Australia, Belgium, Brazil, Canada, China, France, Germany, Hong Kong SAR, India, Indonesia, Italy, Japan, Korea, Luxembourg, Mexico, the Netherlands, Russia, Saudi Arabia, Singapore, South Africa, Spain, Sweden, Switzerland, Turkey, the United Kingdom, and the United States. The task of this committee is to create standards and guidelines, and a set of best practices for member nations to establish in their respective jurisdictions (Bank for International Settlements n.d.). In the context of counterterrorist financing, the committee issued a report, "Customer Due Diligence for Banks," in October 2001, which was

Table 3.1   Types of Bank Accounts

Legitimate accounts: There are instances where individuals have had a number of accounts with different banks. Accounts with one bank are to be used for domestic purposes, receiving salaries and benefits, while those at another bank are for business purposes. The latter accounts will receive money transfers and check payments.

Dormant accounts: Accounts with small balances can be held with a number of banks, with the intention of activating them when funds are required, e.g., for the purchase of terrorist material. They will then be emptied fairly quickly by a series of cash withdrawals. Dormant accounts have also been used as the basis for obtaining bank loans not subsequently repaid.

Telegraphic transfers: Certain wire companies are said to be used in preference to others. The key factors appear to be the ease of sending and receiving money, the extent to which documentation is required, and the location of the outlet.

Money service businesses: *Bureaux de change*, money changers, and other dealers in foreign currency are often a channel for funds, with funds often passing through several jurisdictions before they reach their final destination.

Source: Guideline notes issued by the U.K. Joint Money Laundering Steering Group (JMLSG), December 2001.

reinforced in 2003 by a "General Guide" that outlined the following elements (Bank for International Settlements):

- Customer acceptance policy
- Customer identification
- Ongoing monitoring of higher risk accounts
- Risk management

The private sector has been just as active through the efforts of the Wolfsberg Group, which comprises 12 prominent banks around the world, namely, ABN Amro Bank N.V. (the Netherlands); Santander Central Hispano, S.A. (Spain); Bank of Tokyo Mitsubishi, Ltd. (Japan); Barclays (United Kingdom); Citigroup (United States); Credit Suisse Group (Switzerland); Deutsche Bank AG (Germany); Goldman Sachs (United States); HSBC (China); J. P. Morgan Chase (United States); Societé Generale (France); and UBS AG (Switzerland). In 2000, this group released a set of compliance norms known as the Wolfsberg Principles that engage banks in identifying account holders' true identities and the sources of their funds as well as monitoring accounts for suspicious transactions or patterns (Anonymous 2001).

The philosophy behind the Wolfsberg Principles is encompassed in guidelines and legislation aimed at the financial services sector in the many countries involved in the antiterrorism fight. The Financial Services Authority (FSA) in the United Kingdom published a consultation paper "Reviewing the FSA Handbook" right after the London bombings that is expected to take the fight against financial crime to a higher level (Financial Services Authority 2005). With Consultation Paper 142, "Operational Risk Systems and Controls," the FSA established a framework for risk management and compliance for financial services in the United Kingdom (Haynes 2004). In the United States, Sections 314 and 326 of the USA PATRIOT Act of 2001 (which fortifies the Bank Secrecy Act) lay down specific requirements for banks. Section 314 calls for banks to inspect their client records for suspected terrorists and money launderers forwarded to them by law enforcement agencies. Section 326 requires banks to be more diligent in obtaining client identification as part of the new "know your customer" (KYC) policy requirement (Anonymous 2004). Australia passed similar legislation in the form of Resolution 1373 in September 2001 and the Suppression of the Financing of Terrorism Act of 2002 (Latimer 2004).

An emerging issue in financial crime with respect to banking is the misuse of correspondent banking relationships. Correspondent banking involves one bank entering into an agreement with another bank to provide services such as moving funds, exchanging currencies and carrying out other financial transactions. It is possible that one of these banks is engaged in or has clients who are engaged in criminal activity, "shell banks, offshore banks,

Table 3.2   Examples of Financial Crime through Correspondent Banking

The following types of financial crime associated with correspondent banking have been documented:

- Laundering illicit proceeds and facilitating crime by accepting deposits or processing wire transfers involving funds that the high-risk foreign bank knew or should have known were associated with drug trafficking, financial fraud, or other wrongdoing
- Conducting high-yield investment scams by convincing investors to wire-transfer funds to the correspondent account to earn high returns, and then refusing to return any monies to the defrauded investors
- Conducting advance-fee-for-loan scams by requiring loan applicants to wire-transfer large fees to the correspondent account, retaining the fees, and then failing to issue the loans
- Facilitating tax evasion by accepting client deposits, commingling them with other funds in the foreign bank's correspondent account, and encouraging clients to rely on bank and corporate secrecy laws in the foreign bank's home jurisdiction to shield the funds from U.S. tax authorities
- Facilitating Internet gambling, illegal under U.S. law, by using the correspondent account to accept and transfer gambling proceeds

Source: L. Gustitus, Elise Bean, and Robert Roach, "Correspondent Banking: A Gateway for Money Laundering," *Economic Perspectives*, May 2001.

and banks in jurisdictions with weak anti-money-laundering controls [that] carry high money laundering risks. Because these high-risk foreign banks typically have limited resources and staff and operate outside their licensing jurisdiction, they use their correspondent banking accounts to conduct their banking operations" (Gustitus, Bean, and Roach 2001). Table 3.2 presents a brief description of the types of financial crime that are committed through correspondent banking.

In the United States, the failure of banks to perform due diligence of their corresponding partners has increased their exposure to financial crime risk.

High-risk foreign banks that are denied their own correspondent accounts at U.S. banks can obtain the same access to the U.S. financial system by opening correspondent accounts at a foreign bank that already has a U.S. bank account. U.S. banks have largely ignored or failed to address the money laundering risks associated with "nested" correspondent banking (Gustitus, Bean, and Roach 2001).

Wire Transfers

As governments clamp down on the banking system from being misused by financial criminals, other means of transferring funds for terrorism have become prominent. Wire transfers are one such tactic. Box 3.1 provides an example of how this is accomplished.

> ### BOX 3.1 FINANCIAL CRIME PROCEEDS MOVED THROUGH WIRE TRANSFERS
>
> **CASE STUDY**
>
> A terrorist organization in Country X was observed using bank wire transfers to move money in Country Y that was eventually used to pay the rent for safe houses, buy and sell vehicles, and purchase electronic components with which to construct explosive devices. The organization used "bridge" or "conduit" accounts in Country X as a means of moving funds between countries. The accounts, at both ends, were opened in the names of people with no apparent association with the structure of a terrorist organization but who were linked to one another by kinship or similar ties. Thus these apparent family connections could provide a justification for the transfers between them, if necessary.
>
> Funds, mainly in the form of cash deposits by the terrorist organization, were deposited into bank accounts from which the transfers were made. Once the money was received at the destination, the holder either left it on deposit or invested it in mutual funds, where it remained hidden and available for the organization's future needs. Alternatively, the money was transferred to other bank accounts managed by the organization's correspondent financial manager, from where it was distributed to pay for the purchase of equipment and material or to cover other ad hoc expenses incurred by the organization in its clandestine activities.
>
> *Source*: **"Terrorist Financing," Financial Action Task Force, February 29, 2008a.**

It is noteworthy that the 9/11 hijackers wired more than $130,000 in funds to finance their operations (Swartz 2005). While systems in Australia and Canada are considered efficient for collecting information for the detection of suspicious activity through wire transfers, the viability of having a similar system in the U.S. has been under a lengthy process of study. This is due to the sheer volume of international transfers to the United States and the limited resources available at the disposal of the U.S. government (Blackwell 2005).

Financial Instruments—Securities

Financial criminals misuse securities in a number of ways in order to move funds for terrorism. They can raise capital by offering shares of a company

BOX 3.2   FINANCIAL CRIME PROCEEDS MOVED THROUGH FINANCIAL SECURITIES

Offence:	Money laundering
Securities-related predicate offence (if any):	N/A
Jurisdiction:	Israel
Subject:	Individual
Instruments, methods, and techniques:	Front companies, publicly traded shares of a shell company
Indicators:	Use of a public shell company (traded on the stock exchange)
	Use of a front company/straw man to perform the acquisition
	Transferring funds through several accounts
	Use of a money services business (MSB) to transfer funds
	Withdrawing the funds shortly after the acquisition by means of loans and then transferring funds to the same MSB

SUSPICIOUS TRANSACTION/ACTIVITY REPORT INFORMATION

The FIU received an STR from a bank regarding D, a man in his 20s with a student account. The STR stated that D bought a controlling interest in public shell Company X and then proceeded to open a bank account in the name of that company. A few days later, the account received a deposit of approximately USD 2.5 million.

CASE DESCRIPTION

In addition to Company X, D was also the sole owner of a private Company, Y. D used Company Y to purchase a controlling interest in Company X through the over-the-counter (OTC) market. Part of the USD 2.5 million that was credited to Company X was derived from a Company Y account. Company Y received large deposits from several private accounts managed by criminal entities involved in drug trafficking. In one case, the funds were transferred from the person known to be involved in criminal activity through an MSB account to the account of Company X to further distance the source of the funds. The new controlling owners appointed new directors, including family members.

Shortly after the USD 2.5 million was transferred to the account of Company X, it was transferred back to the MSB account. Some of the money was transferred as a loan to Company W, which was associated with the same criminal organization that originally transferred funds to Company Y.

D and his family were well known to the FIU for having acquired public shell companies in the past for money-laundering purposes, including committing other predicate offenses. They were also suspected of fraudulently influencing the movement of the stock share prices of companies owned by them, performing circular transfers of funds, and fraudulently removing funds from the companies.

Source: **"Money Laundering and Terrorist Financing in the Securities Sector," Financial Action Task Force, October 2009.**

where they previously invested their criminal proceeds. They can set up their own investment firms to raise and transfer finances, or they can set up multiple trading accounts to do so. They can use brokerage houses as an intermediary to shift funds from one account to another in different countries, or they can use derivates markets. Due to the high level of liquidity and trading volume involved, it is difficult to trace the source of funds back to the criminals. Corruption of this kind in securities markets is often accompanied by graft, intimidation, and violence against industry participants, unfair competition, investor losses, and an erosion of market integrity and investor confidence. A rise in electronic and private trading, the ease of accessing capital markets all over the world, and the increasingly deregulated nature of the capital markets make these markets increasingly vulnerable to fraud and money laundering (Schneider 2005). Box 3.2 shows how.

A subject of increased debate with regard to financial crime through securities is the regulation of hedge funds. Hedge funds are open for investment usually only to wealthy investors who are exposed to the higher risk but stand to gain from the potentially high returns these investments have to offer. Governments see them as a possible conduit for financial crime, as the account holders' identities are not always known to the investment company. Any new regulation in this area would focus on identifying the client, determining that the client is not a front for someone else, and reporting suspicious activity to the government (Andrews 2002). The issue in the case of hedge funds has been how to regulate them, since the majority of them are offshore (Financial Services Authority 2003). In jurisdictions such as the United States, the debate has been about who should regulate them (Der Hovanesian and Kopecki 2006).

Insurance

Life insurance companies provide a vehicle for financial criminals to clean dirty money through insurance payouts. These criminals can also borrow clean funds against life insurance policies that have been taken out using money earned through illegal means. Additionally, they can exchange dirty money for clean money via annuity contracts that pay out an immediate or deferred income flow (U.S. Department of the Treasury 2005). Box 3.3 discusses an example of life insurance policies bought with drug money in order to clean it.

While insurance companies may have anti-money-laundering (AML) procedures in place, they still face the risk of being exploited for financial crime. This is because those responsible for selling their policies are not always employed directly by them, which might make enforcement difficult. Secondly, the purchaser of the policy might not be the beneficiary, making it difficult for the company to abide by KYC protocols. The involvement of multiple parties and the complicated nature of the business leave the door open for financial criminals to take advantage of the vulnerabilities of the insurance sector (U.S. Department of the Treasury 2005). Box 3.4 describes one such case.

Authorities fear that terrorist financers, like money launderers, might exploit the insurance sector to move money (Lichtblau 2002).

Informal Fund Transfer (IFT) System

The most common type of IFT is known as *hawala*. It is a legitimate remittance system used around the world that serves as an alternative to formal banking. It is based more on the use of connections in the form of family ties or acquaintances, and transactions often take place based on trust rather than the use of a negotiable instrument. It is conducted through a series of steps as depicted in Figure 3.1.

The advantage for the user of choosing *hawala* over traditional methods to transfer funds is that it is less costly (in avoiding charges imposed by banks for changing currency) and more efficient than sending a bank draft or sending money through an international wire transfer (Interpol General Secretariat n.d.). At the same time, it has gained notoriety for being the preferred method for the transfer of funds for illegal activities such as terrorism because it does not leave a paper trail. Some reports have even claimed

BOX 3.3 FINANCIAL CRIME PROCEEDS MOVED THROUGH INSURANCE POLICIES

CASE STUDY

A number of insurance companies, domiciled in the Isle of Man and the Bailiwick of Guernsey, were identified through information received in a narcotics smuggling investigation as having numerous policies that were paid for with drug proceeds. It was determined that narcotics proceeds were deposited into life insurance policies over a substantial period of time prior to 2001. These policies were primarily established by one master broker who operated in Colombia and other South American jurisdictions. Funds were credited to the policies that were identified as containing drug proceeds in several ways. First, and most common, were via third-party wire transfers. These wire transfers often originated from money brokers or *casas de cambio*. In many instances, one bulk wire transfer was sent to the institution on the order of the broker. Once credited to the institution's account, the broker provided detailed information of how to break up the wire and which accounts to credit the funds. The insurer also received payments via third-party checks and structured money orders (to avoid reporting thresholds). Finally, some policies were paid with funds from the commission accounts of the brokers. In this scenario, the brokers accepted cash from the client in Colombia and credited the client's policy with funds from his business operating account or as a piece of his commission check.

Source: **"Money Laundering and Terrorist Financing Typologies 2004–2005," Financial Action Task Force, June 10, 2005.**

that *hawala* was used to funnel money to finance the September 11 attacks (Simpson 2001).

Hawala (Middle East) has different names in different parts of the world: *hue* (Vietnam), *fei-ch'ien* (China), *phei kwan* (Thailand), *hundi* (South Asia), *hui kuan* (Hong Kong), or *cambistas*.

In the Dominican Republic there is a nationwide network of *"cambistas."*[*] These are money changers who operate outside the licensed, regulated money

---

[*] According to a 2010 update, "The Dominican Superintendent of Banks recently took action to shut down the illegal cambistas and has imposed new restrictions on the banks and Agentes de Cambio that support or supported the cambista entities" (LAC expert 2010).

BOX 3.4   FINANCIAL CRIME PROCEEDS MOVED THROUGH INSURANCE COMPANIES

CASE STUDY

In the Russian Federation, a group of persons with interests in home construction effected a payment in favor of construction Company A under contracts connected with their participation in investment construction (at cost price).

Insurance Company P accepted possible financial risks to these contracts under a contract of financial risks insurance and received an insurance premium. At the same time, the insurance Company P entered into a secret agreement with construction Company A providing that the difference between the market cost of housing and the cost price would be transferred in favor of the insurance company as a premium under the contract of financial risks insurance.

When the funds were received by the insurance Company P, they were transferred as an insurance premium under the general reinsurance contract in favor of insurance Company X. By way of fictitious service contracts and commission payments made under an agency contract, insurance Company X channeled the funds to several offshore shell firms. Beneficiaries of the actual profit, being withdrawn abroad, were the owners and directors of the construction Company A.

Source: **"Money Laundering and Terrorist Financing Typologies 2004–2005," Financial Action Task Force, June 10, 2005.**

services business system. There are many licensed *Agentes de Cambio* in the Dominican Republic that are licensed, regulated, have strong AML programs, file currency reports and suspicious activity reports. The *Agentes de Cambio* operate under Dominican Regulations that parallel the AML Program requirements of U.S. money services businesses and include written policies and procedures (that must be approved by the Superintendent of Banks), a designated compliance officer, an independent review of their program, and ongoing training. The *cambistas* operate the same way but without the licensing, regulatory structure, etc. The government knows this but takes no action to shut them down. As a result, there is a black market system that is out of control; it caters to narcotics money and corruption. Many believe the lawmakers have a financial interest in ensuring these *cambistas* stay in business (LAC expert 2010).

While it is difficult to measure the amount of money moved through the global *hawala* network, some economists estimate this amount to be

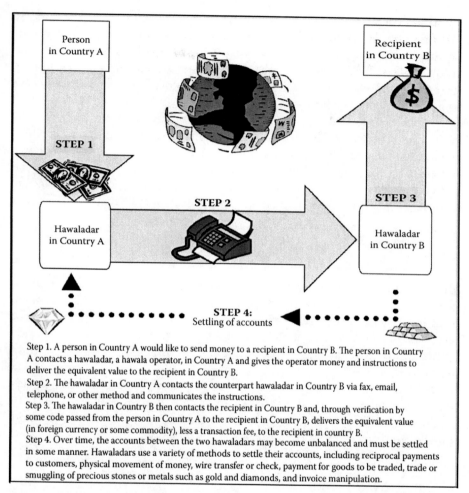

Step 1. A person in Country A would like to send money to a recipient in Country B. The person in Country A contacts a hawaladar, a hawala operator, in Country A and gives the operator money and instructions to deliver the equivalent value to the recipient in Country B.

Step 2. The hawaladar in Country A contacts the counterpart hawaladar in Country B via fax, email, telephone, or other method and communicates the instructions.

Step 3. The hawaladar in Country B then contacts the recipient in Country B and, through verification by some code passed from the person in Country A to the recipient in Country B, delivers the equivalent value (in foreign currency or some commodity), less a transaction fee, to the recipient in country B.

Step 4. Over time, the accounts between the two hawaladars may become unbalanced and must be settled in some manner. Hawaladars use a variety of methods to settle their accounts, including reciprocal payments to customers, physical movement of money, wire transfer or check, payment for goods to be traded, trade or smuggling of precious stones or metals such as gold and diamonds, and invoice manipulation.

Figure 3.1 Steps in informal fund transfers. Steps Involved In a Typical Hawala Transaction. (GAO-04-163: U.S. Agencies Should Systematically Assess Terrorists' Use of Alternative Financing Mechanisms, 2003.)

around $100 billion (Peters 2009, 170). It is believed that much of the dirty portion of this money is moved within the Afghanistan-Pakistan region. The drug money moved through *hawala* in the two Afghan towns of Helmand and Kandahar alone accounts for more than $1 billion. Interestingly, (1) of the money moved through the Pakistani *hawala* system, one-third is related to drugs; (2) the money being remitted into Pakistan via *hawala* is eight times the amount remitted through banks there; and (3) capital flight from Pakistan totals $100 billion. Both, Afghanistan and Pakistan are in the middle of a campaign to register *hawaladars* (the facilitators of *hawala* transactions) and establish ways to identify those who use this system (Weiss 2005).

It has been suggested that making the formal banking system easy to use (by, for example, eliminating high transaction costs and long transaction processing times) would deter people from turning to IFTs to move funds. As one study reports, "Prescribing regulations alone, especially where developing, unstable, and post-conflict countries lack regulatory capacity, will not serve as a panacea for possible abuse of the IFT systems. In that regard, regulators must have appropriate supervisory capacity to enforce regulations. ... (ITFs) cannot be completely eliminated through criminal proceedings and prohibition orders" (Zagaris 2007). While government campaigns to register *hawala* dealers must continue, they must be proactive in addressing weaknesses in the banking sector at the same time. In some countries, this may be impacted by the level of economic development and political stability (Zagaris 2007).

Charity

The crackdown on the funding of terrorist activity after September 11, 2001, has led to the United States and foreign governments identifying charities, both inside and outside the United States, as vehicles for the movement of terrorism funds (Francis 2004). Sometimes this involves the misuse of funds within legitimate charities to commit financial crime. Box 3.5 is a case study of how this is done.

Misuse of charities to commit financial crime could also involve the setting up of sham charities. Box 3.6 provides a case study of this.

In a third case, a terrorist network could set up a charity to raise and transfer funds in support of its cause.

Commodities

Terrorists move funds through commodities that are relatively liquid, easy to conceal, and not subject to standard financial reporting requirements. Commodities that can be smuggled because of the ease in concealing them are also used for this purpose (U.S. GAO 2003). Some of these commodities include gold, illicit drugs, weapons, cigarettes, and precious stones. Box 3.7 and Box 3.8 show how financial criminals use the latter to move funds.

Terrorists also use honey businesses to move funds. Reports suggest that members of the terrorist group al-Qaeda started moving funds through commodities instead of banks when the U.S. government froze $220 million worth of gold deposited in the Federal Reserve system by Taliban and al-Qaeda operatives post-9/11 (Farah and Schultz 2004). On record is the fact that Osama bin Laden used a network of honey stores for the purpose of raising money and smuggling contraband (BBC 2001).

BOX 3.5   FINANCIAL CRIME PROCEEDS MOVED THROUGH LEGITIMATE CHARITIES

CASE STUDY

In Belgium, a suspicious transaction report (STR) was made following an attempt by Individual A to deposit substantial amounts of cash into the account of a charity—over which he had power-of-attorney—with the instruction that it be transferred onward to a notary as an advance for the purchase of real estate.

The investigation revealed that

- Payments into the account consisted of multiple cash deposits (presumably donations) but also payments directly from the account of Individual A. In turn, A's personal account revealed multiple cash deposits that corresponded to donations from private individuals.
- The debit transactions consisted of transfers to the nonprofit organization (NPO) and international transfers to Individual B. Police sources revealed that A had links with individuals that were known for terrorist activities, including B.
- Law enforcement assessed that the charity, which continued to fulfill an important social function, was being exploited both as a front to raise funds and as a means of transmission to divert a portion of them to known terrorist associates of A.

COMMENTARY

This case is indicative of the vulnerabilities to exploitation that arise with weak governance combined with high levels of cash deposits.

Source: **"Terrorist Financing," Financial Action Task Force, February 29, 2008a.**

International Trade

Governments have begun addressing how to close the back door to prevent terrorists from manipulating the international trade system to commit financial crime. While it is difficult to measure the exact amount laundered through international trade, some studies estimate this amount to run in the billions of dollars (U.S. Department of the Treasury 2010). According to one report, the estimated amount of money moved from the United

---

**BOX 3.6   FINANCIAL CRIME PROCEEDS
MOVED THROUGH SHAM CHARITIES**

CASE STUDY

An NPO with an office in Russia came to the attention of the authorities through the submission of STRs by credit institutions on an apparent discrepancy between the stated objectives of the NPO and its actual expenditure. The NPO was also known to have a poor history of reporting to the authorities on tax issues.

An investigation revealed that funds were being transferred from the NPO to apparently fictitious or shell entities and then being withdrawn in cash for onward transmission to illegal armed militants.

Source: "Terrorist Financing," Financial Action Task Force,
February 29, 2008a.

States to the countries appearing on the U.S. Department of State's watch list was about $4.27 billion in 2001. In the same year, approximately $3.65 billion was moved from the United States to the top five countries on this list. The report suggests that some of this money could be used for funding terrorism (Zdanowicz 2004). Some of the ways in which financial criminals exploit the international trade system to move funds are through over/under invoicing and double invoicing of goods, over/under shipment of goods, and falsely describing goods. Boxes 3.9–3.11 encapsulate a discussion about these through case studies.

Financial criminals have even targeted trade financing which has created certain vulnerabilities for banks that are involved through loans, letters of credit, documentary collections etc. In the United States, the Federal Financial Institutions Examination Council (FFIEC) recommends that banks involved in trade financing be aware of certain red flags, such as a business that ships items not related to its business, etc. (FFIEC n.d.). The Financial Crimes Enforcement Network (FINCEN) has also issued an advisory to financial institutions on filing suspicious activity reports for trade-based money laundering (U.S. Department of the Treasury).

There are a number of detection measures against trade-based financial crime. One practice involves engaging in risk profiling by analyzing a country's trade database. This involves monitoring the following:

- Country Risk Index: an index of the most recent 12-month abnormal pricing history of a country's trading partner nations

BOX 3.7 FINANCIAL CRIME PROCEEDS MOVED THROUGH PRECIOUS METALS

CASE STUDY

During the invasion of Afghanistan in 2001, it was widely reported that the Taliban and members of al-Qaeda smuggled their money out of the country via Pakistan using couriers that handled bars of gold. In Karachi, couriers and *hawala* dealers transferred the money to the Gulf Region, where once again it was converted to gold bullion. It has been estimated that during one three-week period in late November to early December 2001, al-Qaeda transferred USD 10 million in cash and gold out of Afghanistan. An al-Qaeda manual found by British forces in Afghanistan in December 2001 included not only chapters on how to build explosives and clean weapons, but on how to smuggle gold on small boats or conceal it on the body.

Gold is often used by *hawala* brokers to balance their books. *Hawala* dealers also routinely have gold, rather than currency, placed around the globe. Terrorists may store their assets in gold because its value is easy to determine and remains relatively consistent over time. There is always a market for gold given its cultural significance in many areas of the world, such as Southeast Asia, South and Central Asia, the Arabian Peninsula, and North Africa.

Source: **"Terrorist Financing," Financial Action Task Force, February 29, 2008a.**

- Product Risk Index: an index of the most recent 12-month abnormal pricing history of products that pass through the country's borders through trade
- Customs District Risk Index: an index of the most recent 12-month abnormal pricing history of transactions within each customs district of that country

These risk indices, which can be updated monthly, are statistical methodologies intended to assist law enforcement and financial institutions mitigate the risk of financial crime committed through international trade (Zdanowicz 2009).

Another financial crime prevention technique involves data mining. The U.S. Customs supercomputer database, the Numerically Integrated Profiling System (NIPS), kept track of financial crime by helping agents access import and export data. However, it was problematic because customs agents could

BOX 3.8   FINANCIAL CRIME PROCEEDS MOVED THROUGH PRECIOUS STONES

CASE STUDY

The financial intelligence unit (FIU) in Country C received several suspicious transaction reports from different banks concerning two persons and a diamond trading company. The individuals and the company in question were account holders at the various banks. In the space of a few months, a large number of fund transfers to and from overseas were made from the accounts of the two individuals. Moreover, soon after the account was opened, one of the individuals received several USD checks for large amounts.

According to information obtained by the FIU, one of the accounts held by the company appeared to have received large U.S. dollar deposits originating from companies active in the diamond industry. One of the directors of the company, a citizen of Country C but residing in Africa, maintained an account at another bank in Country C. Several transfers had been carried out to and from overseas using this account. The transfers from foreign countries were mainly in U.S. dollars. They were converted into the local currency and were then transferred to foreign countries and to accounts in Country C belonging to one of the two subjects of the suspicious transaction report.

Police information obtained by the FIU revealed that an investigation had already been initiated relating to these individuals and the trafficking of diamonds originating from Africa. The large fund transfers by the diamond trading company were mainly sent to the same person residing in another region. Police sources revealed that this person and the individual that had cashed the checks were suspected of buying diamonds from the rebel army of an African country and then smuggling them into Country C on behalf of a terrorist organization. Further research by the FIU also revealed links between the subjects of the STR and individuals and companies already tied to the laundering of funds for organized crime. This case is currently under investigation.

Source: **"Guidance for Financial Institutions in Detecting Terrorist Financing," Financial Action Task Force, April 24, 2002.**

not access this data in real time, as they depended on Customs headquarters to mail it to them (Lehmkuhler 2003). The alternative is a method that estimates the amount of money shifted out of the United States "based on pricing norms, (interquartile range), as specified in the section 482 regulations of the U.S. Internal Revenue Service (Internal Revenue Service) tax code. The

BOX 3.9   FINANCIAL CRIME PROCEEDS MOVED THROUGH OVER/UNDER INVOICING OF GOODS

CASE STUDY

Company A (a foreign exporter) ships 1 million widgets worth $2 each, but invoices Company B (a colluding domestic importer) for 1 million widgets at a price of only $1 each. Company B pays Company A for the goods by sending a wire transfer for $1 million. Company B then sells the widgets on the open market for $2 million and deposits the extra $1 million (the difference between the invoiced price and the "fair market" value) into a bank account to be disbursed according to Company A's instructions.

Alternatively, Company C (a domestic exporter) ships 1 million widgets worth $2 each, but invoices Company D (a colluding foreign importer) for 1 million widgets at a price of $3 each. Company D pays Company C for the goods by sending a wire transfer for $3 million. Company C then pays $2 million to its suppliers and deposits the remaining $1 million (the difference between the invoiced price and the "fair market" price) into a bank account to be disbursed according to Company D's instructions.

Source: **"Trade Based Money Laundering," Financial Action Task Force, June 23, 2006.**

IRS defines suspicious prices as those import prices that exceed the upper quartile import prices and those export prices that are less than the lower quartile export prices" (Zdanowicz 2004). This deviation could possibly signify income tax avoidance/evasion, money laundering, or terrorist financing. This method is one that can be conducted in real time, which helps in determining which transactions to audit and which cargo shipments to inspect (Zdanowicz 2004).

Besides domestic vigilance of abnormal trade practices, initiatives such as Electronic Data Interchange (EDI) and Trade Transparency Units (TTUs) are deployed to improve information sharing. EDI facilitates the electronic exchange of information among authorities in a standardized format (Financial Action Task Force 2008b). On the other hand, TTUs were set up by U.S. Immigration and Customs Enforcement (ICE), with financial assistance from the Departments of State and Treasury, in Colombia, Brazil, Argentina, and Paraguay. Their purpose was to share trade and financial information to detect money laundering committed

BOX 3.10 FINANCIAL CRIME PROCEEDS MOVED THROUGH OVER/UNDER SHIPMENT OF GOODS

CASE STUDY

Company E (a domestic exporter) sells 1 million widgets to Company F (a colluding foreign importer) at a price of $2 each, but ships 1.5 million widgets. Company F pays Company E for the goods by sending a wire transfer for $2 million. Company F then sells the widgets on the open market for $3 million and deposits the extra $1 million (the difference between the invoiced quantity and the actual quantity) into a bank account to be disbursed according to Company E's instructions.

Alternatively, Company G (a foreign exporter) sells 1 million widgets to Company H (a colluding domestic importer) at a price of $2 each, but only ships 500,000 widgets. Company H pays Company G for the goods by sending a wire transfer for $2 million. Company G then pays $1 million to its suppliers and deposits the remaining $1 million (the difference between the invoiced quantity and the actual quantity) into a bank account to be disbursed according to Company H's instructions.

Source: **"Trade Based Money Laundering," Financial Action Task Force, June 23, 2006.**

by manipulating trade data (U.S. Department of ICE 2006). On the international level, the World Customs Organization (WCO) is at the center of international cooperation in fighting financial crime; it works with partner organizations such as the FATF, Interpol, and Europol (World Customs Organization n.d.).

A widely used method of money laundering in the Americas through international trade is conducted via the Colombian Black Market Peso Exchange (BMPE). It is used by Colombian drug traffickers through a series of steps to avoid the risk of smuggling bulk currency across international borders (U.S. Department of State 2003). Table 3.3 goes through these steps, while Box 3.12 provides a case study.

Financial criminals also take advantage of free trade zones (FTZs) where customs controls tend to be relaxed. Due to this, FTZs remain ripe with the possibility of exploitation for moving terrorist funds. Box 3.13 describes this further.

Government agencies in the United States and Colombia actively seek to counter these methods, which are generally used by importers to pay their international debts using drug money. The IRS-CI has a number of programs

BOX 3.11   FINANCIAL CRIME PROCEEDS MOVED THROUGH FALSELY DESCRIBED GOODS

CASE STUDY

Company I (a domestic exporter) ships 1 million gold widgets worth $3 each to Company J (a colluding foreign importer), but invoices Company J for 1 million silver widgets worth $2 each. Company J pays Company I for the goods by sending a wire transfer for $2 million. Company J then sells the gold widgets on the open market for $3 million and deposits the extra $1 million (the difference between the invoice value and the actual value) into a bank account to be disbursed according to Company I's instructions.

Alternatively, Company K (a foreign exporter) ships 1 million bronze widgets worth $1 each to Company L (a colluding domestic importer), but invoices Company L for 1 million silver widgets worth $2 each. Company L pays Company K for the goods by sending a wire transfer of $2 million. Company K then pays $1 million to its suppliers and deposits the remaining $1 million (the difference between the invoiced value and the actual value) into a bank account to be disbursed according to Company L's instructions.

Source: **"Trade Based Money Laundering," Financial Action Task Force, June 23, 2006.**

like the Illegal Source Financial Crimes Program and the Narcotics Related Financial Crimes Program. Along with other agencies, like the ICE Agency and the Drug Enforcement Administration, "(it) seeks to disrupt a trade-based money laundering methodology that aims to legitimize the proceeds of narcotics trafficking by exchanging funds for trade items often found in the untaxed underground economy" (U.S. Department of State 2003).

Offshore Tax Havens and Financial Centers

A tax haven is a country that

> provides a no-tax or low-tax environment. In some offshore jurisdictions, the reduced tax regime is aimed towards entities organized in the country with all operations occurring outside the country. These countries seek to encourage investment and make up revenue losses by charging a variety of fees for the start up of the entity and on an annual basis (U.S. IRS n.d.).

Table 3.3   Steps Involved in a Black Market Peso Exchange

The mechanics of a simple black market peso arrangement can be set out in the following steps:

- First, the Colombian drug cartel smuggles illegal drugs into the United States and sells them for cash.
- Second, the drug cartel arranges to sell the U.S. dollars, at a discount, to a peso broker for Colombian pesos.
- Third, the peso broker pays the drug cartel with pesos from his bank account in Colombia (which eliminates the drug cartel from any further involvement in the arrangement).
- Fourth, the peso broker structures or "smurfs" the U.S. currency into the U.S. banking system to avoid reporting requirements and consolidates this money in his U.S. bank account.
- Fifth, the peso broker identifies a Colombian importer that needs U.S. dollars to purchase goods from a U.S. exporter.
- Sixth, the peso broker arranges to pay the U.S. exporter (on behalf of the Colombian importer) from his U.S. bank account.
- Seventh, the U.S. exporter ships the goods to Colombia.
- Finally, the Colombian importer sells the goods (often high-value items such as personal computers, consumer electronics, and household appliances) for pesos and repays the peso broker. This replenishes the peso broker's supply of pesos.

Source: Financial Action Task Force, "Trade Based Money Laundering," June 23, 2006.

Funds channeled through tax havens for possible financing of terrorism and related activities have received special attention from international organizations like the Organization for Economic Cooperation and Development (OECD), which publishes a list of Uncooperative Tax Havens. OECD principles are not enforced on countries but by choosing to cooperate, they commit to transparency of operations and the exchange of information resulting in a more coordinated effort to counter financial crime (Owens 2002). Box 3.14 draws an example of steps financial criminals take in using tax havens to move funds.

Offshore financial centers (OFCs) and shell corporations are often mentioned in association with tax havens. When referring to a country, OFC

means a jurisdiction that offers financial secrecy laws in an effort to attract investment from outside its borders. When referring to a financial institution, "offshore" refers to a financial institution that primarily offers its services to persons domiciled outside the jurisdiction of the country in which the financial institution is organized (U.S. IRS n.d.).

A shell corporation refers to

limited liability companies and other business entities with no significant assets or ongoing business activities. Although publicly traded shell companies can

BOX 3.12   FINANCIAL CRIME PROCEEDS MOVED THROUGH BLACK MARKET PESO EXCHANGE

CASE STUDY

This case involved criminal structures operating in Colombia, Central and South America, Europe, Asia, the Middle East, Mexico, and the United States. The investigation uncovered multi-ton quantities of cocaine being shipped to various locations worldwide and uncovered a massive Colombian/Lebanese drug trafficking and money laundering cell operating globally with direct links to the Islamic extremist organization Hezbollah in Lebanon. A portion of the drug proceeds sold in the Middle East was directed to Hezbollah leaders operating in Lebanon to ensure that the traffickers could operate in certain areas in the Middle East.

The network also had a central money laundering operation based in Country I's Asian-based commodities trade. The network utilized Asian-based financial institutions and trading companies to launder in excess of USD 15 million monthly in narcotics proceeds to Colombia via the black market peso exchange (BMPE). Proceeds were sent to Country I–based business accounts that were controlled by Colombian business owners who would purchase the currency from peso brokers and ship the goods to South America. Traffickers would receive the money up front or subsequent to the sale of goods. The network was able to funnel narcotics proceeds through Country I back to Colombia to the drug trafficking source. A number of businesses in the Colon Free Zone (CFZ) in Panama participated in this scheme, and the zone was a central point of delivery for bulk cash proceeds of drugs.

There was also a related BMPE scheme based in Miami. Electronics companies in Miami would accept drug money from U.S. bank accounts and purchase computer and electronics parts that were shipped to Colombia. The Colombian business owner would sell the parts and transfer the proceeds to the trafficker less a commission.

Transactions between companies in the zone as well as import and export records are maintained on paper, and the CFZ administration and Panamanian customs systems are therefore not integrated, making it very difficult for accurate and up-to-date tracking of shipments in the zone. The lack of transparency of transactions taking place in the zone makes it very difficult to track shipments to and from the zone as well as between companies in the zone, particularly given the size of the CFZ. The zone administrator is currently in the process of updating the system to require companies within the zone to file transactions electronically, and there is also a plan for this to be integrated with the customs system.

Some businesses in the CFZ routinely accept large volumes of cash for wholesale quantities of merchandise. The presence of financial institutions including banks and money services businesses provides further opportunity for the integration of cash into the financial system. Within the CFZ, filing cash transaction reports (CTRs) and suspicious transaction reports (STRs) is required of all businesses; however the practice of filing is not enforced, and customers paying in cash for goods in the zone are not subject to any customer due-diligence procedures. All STRs and CTRs filed in the zone go first to the zone administrator, who forwards them on to the financial intelligence unit.

Source: **"Money Laundering Vulnerabilities of Free Trade Zones,"**
Financial Action Task Force, March 2010.

be used for illicit purposes, the vulnerability of the shell company is greatly compounded when it is privately held and beneficial ownership can more easily be obscured or hidden. Lack of transparency of beneficial ownership can be a desirable characteristic for some legitimate uses of shell companies, but it is also a serious vulnerability that can make some shell companies ideal vehicles for money laundering and other illicit financial activity (U.S. Department of the Treasury 2006).

Box 3.15 explains this with the help of a case study (U.S. Department of the Treasury 2006).

Besides the OECD, another international organization active in this regard is the International Monetary Fund (IMF), which oversees the OFC assessment program.* This program evaluates the compliance by OFCs to international standards against financial crime (Morais 2002).

A report from the Bureau for International Narcotics and Law Enforcement Affairs of the U.S. Department of State (1998) offered the following thoughts on tackling financial crime committed via OFCs:

We should be moving towards an international system where "offshore" means the same as "onshore," requiring the same regulations, the same access to records, the same law enforcement. Over time, jurisdictions that continue to offer under-regulated "offshore" services will develop reputational problems

---

* This is a voluntary program.

BOX 3.13   FINANCIAL CRIME PROCEEDS MOVED THROUGH FREE TRADE ZONES (FTZS)

CASE STUDY

A U.S. company received shipments of alcohol and tobacco from domestic and international suppliers at customs-bonded warehouses (CBWs) and FTZs. The company would repackage the merchandise and ship it out under the name of another company to other CBWs and FTZs, ultimately smuggling it into markets for sale. The proceeds were laundered primarily through the purchase of real estate in various jurisdictions. Investigators were able to determine that the company behind the criminal activity used double invoicing, false customs forms, a counterfeit customs stamp, and forged signatures of customs officials to facilitate the smuggling, transshipment, and sale of the untaxed cigarettes. One element of the scheme was to sell to foreign diplomats.

During the execution of a search warrant at the U.S. company business location, law enforcement seized USD 947,195 worth of untaxed alcohol and cigarettes that had been prepared to be smuggled out of the United States. The investigation resulted in the arrests and convictions of 12 people who were also involved in an illegal weapons and drug distribution organization associated with the Abu Sayyaf Group, a terrorist organization based in the Philippines.

This case exposed two main vulnerabilities in FTZs and CBWs. First is the lack of processing standards and associated due diligence. Ports operate differently and apply different standards. Some ports require that ship handlers must receive preapproval in person with all relevant documentation prior to making deliveries. Other ports require that the delivery take place first and only then are some of the relevant forms supplied. The lack of a standard requirement exposes a vulnerability in the system.

Second, all transactions are initially conducted via paper, and the entry into an automated system is not standard in all ports. This makes it easier to facilitate the diversion. Some ports input the movement of bonded merchandise, but other ports do not, exposing the vulnerability of some ports.

The last vulnerability involves repackaging and smuggling within FTZs. Activities within zones are not closely monitored. Containers and shipments enter the zone and a company warehouse where repacking and labeling may take place as it does in this example. This provides a way to change the country of origin, company name, contents, quantity and price. Lack of oversight may also provide an opportunity to smuggle goods into or out of FTZs or CBW.

Source: **"Money Laundering Vulnerabilities of Free Trade Zones,"**
Financial Action Task Force, March 2010.

BOX 3.14   FINANCIAL CRIME PROCEEDS MOVED THROUGH TAX HAVENS

CASE STUDY

The money laundering method of the regional liberation movement is identical to that of traditional criminal groups. First, the money is deposited into various banks of the region, where the issue of certificates of deposit takes place. Then, these certificates are deposited through intermediary companies in numbered accounts in banks at offshore tax havens, which may only be accessed by code. In the third phase, some of this money is transferred to several European banks from which checks or payment orders are issued from differing current accounts. Finally, the money is transferred to accounts without arousing suspicion in the territory where the liberation movement is active.

Source: **"Report on Money Laundering Typologies, 2000–2001,"**
Financial Action Task Force, February 2001.

---

that drive off legitimate businesses. In the meantime, to protect ourselves (the U.S.) from the consequences of the abuses inherent in offshore financial services, firms based in OFC jurisdictions, which are inadequately regulated, could be subjected to additional due diligence by major clearinghouse banks.

The report also offers recommendations on tackling financial crime committed via tax havens:

The generally accepted principle that there is nothing wrong with handling mere "tax evasion" money offshore has created a swamp in which financial criminals breed. Jurisdictions could eliminate the "tax evasion" loophole through two techniques: including tax evasion among the grounds for the elimination of bank secrecy in the provision of documents to law enforcement and amending mutual legal assistance agreements to include tax offenses. If such an approach became generally accepted, jurisdictions that continued to

BOX 3.15 FINANCIAL CRIME PROCEEDS MOVED THROUGH SHELL CORPORATIONS

CASE STUDY

This case involved 19 individuals in the medical service industry, one being both a lawyer and an accountant. This dossier submitted for prosecution contained 123 violations involving conspiracy, false claims, wire fraud, and money laundering. The false claims involved fictitious patient claims and claims for services that were not provided.

The two primary subjects employed the lawyer's services to set up four interrelated shell corporations as the controlling entities. In addition, eight nominee corporations were created to generate fictitious health care service records reflecting in-home therapy and nursing care. Health care providers including therapists, registered nurses, and physicians operated the nominee corporations. To keep the health care billing, tax return filings, and bank account records synchronized, the two main subjects relied on the lawyer/accountant defendant.

In excess of USD 4 million was laundered through bank accounts in cities of the north and southeast of the country and through suspected offshore accounts. Numerous accounts were created at four or five separate banks for purposes of amassing and moving these funds. Cashier's checks often were purchased and even negotiated through the lawyer/accountant's trust account to conceal property acquisition. This defendant was sentenced to two years in exchange for his cooperation.

Both primary defendants were ordered to forfeit real and personal property, including the USD 4 million and purchased property. They received five- and two-year prison sentences, respectively. Two additional related case defendants (one being an elected official) laundered an additional USD 2 million and were charged with 33 violations of the law in a separate case. They were ordered to forfeit USD 95,000 in currency. The former elected official received a five-year prison sentence.

Source: **"Report on Money Laundering Typologies, 2000–2001,"
Financial Action Task Force, February 2001.**

make themselves available for tax evasion aimed at other jurisdictions might well find that the potential damage to their reputation from remaining outside this new system outweighed the potential income from continuing to offer these services. The G-7 initiative to coordinate, where appropriate, fiscal fraud and anti-money laundering enforcement efforts is a welcome step in this direction (U.S. Department of State 1998).

Alternative Remittance Systems (ARS)

Other fund transfer methods that financial criminals make use of are stored-value cards, the Internet, digital currency, cash couriers and smugglers, casinos, and real estate (Financial Action Task Force 2005). Box 3.16 contains a commentary summarizing these, while Box 3.17 contains a related example.

Stored-Value Cards

Unlike cash, these cards make it easy to move large sums of money across borders and eliminate the need for financial intermediaries. They are untraceable because they can be purchased without identification and by using fake names. They are convenient in the sense that they can be recharged in different places and are easy to carry. Hence, tracking financial criminals who use them is practically impossible (Emerson 2005).

Stored-value cards (or prepaid cards) are of different types: open systems (usually issued by financial intermediaries such as the Visa cash passport card), semi-open systems (used to make purchases, such as the NETS CashCard, but not cash withdrawals at ATM machines), closed systems or closed-loop systems (retail gift cards that can only be used to buy goods or services from the business that issues the card), and semi-closed systems (issued on behalf of a group of selected businesses like the FlyBuys gift card) (Choo 2008). Prepaid cards are "pay early" cards unlike credit cards, which are "pay later" cards, and debit cards, which are "pay now" cards (Sienkiewicz 2007). Box 3.18 presents a case study to show how money can be moved with the help of a prepaid card.

Both government and the private sector have attempted to clamp down on misuse of prepaid cards wherever possible. The private sector monitors usage patterns of these cards, for example, the frequency with which they are reloaded (Sienkiewicz 2007). In some jurisdictions, businesses are required to report information to the government on prepaid cards that are used over a certain monetary threshold (Choo 2008). Some retailers use data mining technology to detect if a cashier is refunding an unusual amount of cash. This is to detect fraud whereby cashiers ring up refunds on gift cards that they then walk away with, in some cases, to fund criminal activity including, possibly, terrorism (Greenhouse 2009).

The Internet and Digital Currency

In the simplest terms, Internet fraud is committed by first setting up an account with an Internet service provider without providing identification or providing false information such as a fictitious name or location.

BOX 3.16   ALTERNATIVE REMITTANCE SYSTEMS (ARS)

COMMENTARY

ARS operators are flexible and progressive in finding new, profitable, and efficient methods of transmitting money. It is important to note that these services are being developed to respond to a particular consumer demand and for the most part have not been designed to circumvent existing AML/CFT measures.

For example, ARS and credit card companies are developing new products allowing debit cards to be bought for cash and then the value moved or paid out via automated teller machines (ATM) and purchases by anyone holding the personal identification number (PIN). This is an efficient way to move money securely and provides a flexible way for the money to be stored and retrieved. The card providers place limits on the value that can be stored in the cards, some of which can only be loaded with value once. AML measures are limited to the card purchaser.

In Africa, bus companies with scheduled routes are, in some cases, furnishing remittance services. The drivers use cash received for tickets to pay out remittances. This gives the bus operators extra revenue and improves security for drivers who previously had to carry the cash proceeds of ticket sales. In other countries taxi firms operate similar systems, delivering money to customers' homes.

Mobile phone companies are using the ability of SIM cards to be loaded with value and have that value removed to use phones as a method of storing, exchanging, and remitting value in countries with developing mobile phone infrastructure.

INTERNET-BASED REMITTANCE SERVICES

At least one Internet-based remittance agency (IBR) has been encountered by the authorities in Hong Kong, China. The IBR in question is based in the United States and uses the global Integrated Funds Transfer System (GIFTS). In conjunction with a major credit card service provider, it provides for the transfer of funds to any beneficiary worldwide through the issuance of an ATM card, and settlement for the transactions occurs by direct debiting of the nominated credit card of the remitter.

Remitters simply open an account with the Web-based service provider. The service provider dispatches an ATM debit card to the nominated beneficiary in any one of 130 countries. The ATM debit card can be utilized at any ATM carrying the service of the major credit card or used to make purchases worldwide within seconds of being credited by the remitter.

The remitter simply enters a secure area of the IBR Web site and authorizes the transfer of funds to the beneficiary's account. The funds are then immediately available to the beneficiary anywhere in the world through the worldwide ATM network. IBR even allows for beneficiaries to request money from the remitter via the IBR Web site. The beneficiary simply completes a request message, and then the system automatically forwards an e-mail to the remitter requesting that he or she authorize the further remittance of funds.

The ATM cards used in this process are easily transferable, thus allowing for greater anonymity than the more traditional use of supplementary credit cards. Regulators and investigators face great difficulty in monitoring such activities, and there is an obvious potential for misuse by criminals and terrorists.

For example, even in jurisdictions where regulated ARSs exist, individuals in one jurisdiction can make remittances to a second jurisdiction without leaving easily traceable records that could be used by competent authorities. The only information available is credit card activity relating to the remitter in the sending country, which will only reflect payments to the Web-based remittance agent. Checks on the beneficiary would then have to be routed through many agencies in a number of jurisdictions, including the sending and receiving jurisdictions as well as the location in which the Internet-based transfer service is located.

Source: **"Money Laundering and Terrorist Financing Typologies 2004–2005," Financial Action Task Force, June 10, 2005.**

The fraudster is then required to book an Internet domain, which costs a reported $70 at the most. He or she may proceed to set up a public relations agency that will send e-mails (by possibly buying a mailing list of potential clients) to promote a product (Morris-Cotterill 1999). Once this is done, the fraudster can commit financial crime in a number of ways, as described in Boxes 3.19–3.22.

1. Selling counterfeit goods
2. Selling goods illegally (avoiding tax obligation)
3. Fraudulent sales
4. Sale of fictitious goods

BOX 3.17   FINANCIAL CRIME PROCEEDS MOVED USING PERSONAL IDENTIFICATION NUMBERS (PINS)

CASE STUDY

An investigation of individuals operating an ARS revealed a method for converting large amounts of funds into commodities. Funds were collected in the United States, placed into a corporate account with a U.S. communications company, and used to purchase prepaid telephone calling card personal identification numbers (PINs). The PIN numbers were then sold in Bangladesh, thus converting the commodity back to cash prior to distribution to the intended recipients. Storing the funds as a commodity via the corporate account allowed for the movement of funds without utilizing the formal banking system in Bangladesh.

The subject of the investigation wired the collected funds from the bank account into a corporate account with a large U.S. telecommunications company on behalf of the ARS operator's Bangladeshi counterpart. The Bangladeshi counterpart controlled the corporate account. The Bangladeshi had set up the account based on a previously established business relationship with the U.S. telecommunications company to sell phone card PIN numbers in Bangladesh. The Bangladeshi counterpart used the funds that the ARS operator deposited into the corporate account to purchase phone card PIN numbers from the U.S. telecommunications company. The Bangladeshi then sold the PIN numbers in Bangladesh, thereby generating cash in Bangladesh for distribution to the intended recipients of the money service transfers originating in the United States. The scheme involved the transfer of USD 200,000 to USD 400,000 per month.

Source: **"Money Laundering and Terrorist Financing Typologies 2004–2005," Financial Action Task Force, June 10, 2005.**

Financial crime via the Internet, telephone, and digital currency is on the rise and is described as

the money laundering and financial risk landmine of the future. Moving value by phone, through internet banking, via cyber-value like E-Gold (now out of business), CashU and other systems—will be a strong barrier for the gathering of evidence to trace assets and make cases in money laundering or terrorist financing. This must be a high priority for law makers (LAC expert 2010).

BOX 3.18　FINANCIAL CRIME PROCEEDS MOVED THROUGH PREPAID CARDS

CASE STUDY

Two banks in a European country (Country C) reported a series of STRs related to unusual deposits of cash made by the director of a domestic limited company involved in the trade of prepaid international telephonic cards in Country C and an African country (Country D). The cash funds, credited at regular intervals of time also by means of managers' relatives, were periodically transferred to a small company registered in another country (Country E), which was supposed to be the seller of the mentioned telephonic cards.

From research carried out by the FIU in Country C, the Country E–registered company seemed to be a shell company without any real economic activity. On this premise, in order to investigate further on the matter, the FIU contacted the FIU in Country E. Thanks to the cooperation between the two FIUs, it has been disclosed that:

1. The competent authorities in Country E were already conducting an independent investigation of the Country E company for suspicious financial transactions.
2. The nature of the shell company of the mentioned company could be confirmed.
3. The Country D partner of the Country C company was under investigation by the Country E customs authority for narcotics trafficking.

At present, all the documents related to the STR mentioned here are now under investigation by the national public prosecutor in Country C.

Source: **"Report on Money Laundering Typologies, 2000–2001," Financial Action Task Force, February 2001.**

However, this type of financial crime is hard to track, "Prior to trading online, individuals establish online accounts by providing their names, email addresses and physical addresses. The required identification, however, can be easily fabricated. Some digital precious metals also allow users to establish anonymous accounts" (Choo 2009). Box 3.23 expounds on this method with the help of a case study.

BOX 3.19   FINANCIAL CRIME PROCEEDS MOVED THROUGH THE SALE OF COUNTERFEIT GOODS OVER THE INTERNET

CASE STUDY

A bank reports the suspicious transactions of a young girl. From January 2005 to August 2005 (eight months), the bank account of the young girl student, was credited by wire transfers and checks written out by individuals located all over France. The amount of each check was rather small (EUR 20 to 40). Regarding the debiting operations, the girl made cash withdrawals and wire transfers bearing the mention "Internet payment provider bills." The purchases amounted to a total of EUR 6,340 split into 43 operations.

In September 2005, she began to use a credit card so that it became more difficult for the bank to understand and analyze her transactions. Only a global amount of payments is registered monthly on her bank account.

Investigations showed that, from September 2005 to March 2006 (eight months), she made 63 purchases online for a total amount of EUR 39,282.24. The young lady was selling counterfeit pearls of a famous brand at half price. She was using a provider in another European country that sold her parcels used to send the goods she had sold online. Over 16 months, she earned more than EUR 43,000, roughly more than EUR 2,800 per month.

Source: **"Money Laundering and Terrorist Financing Vulnerabilities of Commercial Websites and Internet Payment Systems," Financial Action Task Force, June 18, 2008b.**

Some countries, including the United States, have taken a proactive role in addressing this problem. For example, the American government has charged some online money remitters doing business with American citizens for not being registered with them. They have also asked some Web service providers to shut down culprit sites. Other countries have not been as proactive as the United States for various reasons such as technical shortcomings, lack of consensus on suitable measures with other countries, etc. (Jacobson 2009)

Cash Couriers/Smugglers

Cash couriers are considered a major developing problem in financial crime as a means of transporting funds to terrorist financers around the world

BOX 3.20   FINANCIAL CRIME PROCEEDS MOVED THROUGH THE ILLEGAL SALE OF GOODS OVER THE INTERNET

CASE STUDY

The persons under investigation were directors of a company involved in purchasing large quantities of duty-free cigarettes and alcohol to sell on the domestic market contrary to their export-duty free status, thus avoiding tax obligations. By not paying any tax on the goods, the company was able to markedly increase profits. The syndicate also generated false receipts that purported to come from an export company detailing their alleged cigarette exports. Investigations with the purported company confirmed that no such exports had ever been made. Upon the arrival of the cigarettes, payment was made to the delivery driver on a cash-on-delivery basis.

A large portion of the company's sales occurred over the Internet from customers paying via credit card. A majority of the sales on the Internet were illegitimate and came from three different email addresses. Payments for these orders were made from one of two credit cards linked to Belize bank accounts. One of these cards was held in the company's name. The money in the Belize bank account was sent there by one of the directors using several false names from not only Australia but Belize, Hong Kong, and Vietnam. The director conducted structured wire transfers under false names and front-company accounts. The funds were purchased at well-known banks, with multiple transactions occurring on the same day at different bank locations, and all of the cash transfers conducted in amounts of just under AUD 10,000 to avoid the reporting threshold.

Source: **"Money Laundering and Terrorist Financing Vulnerabilities of Commercial Websites and Internet Payment Systems," Financial Action Task Force, June 18, 2008b.**

(Scott-Joynt 2004). Because these couriers often cross international borders to carry out bulk cash transfers, nations around the world have collaborated to tackle the problem. In 2009, a multilateral operation resulted in the confiscation of $3.5 million through 81 cash seizures. One of the focuses of this operation was the airways, which is the preferred choice of transportation for cash couriers due to its convenience and timeliness. This segment of the operation yielded another $4.2 million at ports of entry around the globe, "In addition to intelligence sharing, airports in many G-8 countries employed a

---

BOX 3.21   FINANCIAL CRIME PROCEEDS MOVED THROUGH THE FRAUDULENT SALE OF GOODS OVER THE INTERNET

CASE STUDY

The Belgian FIU received several STRs from banks in Belgium concerning bank accounts credited by wire transfers, apparently related to or justified by sales on commercial Web sites, and followed by cash withdrawals.

The majority of the wire transfers are of small amounts (maximum EUR 800), originate from various senders, and, following the message accompanying the payment, should be related to sales on a commercial Web site, sometimes involving the sales of luxury goods. Payments are not made through an Internet payment service provider but, rather, originate from the bank account of the buyer and are credited to the bank account of the seller. The wire transfers are followed by instant withdrawals in cash.

The goods are never delivered to the buyer (victim of a nondelivery fraud).

In some reports, the wire transfers are not followed by cash withdrawals but by transfers in a country known for producing counterfeit products (in cases related to the sale of counterfeit goods).

The fraudulent bank account is used only during a short period (because of buyer's complaints).

Investigation showed that false names are used on the commercial Web site and the name of the bank account holder where the payment is made are different. (The name used by the seller on the commercial Web site is a fictitious name.) In one file, information received from law enforcement indicated that the subject was known for using different names on the commercial Web site. In another file, the subject was using two different passports and different names.

Source: **"Money Laundering and Terrorist Financing Vulnerabilities of Commercial Websites and Internet Payment Systems," Financial Action Task Force, June 18, 2008b.**

---

variety of methods to detect cash carried in baggage, on travelers, or in shipments. Detection methods included the use of currency detector dogs, X-ray and gamma-ray equipment, body searches and ion mobility scanners" (U.S. Department of ICE 2009). The case study in Box 3.24 reveals the method of operation of cash couriers.

BOX 3.22   FINANCIAL CRIME PROCEEDS MOVED THROUGH THE SALE OF FICTITIOUS GOODS OVER THE INTERNET

CASE STUDY

The National Bureau of Investigation Money Laundering Clearing House was investigating an aggravated fraud and money laundering case. The two main suspects in Finland were acting as Western Union agents in Finland. The offices of the agents were closed on March 27, 2007, and the suspects were taken into custody.

People from countries other than Finland were fooled into buying fictitious goods (in this case, cars or other vehicles) on commercial Web sites and sending the payment to fictitious persons in Finland via Western Union.

The two Western Union agents in Finland picked up the money with the identities of the fictitious persons. Furthermore, the agents forwarded, again with fictitious identities, the money as Western Union transactions outside of Finland.

The two suspects in Finland received text messages from two persons (money flow managers) using mobile phone numbers including:

- Information about the victims abroad (their name, the expected receiver of the money, the amount sent, and the money transfer control number [MTCN])
- Instructions for forwarding the money abroad (the name of the receiver, the amount, and the country where the money was to be sent)

The money flow managers are living in European countries.

The total number of victims is over 300, and the total loss for the victims is about EUR 1.07 million. The main source countries for the assets were the United States and the United Kingdom, but there were also a number of other source countries (about 25 countries).

The two Western Union agents in Finland say that they received 10 percent of the money picked up by them. They also say that both the money flow managers visited Finland during the activity and took with them a significant amount in cash.

Based on the investigations, at least one of the money flow managers seems to have similar arrangements with local Western Union agents in a number of other European countries.

Searches were conducted at the Western Union offices and the homes of the agents, and arrests were made on March 27, 2007.

An investigation of the phones, SIM cards, and PCs used in the scheme provided good evidence. Hundreds of text messages as well as a few e-mail messages were found in which instructions were given to the Western Union agents concerning the fraud cases and the money transactions.

To support the investigation and the case in court, information is needed about as many predicate offences abroad as possible. Therefore, requests (FIU, Interpol, or Mutual Legal Assistance) have been sent to 24 countries.

To date, information on 181 fraud cases from 19 different countries has been received.

Source: **"Money Laundering and Terrorist Financing Vulnerabilities of Commercial Websites and Internet Payment Systems," Financial Action Task Force, June 18, 2008b.**

Casinos

Criminals reportedly exchange illicit cash for gambling chips at casinos and then hold them before cashing them in for a check from the casino, or requesting the casino to wire the money to some account, or passing on the chips to drug dealers as payment in exchange for narcotics, or using the chips to produce certifiable winnings through gambling. Casinos may also be used as a medium for laundering counterfeit money and large currency notes that would be conspicuous anywhere else (U.S. Department of the Treasury 2005). Box 3.25 discusses one such scheme.

Real Estate

Criminals use mortgages and loans on real estate to move illegal funds. Factors such as premature repayment of the money loaned out are potential warning signs for financial institutions. Another is the repayment of a mortgage loan in sums that are disproportionate to the declared income of the borrower (CTIF-CFI 2007). Box 3.26 details a case study about this method.

While intelligence agencies around the world have committed to transnational cooperation, this commitment is hard to put into action, as evidenced by past performance. In the opinion of some critics, government departments are plagued by a high degree of bureaucratic inefficiency and a tendency to resist cooperation with other agencies. Governments' performance

BOX 3.23   FINANCIAL CRIME PROCEEDS MOVED THROUGH INTERNET PAYMENT SYSTEMS

CASE STUDY

On April 27, 2007, a federal grand jury in Washington, D.C., indicted two companies operating a digital currency business and their owners. The indictment charged E-Gold Ltd., Gold and Silver Reserve, Inc., and their owners with one count each of conspiracy to launder monetary instruments, conspiracy to operate an unlicensed money transmitting business, operating an unlicensed money transmitting business under federal law, and one count of money transmission without a license under D.C. law. According to the indictment, persons seeking to use the alternative payment system E-Gold were only required to provide a valid e-mail address to open an E-Gold account; no other contact information was verified. According to the U.S. Department of Justice, the indictment is the result of a 2½-year investigation by the U.S. Secret Service with cooperation among investigators, including the Internal Revenue Service (IRS), the Federal Bureau of Investigation (FBI), and other state and local law enforcement agencies. According to Jeffrey A. Taylor, U.S. attorney for the District of Columbia, "the defendants operated a sophisticated and widespread international money remitting business, unsupervised and unregulated by any entity in the world, which allowed for anonymous transfers of value at a click of a mouse. Not surprisingly, criminals of every stripe gravitated to E-Gold as a place to move their money with impunity."

Source: **"Money Laundering and Terrorist Financing Vulnerabilities of Commercial Websites and Internet Payment Systems,"** Financial Action Task Force, June 18, 2008b.

in stopping the movement of funds used to commit terrorism can be improved with efforts such as information sharing and the hiring of outside consultants. However, past performance serves as a reminder that governments must pay closer attention to the specifics. For example, the improvement of trade data could lead to a higher rate of success in catching financial criminals. In the United States, there are 17,000 codes for products imported and 8,000 codes for products exported. If there was one code for each product, it would make the detection of financial crime easier. Moreover, there may be too few product codes to track the goods traded in and out of the United States; Wal-Mart Stores, Inc., alone has more product codes for its

BOX 3.24   FINANCIAL CRIME PROCEEDS MOVED THROUGH CASH COURIERS

CASE STUDY

An investigation was conducted based upon the filing of four suspicious transaction reports on A Inc. of USA, a licensed ARS service provider operating in New Jersey. Although A Inc. of USA was a licensed service provider, the owners and operators of the service conspired with four unlicensed money remitters (couriers) operating out of New York to commit the criminal acts. The four couriers brought large sums of cash to A Inc. that were deposited into the business's bank accounts and then wired to the Middle East. A Inc. operated with a very limited number of clients, but was responsible for over USD 100,000,000 in cash deposits over a 30 month period, all of which was ultimately transferred to Pakistan. A Inc. failed to complete the appropriate currency transaction reports and created fraudulent foreign exchange records. An unidentified employee attempted to deposit over USD 10,000 in cash and refused to provide identification when requested by a bank official. The bank then contacted the ARS owner and advised him of U.S. Bank Secrecy Act regulations and bank policy.

Source: **"Money Laundering and Terrorist Financing Typologies 2004–2005," Financial Action Task Force, June 10, 2005.**

retail goods. By addressing even the minutest of details, government would go a long way in stopping or intercepting funds meant to finance a major catastrophe. The success of this can be measured by putting a price or value on neutralizing one terrorist, that is, the potential physical costs and costs of human life incurred in a terrorist act factored in with the number of terrorists stopped who were plotting the attack. The greater this value, the greater the success of government in countering terrorism (Nontraditional financial crime expert 2010). This emphasizes the need for better performance measurement and risk management.

BOX 3.25   FINANCIAL CRIME PROCEEDS MOVED THROUGH CASINOS

CASE: LARGE MONEY-LAUNDERING CONSPIRACY

Offence: Money laundering, VAT fraud, counterfeiting, credit card fraud, drug trafficking
Jurisdiction: United Kingdom, Dubai
Technique: Use of casino accounts, placement via gambling
Mechanism: Bank, casino
Instrument: Cash

The money laundering conspiracy involved millions of U.K. pounds from organized criminal gangs being laundered by a group of men from West Midlands. The laundered money included the profits from a number of activities including drug trafficking, multimillion-pound VAT conspiracies in the mobile phone industry, counterfeiting, and credit card fraud. The monies were a mixture of Scottish and English notes. The defendants would transfer large amounts of money to a bank account in Dubai, which would then be accessed by their associates. The defendants received the proceeds of crime in the United Kingdom and made equivalent amounts of criminal monies available in Dubai. They then used the gambling industry to launder the money. Money was placed on a deposit at a casino and withdrawn a day or so later. Other sums would be gambled. Thousands of pounds would be passed over the tables to disguise the original source of the banknotes. Monies gambled or exchanged at the casino provided the defendants with an apparently legitimate explanation as to their source.

Source: **"Vulnerabilities of Casinos and Gaming Sector," Financial Action Task Force, March 2009b.**

BOX 3.26   FINANCIAL CRIME PROCEEDS MOVED THROUGH REAL ESTATE

CASE STUDY (PREDICATE OFFENSE: MONEY LAUNDERING, FORGED LOAN AGREEMENT)

The parents of Mr. X (Mr. and Mrs. Y) purchased a residential property and secured a mortgage with a Canadian bank. In his mortgage application, Mr. Y provided false information related to his annual income and his ownership of another property. The property he had listed as an asset belonged to another family member.

Mr. and Mrs. Y purchased a second residence and acquired another mortgage at the same Canadian bank. A large portion of the down payment came from an unknown source (believed to be Mr. X). The monthly mortgage payments were made by Mr. X through his father's bank account. This was the primary residence of Mr. X. Investigative evidence shows that Mr. X made all mortgage payments through a joint bank account held by Mr. and Mrs. Y and Mr. X.

Mr. X then purchased a residential property and acquired a mortgage from the same Canadian bank. Mr. X listed his income (far higher than the amounts he had reported to Revenue Canada) from Company A and Company B. Mr. X made the down payment and monthly payments. Over two years, Mr. X paid approximately CAD 130,000 towards the mortgage. During this time his annual legitimate income was calculated to be less than CAD 20,000.

Mr. X also used his brother Mr. Z as a front man (nominee) on a title to purchase an additional property. Investigators discovered that Mr. Z had stated an annual income of CAD 72,000 on his mortgage application listing his employer as Mr. X, although Mr. Z had never worked for his brother, and his total income for two years was less than CAD 13,000.

Mr. X made the down payment on this property, and his tenants, who were members of Mr. X's drug trafficking enterprise, paid all the monthly mortgage payments. A total of CAD 110,000 was paid toward this property until Mr. X and his associates were arrested.

Mr. X and his father purchased a fifth property. The origin of the down payment, made by Mr. Y, was unknown but is believed to be the proceeds of Mr. X's drug enterprise. Monthly payments were made by Mr. X.

The use of real estate was one of many methods Mr. X employed to launder the proceeds from his drug enterprise. Recorded conversations between Mr. X and his associates revealed that he felt it was a foolproof method to launder drug proceeds.

Mr. X was convicted in 2006 of drug trafficking, possession of the proceeds of crime, and laundering the proceeds of crime in relation to this case.

Indicators and methods identified in the scheme:

- The use of real estate was one of many methods Mr. X employed to launder the proceeds from his drug enterprise. Recorded conversations between Mr. X and his associates revealed that he felt it was a foolproof method to launder drug money.
- The only problem he faced was securing a mortgage alone, so he had to use a nominee to secure the mortgage or to cosign on the mortgage. A problem surfaced in this investigation when various properties were sold prior to a restraint order being served. This resulted in a portion of the funds being secured in a lawyer's trust account, which could not be restrained. It was the investigator's belief that up to CAD 500,000 was being held in this trust account.

Source: **"Money Laundering and Terrorist Financing through the Real Estate Sector," Financial Action Task Force, June 29, 2007.**

References

Andrews, E. L. 2002. "Threats and responses: Money trail; U.S. proposes hedge fund rules to prevent terrorist financing." *New York Times*, September 18.

Anonymous. 2001. "Anti-laundering plan criticized." *American Banker* 166 (January 10): 4.

Anonymous. 2004. "Two and a half years after 9/11, terrorism remains a key concern for banks." *EFT Report* 28: 1.

Bank for International Settlements. n.d. "Bank Committee on banking supervision." http://www.bis.org/publ/bcbs110.htm.

Bank for International Settlements. 2003. "Consolidated KYC risk management." http://www.bis.org/publ/bcbs110.htm.

BBC. 2001. "Bin Laden's honey connection," October 11. http://news.bbc.co.uk/2/hi/business/1594143.stm.

Blackwell, Rob. 2005. "A sharp split on 'report all wires' idea." *American Banker* 170: 1.

Choo, Kim-Kwang Raymond. 2008. "Money laundering and terrorism financing risks of prepaid cards instruments?" *Asian Journal of Criminology* (March): 23.

Choo, Kim-Kwang Raymond. 2009. "Digital trading in precious metals: Combating fraud." *E-Finance and Payments Law and Policy* (April).

CTIF-CFI. 2007. "Money laundering indicators," April. http://www.ctif-cfi.be/doc/en/typo_ctif_cfi/NL1175eENG.pdf.

Der Hovanesian, M., and Dawn Kopecki. 2006. "Where's the heat on hedge funds?" *Businessweek*, June 19.

Emerson, Steven. 2005. "Money laundering and terror financing issues in the Middle East." Testimony of Steven Emerson before the U.S. Senate Committee of Banking, Housing, and Urban Affairs, June 10. http://www.steveemerson.com/docs/testimony/2005-07-13%20Testimony.pdf.

Farah, Douglas, and Richard Schultz. 2004. "Al Qaeda's growing sanctuary." *Washington Post*, July 14, A19.

FATF. 2001. "Report on Money Laundering Typologies, 2000–2001." February.

FATF. 2002. "Guidance For Financial Institutions In Detecting Terrorist Financing." April 24.

FATF. 2005. "Money laundering and terrorist financing typologies, 2004–2005," June 10. http://www.apgml.org/frameworks/docs/8/FATF%20Yearly%20typol%2004-05_incl%20typologies.pdf.

FATF. 2006. "Trade Based Money Laundering." June 23.

FATF. 2007. "Money Laundering and Terrorist Financing Through The Real Estate Sector." June 29.

FATF. 2008. "Best practices paper on trade based money laundering," June 20, 2008. http://www.fatf-gafi.org/dataoecd/9/28/40936081.pdf.

FATF. 2008a. "Terrorist Financing." February 29.

FATF. 2008b. "Money Laundering And Terrorist Financing Vulnerabilities Of Commercial Websites And Internet Payment Systems." June 18,

FATF. 2009a. "Money Laundering and Terrorist Financing In The Securities Sector." October.

FATF. 2009b. "Vulnerabilities Of Casinos And Gaming Sector." March.

FATF. 2010. "Money Laundering Vulnerabilities Of Free Trade Zones." March.

FFIEC n.d. Bank Secrecy Act/Anti-Money Laundering InfoBase. Available online: http://www.ffiec.gov/bsa_aml_infobase/pages_manual/OLM_103.htm <http://www.ffiec.gov/bsa_aml_infobase/pages_manual/OLM_103.htm>

Financial Services Authority. 2005. "Fighting money laundering and terrorist financing more effectively—proposals in our consultation paper, reviewing the FSA handbook," July 12. http://www.fsa.gov.uk/pubs/other/letter_jmlsg.pdf.

Financial Services Authority. 2003. "Hedge funds and the FSA: Feedback statement on DP 16," March. http://www.fsa.gov.uk/pubs/discussion/fs16.pdf.

Francis, David. 2004. "The war on terror money: Will nations' efforts to cut off terrorists' financing stop future attacks?" *Christian Science Monitor*, April 8, 14.

Greenhouse, Steven. 2009. "Gift-card fraud by employees up sharply, retailers say." *Toronto Star*, December 31, B6.

Gustitus, L., Elise Bean, and Robert Roach. 2001. "Correspondent banking: A gateway for money laundering." *Economic Perspectives* (May): 26–29.

Haynes, Andrew. 2004. "The Wolfsberg principles: An analysis." *Journal of Money Laundering Control* 7: 207–217.

Interpol General Secretariat. n.d. "The Hawala alternative remittance system and its role in money laundering." http://www.interpol.int/Public/FinancialCrime/MoneyLaundering/Hawala/default.asp.

Interview with LAC expert, February 19, 2010.

Interview with nontraditional financial crime expert, April 13, 2010.

Jacobson, Michael. 2009. "Terrorist financing on the Internet," *CTC Sentinel*, The Washington Institute (June 2009).

Latimer, Paul. 2004. "Bank secrecy in Australia: Terrorism legislation as the new exception to the Tournier rule." *Journal of Money Laundering Control* 8: 56–65.

Lehmkuhler, Sina. 2003. "Countering terrorist financing: We need a long-term prioritizing strategy," April. http://www.homelandsecurity.org/journal/articles/Lehmkuhler.html.

Lichtblau, E. 2002. "New hiding place for drug profits: insurance policies." *New York Times*, December 6.

Morais, Herbert. 2002. "The war against money laundering, Terrorism and the financing of terrorism." *Lawasia* 23.

Morris-Cotterill, Nigel. 1999. "Use and abuse of the Internet in fraud and money laundering," *International Review of Law, Computers & Technology* (August): 211.

Napoleoni, L. 2003. "Rapid rise of the economy of terror." *Guardian* (November 3).

Owens, Jeffrey. 2002. "The OECD work on tax havens." OECD Center for Tax Policy and Administration, The Friedrich Ebert Foundation Conference on Money Laundering and Tax Havens—The Hidden Billions for Development, July 8–9.

Peters, Gretchen. 2009. *Seeds of terror: How heroin is bankrolling the Taliban and Al Qaeda*. New York: Thomas Dunne Books.

Schneider, S. 2005. "Money laundering through securities: An analysis of Canadian police cases." *Asper Review of International Business and Trade Law*, 169–184.

Scott-Joynt, Jeremy. 2004. "Cash couriers reveal terror fund challenge." BBC News, May 12.

Sienkiewicz, Stanley. 2007. "Prepaid cards: vulnerable to money laundering?" Federal Reserve Bank of Philadelphia Discussion Paper. February 2007. http://www.philadelphiafed.org/payment-cards-center/publications/discussion-papers/2007/D2007FebPrepaidCardsandMoneyLaundering.pdf.

Simpson, G. 2001. "Hawala played a global role in criminal acts—Before links to terrorism, money-transfer system was cited by Interpol." *Wall Street Journal*, November 13.

Swartz, Nikki. 2005. "U.S. wants international bank record access." *Information Management Journal* 39: 12–14.

U.K. 2001. Joint Money Laundering Steering Group Guideline notes. December.

U.S. Department of ICE. 2006. "ICE assists Brazilian officials in dismantling $200 million trade fraud scheme," Immigration and Customs Enforcement, August 18. http//www.datamininginternational.com/OperationDelugeBrazil_060818dc.pdf.

U.S. Department of ICE. 2009. "Global G-8 operation targeting cash couriers nets $7 million plus." *Imperial Valley News*, July 11. http://imperialvalleynews.com/index2.php?option=com_content&do_pdf=1&id=6214.

U.S. Department of State. 1998. "1998 International narcotics control strategy report." http://www.state.gov/p/inl/rls/nrcrpt/1998/vol2/html/29910.htm.

U.S. Department of State. 2003. "2003 International narcotics control strategy report," March 2004. http://www.state.gov/p/inl/rls/nrcrpt/2003/vol2/html/29910.htm.

U.S. Department of the Treasury. 2005. "U.S. money laundering threat assessment," December. http://www.ustreas.gov/offices/enforcement/pdf/mlta.pdf.

U.S. Department of the Treasury. 2006. "The role of domestic shell companies in financial crime and money laundering," FINCEN, November. http://www.fin-cen.gov/news_room/rp/files/LLCAssessment_FINAL.pdf.

U.S. Department of the Treasury. 2010. "Advisory to financial institutions on filing suspicious activity reports regarding trade-based money laundering," FINCEN Advisory, FIN-2010-A001, February 18. http://www.fincen.gov/statutes_regs/guidance/pdf/fin-2010-a001.pdf.

U.S. GAO. 2003. "U.S. agencies should systematically assess terrorists' use of alternative financing mechanisms," Government Accountability Office, GAO-04-163, November.

U.S. IRS. n.d. "Abusive offshore tax avoidance schemes," Internal Revenue Service. http://www.irs.gov/businesses/small/article/0,,id=106572,00.html.

Weiss, M. A. 2005. "Terrorist financing: The 9/11 Commission recommendation," CRS Report for Congress 21902, updated February 25.

World Customs Organization. n.d. "Enforcement and compliance." http://www.wcoomd.org/home_wco_topics_epoverviewboxes_responsibilities_epmoney-laundering.htm.

Zagaris, B. 2007. "Problems applying traditional anti-money laundering procedures to non-financial transactions, 'parallel banking systems' and Islamic financial systems." *Journal of Money Laundering Control*, 157.

Zdanowicz, John. 2004. "Detecting money laundering and terrorist financing via data mining." *Communications of the ACM* (May): 53–55.

Zdanowicz, John. 2009. "Trade-based money laundering and terrorist financing." *Review of Law and Economics*.

Performance Measurement, Risk Management, and Managing Performance Using the Balanced Scorecard

4

One of the objectives of this book is to measure the outcomes of the efforts of Financial Intelligence Unit (FIUs). Outcome monitoring is defined as "the regular (periodic, frequent) reporting of program results in ways that stakeholders can use to understand and judge those results" (Affholter 1994). It creates an accountability framework for programs by compelling organizations to answer questions such as what they should measure, what measures to use, and how to present performance results (Affholter 1994). A Congressional Research Service report stated that "the parameters used to measure progress can set the framework for the measurement of failure" (Perl 2005), which has forced some organizations to shy away from measuring the impact of their programs. In the context of the fight against terrorism, governments have generally focused overwhelmingly on quantitative measures, "those which may correlate with progress but not accurately measure it, such as the amount of money spent on anti-terror efforts" (Perl 2005).

Outcome monitoring is just one aspect of organizational performance management. Table 4.1 provides a step-by-step understanding of this concept.

Practical evidence underscores the utility of performance management to organizations:

An effective performance management system is a vital tool for aligning the organization with desired results and creating a "line of sight" showing how team, unit, and individual performance can contribute to overall organizational results. In addition, to be successful, transformation efforts, such as the one envisioned for the intelligence community, must have leaders, managers, and employees who are capable of integrating and creating synergy among the multiple organizations involved. A performance management system can help send unmistakable messages about the behaviors that the organization values and that support the organization's mission and goals, as well as provide a consistent message to employees about how they are expected to achieve results. Thus, as transformation efforts are implemented, individual performance and contributions are evaluated on competencies such as change

Table 4.1   A Step-by-Step Guide to Performance Management

1. Align individual performance expectations with organizational goals. An explicit alignment helps individuals see the connection between their daily activities and organizational goals.

2. Connect performance expectations to crosscutting goals. Placing an emphasis on collaboration, interaction, and teamwork across organizational boundaries helps strengthen accountability for results.

3. Provide and routinely use performance information to track organizational priorities. Individuals use performance information to manage during the year, identify performance gaps, and pinpoint improvement opportunities.

4. Require follow-up actions to address organizational priorities. By requiring and tracking follow-up actions on performance gaps, organizations underscore the importance of holding individuals accountable for making progress on their priorities.

5. Use competencies to provide a fuller assessment of performance. Competencies define the skills and supporting behaviors that individuals need to effectively contribute to organizational results.

6. Link pay to individual and organizational performance. Pay, incentive, and reward systems that link employee knowledge, skills, and contributions to organizational results are based on valid, reliable, and transparent performance management systems with adequate safeguards.

7. Make meaningful distinctions in performance. Effective performance management systems strive to provide candid and constructive feedback and the necessary objective information and documentation to reward top performers and deal with poor performers.

8. Involve employees and stakeholders to gain ownership of performance management systems. Early and direct involvement helps increase employees' and stakeholders' understanding and ownership of the system and belief in its fairness.

9. Maintain continuity during transitions. Because cultural transformations take time, performance management systems reinforce accountability for change management and other organizational goals.

Source: J. C. Mihm, "Intelligence Reform: Human Capital Considerations Critical to 9/11 Commission's Proposed Reforms," Government Accountability Office, September 14, 2004.

management, cultural sensitivity, teamwork, collaboration, and information sharing. Leaders, managers, and employees who demonstrate these competencies are rewarded for their successful contributions to the achievement of the transformation process (Mihm 2004).

Imperative to achieving this are the tenets of performance management including performance measurement, risk management, and the balanced scorecard.

A Primer on Performance Measurement

The adoption of performance measurement in government follows the lead set by the private sector to do more with less, that is, maximizing the value of each tax dollar. This stems from the principles of New Public Management, which embodies the salient elements of performance measurement (Australian Department of Finance and Administration 2000):

- What government wants to achieve, i.e., outcomes
- How government achieves this, i.e., outputs produced
- How government can be held accountable for delivering outputs and outcomes, i.e., a measure of its effectiveness

Spurred by the motive to reinvent government, performance measurement helps streamline practices and processes within the public sector by setting specific targets to reach goals and a plan to meet these targets (D'Souza 2005). In keeping with its results-oriented approach, it calls for governments to engage in cross-jurisdictional comparisons. A forum conducted by the U.S. Government Accountability Office (GAO) involving practitioner and academic participants revealed that "to sustain a focus on results, high-performing organizations continuously assess and benchmark performance and efforts to improve performance" (U.S. GAO 2004). Together, these assist in making progress toward organizational objectives such as the elimination of redundancy, reduced costs, a well-directed workforce, and satisfied customers (U.S. GAO 2004).

The thrust of a sound performance system comes from metrics, that is, what an organization should measure. Table 4.2 elaborates on this.

Follow-up measures include establishing accountability for performance within the organization that is "making managers and employees alike 'buy in' to performance measurement by assuming responsibility for some part of the process," gathering and analyzing performance data to determine if organizational goals are being met, and reporting and using performance information to assist in deciding if and what corrective actions or changes are needed in the performance measurement system to the measures themselves or to the achievement of the organization's goals (Gore 1997).

These practices in performance measurement can only be effective if they are strongly supported by leadership and if the right message cascades from the top to the bottom of the organizational hierarchy. "Measuring performance and documenting outcomes and results can be a daunting task. The measurement challenge is complicated by multiple and competing demands, programs and services that seem to defy measurement, limited resources, political expectations, and networked delivery systems" (Callahan and Kloby 2009).

Table 4.2   Best Practices in Establishing Organizational Performance Measures

Ensure a Narrow, Strategic Focus

The measures and goals that an organization sets should be narrowly focused to a critical few. It is neither possible nor desirable to measure everything. In addition, mature performance measurement systems are linked to strategic and operational planning. World-class organizations know where they are headed through effective customer-driven strategic planning. They know where they are by measuring performance against corporate goals and objectives. The organizational strategy, correctly developed and modeled by senior management, provides a framework within which business units, teams, and individuals can implement a performance measurement system.

Measure the Right Thing

Before deciding on specific measures, an organization should identify and thoroughly understand the processes to be measured. Then, each key process should be mapped, taken apart and analyzed to ensure (1) a thorough, rather than assumed, understanding of the process; and (2) that a measure central to the success of the process is chosen. In some cases, targets, minimums, or maximums are defined for each measure.

Be a Means, Not an End

In a best-in-class organization, employees and managers understand and work toward the desired outcomes that are at the core of their organization's vision. They focus on achieving organizational goals by using performance measures to gauge goal achievement, but do not focus on the measures per se. Performance measurement is thus seen as a means, not an end.

What to Measure?

Regardless of size, sector, or specialization, organizations tend to be interested in the same general aspects of performance:

> Financial considerations
>
> Customer satisfaction
>
> Internal business operations
>
> Employee satisfaction
>
> Community and shareholder/stakeholder satisfaction

Attention to, and establishment of, measurements in these areas is thus a significant part of a successful performance measurement system.

Table 4.2   Best Practices in Establishing Organizational Performance Measures (continued)

Determining a Baseline and Goals

Once an organization has decided on its performance measures, the next step in the process is to determine a baseline for each of the measures selected. Once data are collected for the first time on a particular measurement, the organization then has baseline data. Determining appropriate goals for each measure after these baseline data are collected can be accomplished in several ways. Most organizations use various statistical analysis techniques as well as benchmarking to set goals for future performance. A common practice is to set goals that will force the organization to stretch to exceed its past performance. By benchmarking measures, an organization can validate the fact that the goals are still attainable. For example, a goal of 100 percent customer satisfaction may be an admirable goal for any organization. However, if industry standards have been at 80 percent, a goal of 100 percent may not be realistically attainable. In such a case, setting a 100 percent goal can easily demotivate employees by giving them an essentially impossible target. In this regard, one organization noted that setting a quality standard with zero tolerance for human error undermines morale and makes goals appear unattainable. Organizations should instead set goals that excite an employee's interest and elicit commitment. To this end, it is important to provide information on performance goals and results to employees. This increases employee understanding of the organization's mission and goals and unifies the workforce behind them. It also helps emphasize a team philosophy rather than fostering individual competition.

Reviewing Measures

An important aspect of performance measurement is its iterative quality. Organizations should continually assess whether their current measures are sufficient or excessive, are proving to be useful in managing the business, and are driving the organization to the right result. This review lets the organization make sure that it is maintaining the right measures. When measures become obsolete, they should be discarded and replaced with something relevant. Performance analysis also lets organizations change the priority of specific measures over time. Some performance goals, for instance, are intended to influence behavior and should be deemphasized once target performance is achieved. Continuous and regular review of measures as they relate to the corresponding goals and the organization's strategic plan are key to success in performance measurement. This not only helps in deciding the right things to measure, but provides needed information to assess progress toward reaching goals of all levels within the organization. Performance measurement has no purpose if data are not used to improve organizational performance.

Source: "Benchmarking Study Report," *National Performance Review,* June 1997.

The Role of Performance Measurement in Countering Terrorism and Terrorist Financing

Performance measurement plays a vital role in organizations combating terrorism and terrorist financing. Counterterrorism program and policy initiatives, post-9/11, have cut across different levels of government, sectors, and national boundaries. The global fight against terrorism has resulted in new fiscal pressures on government, and thus highlights the crucial need for "performance measurement [which] plays an important role in identifying funding alternatives and establishing service funding levels" (Frank and D'Souza 2004). Among the various security measures initiated and upgraded by government, the role and performance of intelligence agencies has been brought to the forefront. In recommending an appropriate performance system for these agencies in the United States, a recently published GAO report cited the central theme of the 9/11 Commission report that "one of the major challenges facing the intelligence community is moving from a culture of a 'need to know' to a 'need to share'" (U.S. GAO 2004). Performance measurement can particularly assist decision makers in assessing proximate outcomes in prosecuting the fight against terrorism. Proximate outcomes, in this context, are those policies that are perceived to best limit the flow of funds to terrorists. Ultimate outcomes would be the prevention of terrorist acts (Frank and D'Souza 2005).

Part of the process of measuring outcomes of counterterrorism operations is having a strategic vision of the roles and missions of counterterrorism agencies (Carroll 2003).

> How one perceives and measures progress is central to formulating and implementing anti-terror strategy. The perception of progress has a major impact on establishing priorities and allocating resources. The parameters used to measure progress can also set the framework for measurement of failures. To better define the parameters of success, it is important to determine what both the terrorists, and those who fight them, see as their goals and priorities (Perl 2005).

Successful performance measurement is linked to having an effective strategy. Strategy in the fight against terrorism depends on the terrorist threat and its potential risks and impacts. How a country measures progress here could depend on the strategy it chooses to implement. A strategy utilizing different tactics can achieve a positive outcome. For example, some countries may choose aggressive tactics against terrorists such as drone attacks, while others might adopt a hands-off approach. In other words, there is no set list of criteria against which to measure progress, which makes it difficult to measure performance (Perl 2005).

There are a range of measures for evaluating progress in the fight against terrorism.

> Success at each stage of the process can be measured in various ways, including relatively continuous metrics such as the number of recruits, the dollars expended, the economic value of targets, the number of casualties inflicted, etc. Similar assessment categories can be developed for other pertinent factors, such as societal or environmental aspects of terrorism. Related factors may sometimes be grouped for convenience of discussion or to render them more amenable to certain mathematical treatment. Measurements may be compared at various points in time or otherwise analyzed inferentially (Perl 2005).

Perception plays an important role in determining if counterterrorism operations are successful.

> Progress may be defined differently by the terrorists and those who oppose them. Hence both can claim progress, and both can be correct in their assessments. How can this be reconciled? How can measurements of progress be established which are not politicized or biased? In this regard, one must be cautious that success is not defined retrospectively, with goals reformulated after the fact to correspond with the known outcomes. Arguably, measurements of progress have greater validity if strategies are established before, and not after, taking action (Perl 2005).

Secondly, a lull in terrorist activity should not be viewed as progress made in the fight against terrorism. Terrorists could possibly base the success of their actions on political, social, or economic outcomes. For example, if their terrorist activity results in a country spending heavily on counterterrorism measures, thereby increasing its deficit, then the outcome could be viewed as a success. A slowdown of terrorist strikes could also mean that terrorists are reorganizing and waiting for the right time to strike. There is also the matter of how to measure the opportunity cost of a country's actions to fight terrorism. This includes the diversion of resources from other government programs, an increase in government expenditures, and the curbing of individual freedoms (Perl 2005).

Similarly, with counterterrorist financing, freezing assets or confiscating funds valued at a certain amount gives no indication of how it has impacted terrorists' ability to raise or transfer funds in sponsorship of their terrorist activities. Terrorists might measure success in terms of the burden and cost imposed on governments to impede the relatively smaller amounts of money that it takes to finance an act of terrorism. The number of suspicious reports received by FIUs from reporting entities annually is reported by the media every year. This does not necessarily translate into success in stopping financial criminals.

> In attempting to measure incidents, some [countries] tend to define success in familiar ways: body counts and numbers. In a western, science-and technology-oriented society, many feel that if a problem can be quantified, it can be solved. However, a common pitfall is overreliance on quantitative data at the expense of its qualitative significance (Perl 2005).

For an organization's performance management plan to succeed, it must embrace risk management. "As it is popularly described in the media, performance management, whether defined narrowly or ideally, more broadly, does not currently embrace risk governance. It needs to" (Information Management 2005).

Risk Management

Strategic risk management is planning how to allocate resources to counter risk. In the context of terrorism, it asks how much resources to allocate to protect the homeland against the threat and hazards of terrorism and how to spread these across the board. For example, should more resources be allocated to border security to prevent terrorists from entering the country, or should more be spent on protecting critical infrastructure. To help analyze and manage risks, the U.S. Department of Homeland Security (DHS) has developed a tool called the Risk Assessment Process for Informed Decision-Making (RAPID). According to one report,

> RAPID has identified 85 risk reduction areas (such as screening cargo for nuclear material) and mapped them against the priority goals identified in the DHS strategic plan. DHS's programs were then surveyed to identify the risk reduction areas that each program addressed. This tool is intended to provide a means to identify gaps in programming and allocate resources to programs when new strategic goals are developed or strategic priorities are shifted. It also provides a framework for program managers to justify their budgets in terms of how they contribute towards DHS risk reduction areas and strategic objectives (Schanzer and Eyerman 2009).

Risk management, in the case of terrorist financing, is more a case of using intuition rather than risk calculation to determine and sort out the suspect from the legitimate and the normal from the abnormal. The European Union has been at the forefront of fighting financial crime, which is a non-violent and technologically sophisticated way of fighting terrorism compared with the military-intervention approach adopted by the United States. Methods of risk management, in this context, include asset freezing, regulation, and mining of financial data. "Money trails don't lie and ... following the money has the ability to reveal the structure of terrorist networks" (de Goede 2008, 98).

Asset freezing is a financial-crime-prevention tool used by most countries in lieu of a court trial. In other words, it is designed to enable governments to take action on security matters outside of the courts and is a commonly used measure of performance in countering financial crime. "Success is the ability of the FIU to turn into intelligence information that can be passed on to law enforcement that would lead to seizing assets and result in convictions. How often is this done?" (Global financial crime expert3 2008). The fight against financial crime was strongly supported by then-U.K. prime minister Gordon Brown, who stated that "financial information is to be a key asset in breaking the contemporary code of international terrorism" (de Goede 2008, 98). In accordance with this, the U.K. Treasury Department adopted a policy of freezing the assets and money flows to anyone in the United Kingdom suspected of planning or engaging in terrorism. In a sense, the Treasury served as a branch of the department of national security. The Netherlands too has taken similar action against a local terrorist network, *Hofstadgroep*. The Dutch government has frozen the assets of not only convicted members of this group, but also those who have been acquitted or released from prison. The need for such measures was justified because "a terrorist will always be a terrorist" irrespective of the restrictions imposed by standard criminal procedures (de Goede 2008, 98).

Governments also use regulatory instruments as a tool to clamp down on financial criminals. The purpose of the Third Money Laundering Directive of the European Union was for member countries to incorporate the anti-terrorist financing stipulations of the Financial Action Task Force. In the United States, Title III of the USA PATRIOT Act required financial institutions to report unlawful or suspicious transactions—"not the sort in which a particular customer would normally be expected to engage." Besides being compelled by law to meet certain reporting thresholds, private institutions are permitted to adopt their own models to determine suspicious and abnormal transactions that possibly indicate financial crime. They are encouraged to use a risk-based approach to determine "usual and unusual transaction patterns, to model economic purpose and normality and to determine and report deviations" (de Goede 2008, 102). Of course, risk-based regulatory guidelines come with certain limitations. "The definition of 'what to look for' can never be fully articulated, because it is thought to inform terrorists of what to avoid, and because it leaves authorities vulnerable to charges of discrimination" (de Goede 2008, 102).

Another form of financial crime detection is social network analysis, a process in which "financial data are increasingly mined for suspects' associations and their associations" (de Goede 2008, 106). This process begins with digging for a suspect's name and phone or credit card number "in order to pre-emptively arrest, detain and disrupt those thought to pose a future danger" (de Goede 2008, 106). It tries to identify individuals who "are in the process of plotting terror attacks through their associations and acquaintances. This can be performed with the help of social network analytical software solutions by mapping and measuring nodes in the suspects' network such as the number of associations in the network and their closeness to the suspect. Mathematical concepts and methods can also be used to accomplish this" (de Goede 2008, 105).

Besides investigating suspects through their associations and acquaintances, social network analysis encompasses mining through financial records. This permits the investigator not only to try to implicate suspects and their close associates involved in any conspiracy, but also to weed out the wider network of terrorist plotters who might be directly and indirectly associated with a suspect. While the suspects' close contacts can be confirmed through family members, broader links to other associates can be confirmed through financial records such as wire transfers made or received. Software such as NORA (non-obvious relationship awareness) can be used to "search through different databases and lists in order to ... identify connections through addresses that have bordering backyards, or names that are similar rather than the same" (de Goede 2008, 106).

An investigative apparatus similar to social network analysis is link analysis. The Financial Crime Enforcement Network (FINCEN) has been exploring the possibility of creating a real-time database of wire transfers going in and coming out of the United States. This would enable authorities to conduct a link analysis where "a financial data string may be pulled in order to associate names, phone numbers, social security numbers, credit card numbers and addresses from different databases" (de Goede 2008, 102). Canada and Australia already have this type of data warehouse in place. Sometimes authorities could simply issue subpoenas for financial records as the U.S. Treasury department has done with the Belgian-based Society for Worldwide Interbank Financial Telecommunication (SWIFT) (de Goede 2008, 102).

Social network analysis, while touted to be effective, has also been considered controversial. Firstly, there have been concerns about privacy violations of individuals who have been the target of search investigations. Secondly, there is the case of association by guilt. That is, can someone associated with a terror suspect actually be part of the terror network? In one such case, an American citizen was put on the no-fly list for contributing to a charity many years before it was blacklisted.

Often, such links and connections remain unexamined in courts of law, either because, in the case of blacklisting, criminal standard evidence is neither available nor required as prosecution does not follow the listing procedure. In this way, the "association rules" governing the mathematical logics of social network analysis produce guilt by association—destroying organizations and individual reputations, without, in many instances, juridical recourse. Like the *Schutzhaft* [the "protective" custody system used in Nazi Germany], financial targeting enables security action, and even criminal prosecution, without a link to crime (de Goede 2008, 109).

A Derivative of the Balanced Scorecard

The balanced scorecard provides a framework for organizational performance management and serves as a means for an organization to carry out its strategy more effectively. Developed by Robert Kaplan and David Norton, it looks at an organization from four perspectives and uses metrics to evaluate the organization's performance along the line of these perspectives (Arveson 1998). The first of these perspectives is the business process perspective, which pertains to operational issues like the flow of work processes. The second perspective is the customer perspective, which deals with how an organization can satisfy its customers. The third perspective is the learning and growth perspective, which addresses human resource development issues such as hiring, training, and employee progress and advancement. The final perspective is financial, which includes financial data and investment decisions that are determined by using cost-benefit and risk analysis.

There are differences in applying the balanced scorecard to the public sector. "While you are accountable for the efficient allocation of funds that is not your ultimate aspiration. You exist to serve a higher purpose, for example: 'reducing the incidence of HIV,' 'bringing classical music to your community,' or 'increasing public safety" (Arveson 1998). Table 4.3 further discusses the use of the balanced scorecard in the public sector.

In the public sector, the financial perspective is looked at differently than in the private sector.

In the for-profit domain, the objectives in this perspective represent the end in mind of our strategic story, typically culminating in objectives such as "Increase shareholder value," "Grow revenues," and "Lower costs." In the nonprofit and public sectors, financial objectives ensure we're achieving our results, but doing so in an efficient manner that minimizes cost. Typical examples include: "Expand revenue sources," "Contain costs," and "Utilize assets effectively" (Niven 2003).

Table 4.3   The Balanced Scorecard in the Public Sector

The *business perspective*, like the customer perspective, has a different interpretation in the government than in the private sector. For many organizations, there are actually two separate sets of measures: the *outcomes*, or social/political impacts, which define the role of the agency/department within the government and American society, and the *business processes* needed for organizational efficiency and effectiveness.

Examples of business results

- How do you want your stakeholders and/or customers to view you?
- Are your measures based on outcome/results?
- Are the results something customers care about?
- Do you have real-time data for reporting purposes?

The *customer perspective* considers the organization's performance through the eyes of a customer, so that the organization retains a careful focus on customer needs and satisfaction. For a government entity, this perspective takes on a somewhat different meaning than for a private sector firm, as most public sector organizations have many types of customers. The private sector recognizes the importance of the customer and makes the customer a driver of performance. To achieve the best in business performance, the government, too, must incorporate customer needs and wants and must respond to them as part of its performance planning.

Examples of concerns from the customer perspective

- How do you want your customers to view you?
- Who are your customers? Is there more than one group?
- Are measures based on external customer input?
- Do your measures reflect the characteristics of good service (accessible, accurate, clear, closure, timely, respectful)?

The *employee perspective* focuses attention on the performance of the key internal processes that drive the organization. This perspective directs attention to the basis of all future success—the organization's people and infrastructure. Adequate investment in these areas is critical to all long-term success. Without employee buy-in, an organization's achievements will be minimal. Employees must be part of the team.

Examples of concerns from the employee perspective

- How do you get employees to see the federal government as an employer of choice?
- Focus on issues such as employee development and retention.

Source: "Balancing Measures: Best Practices in Performance Measurement," National Partnership for Reinventing Government, August 1999.

Metrics on the four perspectives are used to measure how well the organization has turned strategy into action (Niven 2003). In this book, the balanced scorecard is used to supplement efforts at meeting the critical need for the development of metrics in the fight against financial crime. Interdicting dirty money is all about process; those prosecuting the fight against financial crime, for example, must ascertain which processes are most effective. A customer orientation comes into play because the government must partner with banks and other private and public institutions in promulgating policies that are effective. The employee learning and growth perspective may be, in some ways, the most critical. As noted at the onset, financial criminals are wily and adaptable. Those fighting them must, therefore, adapt accordingly. Lastly, financial indicators are needed because this fight does not have unlimited resources, and the domestic-international funding balance may need to be shifted (Frank and D'Souza 2005).

Performance Management of Financial Intelligence Units

The backbone of this book is buttressed by interviews conducted with experts in preventing financial crime. These experts included policy think-tank personnel, government policy advisors, independent management consultants and those from some of the Big Four firms, public and private auditors, financial lawyers, money laundering reporting (compliance) officers from financial and nonfinancial institutions, law enforcement and intelligence agency personnel, current and former FIU personnel from the public and private sectors, academicians, a former prosecutor, and a former member of Parliament. In aggregate, eight interviews were conducted with North American experts in financial crime; ten with experts within the European Union; four with Australian experts; one each with experts on India, Latin America and the Caribbean (LAC), and the Middle East and North America (MENA); and current and former personnel from international organizations like the United Nations, World Bank, and the Financial Action Task Force (FATF). The interview questions included an assessment of the organizations being studied, the four balanced-scorecard components, comparison with other FIUs, and specific policy issues dealing with new and emerging trends in financial crime. Interviewees were asked the same set of questions with slight modifications depending on the jurisdiction of the interviewee. The rationale for selection of the questions was as follows.

Introductory Questions

The purpose of the introductory questions was to understand the overall working of the FIUs and to be able to assess their performance from a broad perspective.

1. How would you assess your FIU's performance in fighting financial crime? What has the reaction been from politicians? Citizens? People within the organization?
2. Please discuss your FIU's strengths, weaknesses, opportunities, and threats (SWOT analysis). What steps have been taken to improve its effectiveness and efficiency of operations post-9/11?

3. How does your FIU define success? For example, would you consider it a success if its investigations led to 50% of financial criminals being caught (in the jurisdiction of study)? What are the factors that lead to success for your FIU? What are the impediments to success?

Responses to these questions provide an overall assessment of the FIU under study.

> At a time when "transformation" is underway in defence and other areas of government, intelligence must keep pace or run the risk of increasing irrelevance and potential decline. And, in whatever form change comes, it must ultimately remain focused on the key goal of intelligence—outthinking and outsmarting our adversaries (RAND Corp. 2005).

The first two questions outline this sentiment—the respondent's assessment of the antifinancial crime regime in his or her home jurisdiction to "outthink and outsmart its adversaries" and the respondent's evaluation, with the help of a SWOT analysis, of the FIU's ability to contribute to this. While simplistic in its orientation, SWOT analysis is an essential management tool to evaluate an organization's internal and external environment (Humphrey n.d.).

The third segment is an attempt to quantify outcomes in financial crime detection:

> How one perceives and measures progress is central to formulating and implementing anti-terror strategy. The perception of progress has a major impact on establishing priorities and allocating resources. The parameters used to measure progress can also set the framework for measurement of failures. To better define the parameters of success, it is important to determine what both the terrorists, and those who fight them, see as their goals and priorities (Perl 2005).

Questions Based on the Balanced Scorecard Approaches

This set of questions breaks down the FIU on the basis of role and function and determines metrics for performance in each of these areas.

4. *Business process perspective*: How is your FIU set up to ensure it performs to maximum potential? How do you know it is doing a good job? How would you assess the processes and procedures followed by your FIU? What measures of performance do you think it should use to improve business processes?
5. *Customer satisfaction perspective*: Who does your FIU see as its customers? How does it measure customer satisfaction? What steps should it take to improve customer satisfaction?

6. *Human resource perspective*: How does your FIU assess its staffing needs and how does it train people to meet these needs? What kind of performance appraisal system does it have in place? How does your FIU tie staffing to strategic aims/goals? How would you assess the performance of personnel at your FIU? What measures of performance do you think your FIU should use for personnel?

7. *Financial perspective*: Is your FIU producing expected return on investment? Which area or programs in financial crime detection and prevention is investment needed in? Which areas of your FIU could benefit from increased funding? What measures do you use to determine financial performance? How do you suggest your FIU measure financial performance?

These questions form the crux of the interviews. The balanced scorecard is deployed here as a mechanism for assisting decision makers and analytics in improving antifinancial crime administration, but it may also prove useful in other facets of counterterrorism strategy (Frank and D'Souza 2005).

General Questions

These questions were meant to cover those areas that the interviewee's responses might not have covered in previous segments of the questionnaire.

8. Do you have suggestions for your FIU to improve:
   - implementation
   - information-sharing
   - strengthening its planning process, both short- and long-term?

Lack of coordination, information sharing, and planning have been common complaints against agencies involved in fighting financial crime, both in the United States and abroad. This fragmented approach to fighting financial crime could be a result of the number of financial-crime-fighting agencies involved. In the United States alone, there are several agencies with overlapping responsibilities, as demonstrated in Table 4.4.

Comparative Question

This question weighs the performance of the FIU in one country against an FIU in another country.

Table 4.4   Key U.S. Government Entities Responsible for Deterring Terrorist Financing

Department	Bureau/Division/Office	Role
Central Intelligence Agency		Leads gathering, analyzing, and disseminating intelligence on foreign terrorist organizations and their financing mechanisms; charged with promoting coordination and information sharing between all intelligence community agencies
Homeland Security	Bureau of Customs and Border Protection	Detects movement of bulk cash across U.S. borders and maintains data about movement of commodities into and out of the United States
	Bureau of Immigration and Customs Enforcement (ICE, formerly part of the Treasury's U.S. Customs Service)	Participates in investigations of terrorist financing cases involving U.S. border activities and the movement of trade, currency, or commodities
	U.S. Secret Service	Participates in investigations of terrorist financing cases, including those involving counterfeiting
Justice	Bureau of Alcohol, Tobacco, Firearms, and Explosives (ATF)	Participates in investigations of terrorist financing cases involving alcohol, tobacco, firearms, and explosives
	Civil Division	Defends challenges to terrorist designations
	Criminal Division	Develops, coordinates, and prosecutes terrorist financing cases; participates in financial analysis and develops relevant financial tools; promotes international efforts and delivers training to other nations
	Drug Enforcement Administration (DEA)	Participates in investigations of terrorist financing cases involving narcotics and other illicit drugs
	Federal Bureau of Investigation (FBI)	Leads all terrorist financing investigations and operations; primary responsibility for collecting foreign intelligence and counterintelligence information within the United States
National Security Council		Manages the overall interagency framework for combating terrorism

Table 4.4   Key U.S. Government Entities Responsible for Deterring Terrorist Financing (continued)

Department	Bureau/Division/Office	Role
State	Bureau of Economic and Business Affairs	Chairs coalition subgroup of a National Security Council Policy Coordinating Committee, which leads U.S. government efforts to develop strategies and activities to obtain international cooperation
	Bureau of International Narcotics and Law Enforcement Affairs	Implements U.S. technical assistance and training to foreign governments on terrorist financing
	Office of the Coordinator for Counterterrorism	Coordinates U.S. counterterrorism policy and efforts with foreign governments to deter terrorist financing
Treasury	Executive Office for Terrorist Financing and Financial Crime	Develops U.S. strategies and policies to deter terrorist financing, domestically and internationally; develops and implements the National Money Laundering Strategy as well as other policies and programs to prevent financial crimes
	Financial Crimes Enforcement Network (FINCEN)	Supports law enforcement investigations to prevent and detect money laundering, terrorist financing, and other financial crime through use of analytical tools and information-sharing mechanisms; administers the Bank Secrecy Act
	Internal Revenue Service (IRS) Criminal Investigation	Participates in investigations of terrorist financing cases with an emphasis on charitable organizations
	IRS Tax Exempt and Government Entities	Administers the eligibility requirements and other IRS tax laws that apply to charitable and other organizations that claim exemption from federal income tax
	Office of Foreign Assets Control	Develops and implements U.S. strategies and policies to deter terrorist financing; imposes controls on transactions; and freezes foreign assets under U.S. jurisdiction

Table 4.4   Key U.S. Government Entities Responsible for Deterring Terrorist Financing (continued)

Department	Bureau/Division/Office	Role
	Office of the General Counsel	Chairs Policy Coordination Committee for Terrorist Financing, which coordinates U.S. government efforts to identify and deter terrorist financing; coordinates U.S. government actions regarding implementation of, and imposition of, economic sanctions under Executive Order 13224 with respect to the freezing of terrorist-related assets
	Office of International Affairs	Provides advice, training, and technical assistance to nations on issues including deterrence of terrorist financing

Source: U.S. Government Accountability Office, GAO-04-163, November 2003.

9. How does your FIU compare to those abroad? Better, same, or worse?

The comparison of two organizations is known as benchmarking, a process of "examining best-in-class organizations and attempting to emulate their results" (Niven 2003). This encourages organizations to evaluate their processes and compare them with those of similar organizations to achieve the best results. It potentially leads to the organization serving customers better, in other words, increased customer satisfaction and value on every dollar invested through a more competent workforce (Affholter 1994). However, some critics argue that benchmarking is too time-consuming and expensive (Risher and Fay 1995).

Technical Question

This question determines the performance of FIUs in countering newer methods of financial crime that terrorists use to raise funds.

10. How would you evaluate your FIU's performance in countering financial crime committed through:
    - international trade through false invoicing
    - the use of informal banking systems, credit/debit cards and the Internet

The use of alternative means of committing financial crime have grown in prominence as governments have clamped down on more traditional means such as financial institutions.

An implied intention of these interviews was to probe respondents' perceptions about success and the barriers to achieving it in countering financial crime. Are there cultural differences between jurisdictions, and do these differences, if any, have an influence on performance? The next chapter digs deep for answers.

References

Affholter, Dennis. 1994. *Outcome monitoring: Handbook of practical program evaluation*. San Francisco: Jossey-Bass.

Arveson, P. 1998. "What is the balanced scorecard?" http://www.balancedscorecard.org/basics/bsc1.html.

Australian Department of Finance and Administration. 2000. "The outcomes and outputs framework guidance document," November, 3–4.

Callahan, Kathe, and Kathryn Kloby. 2009. "Moving toward outcome-oriented performance measurement systems," Managing for Performance and Results Series, IBM Center for the Business of Government.

Carroll, James D. 2003. "The domestic security state." *Government Foresight* (September): 22.

De Goede, M. 2008. "Risk, preemption and exception in the war on terrorist financing." In *Risk and the war on terror*, ed. L. Amoore and M. de Goede, 97–111. Boca Raton, FL: Routledge Press.

D'Souza, J. 2005. "Public administration and the new public management: A case study of budgetary reform in the United Kingdom." *Public Administration Management*.

Frank, Howard A., and Jayesh D'Souza. 2004. "Twelve years into the performance measurement revolution: Where we need to go in implementation research." *International Journal of Public Administration* 27 8/9 (July/August): 701–718.

Frank, Howard, and Jayesh D'Souza. 2005. Advancing The War On Terror In The Face Of Budgetary Constraints: Can Performance Enhancement Provide The Solution? Paper presented at the annual conference of the Association for Budgeting and Financial Management, Washington, DC, November.

Gore, A. 1997. "Serving the American public: Best practices in performance measurement." *National Performance Review* (June).

Humphrey, Albert. n.d. "The origin of SWOT analysis." http://www.european-quality.co.uk/Frequently-Asked-Questions/Business-Improvement-definitions/The-origin-of-SWOT-Analysis/.

Information Management. 2005. "The future: Risk-based performance management?" November 3. http://www.information-management.com/news/1041154-1.html.

Interview with global financial crime expert3, September 18, 2008.

Mihm, J. C. 2004. "Intelligence reform: Human capital considerations critical to 9/11 Commission's proposed reforms," Government Accountability Office, GAO-04-1084T, 7, September 14.

National Partnership For Reinventing Government. 1999. "Balancing Measures: Best Practices In Performance Measurement." August.

National Performance Review. 1997. "Benchmarking Study Report." June.

Niven, Paul. 2003. *Balanced scorecard step-by-step for government and nonprofit agencies*. New York: Wiley.

Perl, R. 2005. "Combating terrorism: The challenge of measuring effectiveness." CRS Report for Congress, November 23.

RAND Corp. 2005. "Toward a revolution in intelligence affairs." http://rand.org/pubs/technical_reports/2005/RAND_TR242.pdf.

Risher, Howard, and Charles Fay. 1995. *Managing employees as a source of competitive advantage. The performance imperative: Strategies for enhancing workforce effectiveness*. San Francisco: Jossey-Bass.

Schanzer, David, and D. H. Eyerman. 2009. "Improving strategic risk management at the Department of Homeland Security," Analytics and Risk Management—Tools for Making Better Decisions, IBM Center for the Business of Government.

U.S. Government Accountability Office. 2003. "U.S. Agencies Should Systematically Assess Terrorists' Use of Alternative Financing Mechanisms." GAO-04-163, November.

U.S. Government Accountability Office. 2004. "High-performing organizations: Metrics, means, and mechanisms for achieving high performance in the 21st century public management environment," GAO-04-343SP, February 13.

U.S. Government Accountability Office. 2004. "Intelligence Reform: Human Capital Considerations Critical to 9/11 Commission's Proposed Reforms." GAO-04-1084T, September 14.

An International Focus on the Fight against Financial Crime

5

Criminals are constantly finding new means to circumvent the existing legal framework. The need to counter the high incidence of financial crime has forced jurisdictions to employ mechanisms that outwit financial criminals in an attempt to close these gaps. Countries across the world have been setting up specialist agencies for tackling financial crime. The financial intelligence unit (FIU) "is a central, national agency responsible for receiving (and, as permitted, requesting), analyzing and disseminating to the competent authorities, disclosures of financial information: (i) concerning suspected proceeds of crime and potential financing of terrorism, or (ii) required by national legislation or regulation, in order to counter money laundering and terrorism financing" (Egmont Group n.d.). A number of FIUs work together on issues pertaining to information exchange, training, and the sharing of expertise to counter financial crime. They are part of an informal group called the Egmont Group that transcends national borders for the purpose of international cooperation (OECD 2003). This chapter presents a bird's eye view of individual and collective AML/CTF (anti-money-laundering/counterterrorist financing) initiatives in the following regions around the globe: the European Union, North America, Asia and the Pacific, the Caribbean and Latin America, and the Middle East and Africa. It also introduces FIUs established in selected countries in these regions.

The European Union

The formation of the European Union (EU) created a single market for member countries which has certain economic benefits. On the flip side, there is also the increased possibility of financial crime due to the easing of economic barriers. As a means of protection against this, the Council of Economic and Finance Ministers approved the EU Third Money Laundering Directive to prevent the use of the financial system for the purposes of money laundering or terrorist financing that was passed by the European Parliament in May 2005. It imposes risk management and customer identification and suspicious transaction reporting requirements on financial institutions, lawyers, notaries, accountants, real estate agents, casinos, and trust and company service providers (Europa 1 n.d.).

In 2006, the European Commission set up the EU Financial Intelligence Units' Platform with a view to enhancing cooperation among FIUs of member countries. This followed a council decision of October 17, 2000, that formalized arrangements among member-country FIUs with respect to information sharing (Europa 2 2010). AML/CTF systems in most EU member countries are evaluated by the Financial Action Task Force (FATF). Those EU countries that are not members of the FATF are evaluated by MONEYVAL (Council of Europe n.d.). Three countries have especially come under scrutiny due to terrorist attacks and foiled terrorism plots: Spain, the United Kingdom, and the Netherlands.

Spain

Spain is not only a center for illegal narcotic activity, but also a haven for money launderers. Financial crime in the form of tax evasion and smuggling operations via Gibraltar and Latin America also poses a problem for Spanish authorities. Drug money in Spain is invested in real estate, especially along the coastal areas of the country (Spanish expert 2008). Since 2005, a major money laundering ring involving the coastal cities of Marbella, Ballena Blanca, Hidalgo, and Malaya was in operation. The ongoing investigation tied this financial criminal activity to the construction and tourism industries (Association of Multiple Listing Agents 2009) and estimated dirty money moved within and across Spain's borders at approximately EUR 1 billion (Typically Spanish.com 2009).

Terrorism in Spain is linked to its immigrant population from Morocco and Islamic Africa in general (Spanish expert 2008). Like money laundering, terrorist events have triggered a strong reaction from Spanish authorities. Raids across the country have resulted in a number of arrests since the train bombings in Madrid in March 2004. In January 2008, for example, 14 suspects of Indian and Pakistani origin were taken into custody for allegedly plotting an attack on Barcelona (*New York Times* 2008). The bombing at the Madrid Barajas International Airport, in December 2006, led to the arrest of a number of prominent members of the Basque separatist group ETA over the past three years, crippling its political, social, and military bases (*New York Times* 2009). On June 10, 2008, as part of Operation Submarine, Spanish authorities arrested eight Algerian nationals for alleged terrorist financing activities. Spanish authorities have also increased vigilance over alternative remittance systems such as *locutorios* (communication centers that often offer wire-transfer services) and *hawalas* (Know Your Country 2010).

The Executive Service, or Servicio Ejecutivo de la Comisión de Prevención de Blanqueo de Capitales e Infracciones Monetarias (SEPBLAC), is Spain's FIU. It operates under the auspices of the Banco de España (Bank of Spain). It was originally set up to function as a financial supervisor in charge of investigating breaches of exchange control law, but its powers were later extended to the prevention of money laundering by Law 19/1993 (SEPBLAC n.d.). In response to recent terrorism events, the Spanish government prepared a draft law to include antiterrorist financing measures. Under this, SEPBLAC, among other entities, will be responsible for fighting terrorist financing (Forbes.com 2009). Finally, on April 30, 2010, Law 10/2010 dealing with the prevention of money laundering and the financing of terrorism came into force. In addition, Spain, being a part of the European Union, falls under Directive 2005/60/EC of the European Parliament and Council, which prohibits the use of the financial system for money laundering and terrorist financing.

SEPBLAC's functions include: (a) tackling money laundering/terrorist financing. This involves receiving information through monthly mandatory reporting and analyzing it, responding to requests for information from national authorities, and international information requests; (b) monitoring movements of payment methods such as payments between residents and nonresidents; and (c) acting as supervisor or watchdog of the financial system. This involves conducting field inspections, taking corrective action, and imposing fines on violators (Spanish expert 2008; SEPBLAC 2007). SEPBLAC joined the Egmont Group of financial intelligence units in 1995, and like any other FIU, its functions include receiving, analyzing, and disseminating information to the appropriate authorities: the national court, the antinarcotics public prosecutor's office, the anticorruption public prosecutor's office, the *policía nacional* (national police), and the *guardia civil* (civil guard). It receives funding from the Bank of Spain for carrying out its roles and responsibilities (International Monetary Fund 2007). As shown in Figure 5.1, SEPBLAC is ultimately responsible to the Commission for the Prevention of Money Laundering and Monetary Offences, which is chaired by the secretary of state for economy. SEPBLAC is supported in its functions by Bank of Spain, the National Securities Exchange Commission, or corre-

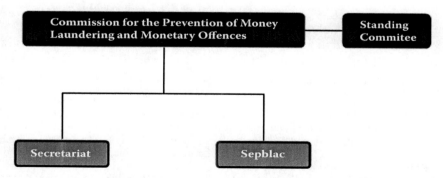

Figure 5.1 Reporting structure for SEPBLAC. (SEPBLAC, 2009.)

sponding regional bodies that provide all necessary information to carry out its investigations and analyses (GRECO 2001).

Spain has relatively stronger anti-financial-crime legislation than other countries that prevent financial criminals from taking advantage of loopholes in the system. For example, it does not allow a person to open an Internet account at a bank without physically opening an account at a branch of the bank. Also, reporting entities are required to check customer identities against a domestic terrorist list as well as a watch list maintained by the Office of Foreign Assets Control (OFAC). Among changes made to strengthen legislation, reporting entities now have to maintain client records for ten years instead of five (Spanish expert 2009). Generally, the nonfinancial sector is not as compliant in fulfilling its reporting obligations as the financial sector (Spanish expert 2008).

Spain is only just in the process of implementing the EU Third Money Laundering Directive. A number of other EU countries implemented this directive in 2007. As Spain gets ready to implement this directive, reporting entities will have five years to depurate their customer databases, which will help them identify high-risk clients and gather relevant information on them (Spanish expert 2009).

United Kingdom

In February 2004, the then-U.K. home secretary, David Blunkett, announced plans for the creation of a U.K.-wide Serious Organized Crime Agency (SOCA).* This was created by merging the National Crime Squad, the National Criminal Intelligence Service, and investigative branches of Customs and the Immigration Service (BBC News 2004). Housed within SOCA is the U.K. Financial Intelligence Unit (UKFIU), which is responsible for receiving, analyzing, and distributing financial intelligence to counter money laundering and terrorist financing (SOCA n.d.). Anti-financial-crime legislation in the United Kingdom is summarized in Tables 5.1 and 5.2.

Besides the legislative apparatus, guidance is available to reporting entities from groups such as the Joint Money Laundering Steering Group (JMLSG). This body is made up of the leading U.K. trade associations in the financial services industry. It advises the financial sector on best practices within the industry and in adhering to AML/CTF procedures using

---

* According to a 2010 update, "The new U.K. government announced that SOCA is to be reorganized and become part of a new larger agency which will be called the National Crime Agency (NCA) from 2013. This will include the U.K. Border Agency also which regulates U.K. borders. It is to be run by a former Chief Constable which reinforces the view that the new government thinks SOCA was too secretive and outside the law enforcement family. The full details of how the new NCA will function are yet to be worked out" (British expert 2008).

Table 5.1   Anti-Money-Laundering Legislation in the United Kingdom

Money Laundering Legislation—POCA 2002

The Proceeds of Crime Act ("the Act") received royal assent on 24 July 2002 and came into force on 24 February 2003. The Act is split into a number of different parts. Part VII of the Act deals with money laundering. The Act expanded, reformed, and consolidated the United Kingdom's criminal money laundering offenses. Most of the offenses under the Act apply to all individuals and businesses in the United Kingdom. However, some of the offenses apply only to those doing business in the "regulated sector." The regulated sector is defined in Schedule 9 of the Act.

The Money Laundering Regulations 2003 ("the Regulations") came into force on 1 March 2004. In general terms, these Regulations impose requirements on those conducting "relevant business" to have systems in place to obtain evidence of the identity of their clients, keep records, train staff, and make internal reports.

Money Laundering Offenses (POCA) 2002

The three principal money laundering offenses are contained in sections 327, 328, and 329 of the Act. These offenses are triable either in a Magistrates' Court or in the Crown Court and are punishable, upon conviction on indictment in the Crown Court, by a maximum of 14 years imprisonment and/or a fine.

> Section 327: An offense is committed if a person conceals, disguises, converts, transfers, or removes from the jurisdiction property that is, or represents, the proceeds of crime that the person knows or suspects represents the proceeds of crime.

> Section 328: An offense is committed when a person enters into or becomes concerned in an arrangement that he knows or suspects will facilitate another person to acquire, retain, use, or control criminal property and the person knows or suspects that the property is criminal property.

> Section 329: An offense is committed when a person acquires, uses, or has possession of property that he knows or suspects represents the proceeds of crime.

All three of the principal money laundering offenses contain certain defenses. For example, in the case of each of these offenses, it is a defense to have made an authorized disclosure to, and obtained appropriate consent from, the authorities before doing the act that would constitute the offense (see sections 335 and 338 of the Act).

Source: SOCA 2009a.

a risk-based approach. The guidance helps entities abide by rules and regulations imposed by industry supervisors such as the Financial Services Authority (FSA) (Transparency International 2009).

The United Kingdom's financial-crime-fighting mechanism received a satisfactory rating in the FATF's third round of mutual evaluations for its strong internal controls and compliance arrangements with financial institutions. However, some issues were pointed out for improvement. First, reporting entities should make use of independent auditors. Also, controls surrounding foreign branches of financial institutions and their subsidiaries should be tightened (FATF 2007a). Although the British government has wide-ranging authority through a number of agencies to fight financial crime, the lack of a central agency to coordinate this effort leaves foreign

Table 5.2   Counterterrorist/Proliferation Financing Legislation in the United Kingdom

The key pieces of legislation for terrorist finance are:

- The Terrorism Act 2000 (TACT)
- The Anti-Terrorism Crime and Security Act 2001 (ATCS)
- Various orders giving effect to United Nations measures

In addition, section 18 of TACT creates an offense of money laundering in relation to terrorist property. TACT defines "terrorist property" as "money or other property" (Section 14[1]), with "property" being defined as "property wherever situated and whether real or personal, heritable or moveable, and things in action and other intangible or incorporeal property" (Section 121).

The obligations placed on the regulated sector by the Money Laundering Regulations 2007 apply to terrorist financing, and TACT contains a mandatory reporting regime and consent provisions together with tipping off offenses, all similar to the provisions in POCA.

The ATCS is designed to cut off terrorist funding and ensure that government departments and agencies can collect and share information required for countering the terrorist threat. The freezing powers in the Act are available wherever funds could be used to finance terrorism. There is a power to seize terrorist cash anywhere in the United Kingdom, and the power to freeze assets at the start of an investigation, rather than when the person is about to be charged, thereby reducing the risk that funds will be used or moved before they can be frozen. ATCS allows the Treasury to freeze the assets of overseas governments or residents who have taken or are likely to take action to the detriment of the United Kingdom's economy or action constituting a threat to the life or property of a national or resident of the United Kingdom. The Act contains information-sharing gateways to ensure that public authorities can disclose information for the purposes of a criminal investigation or proceedings.

EU Regulation on Counter Proliferation Finance, Council Regulation (EC) 1110/2008, was agreed to and came into effect on 12 November 2008. The Regulation was developed in order to implement the vigilance requirements in United Nations Security Council Resolution (UNSCR) 1803 in the European Union. UNSCR 1803 was adopted in March 2008 because of the international community's ongoing concerns about Iran's nuclear development program. The Regulation requires U.K. credit and financial sector firms to apply vigilance to business with Iranian financial sector firms. This includes the reporting of suspicions of proliferation finance.

Source: SOCA 2009b.

governments frustrated, at times, in trying to find the appropriate agency to deal with in matters that require international cooperation (Transparency International 2009). Additionally, there are problems in the United Kingdom when it comes to law enforcement tackling financial crime. The first is that they attend to local concerns, as they are local police forces. For example, the Metropolitan Police Services is based in London and attends to matters in London and not nationally. The second is that fraud and fraud-type offenses are given low priority by these police forces (Transparency International 2009).

Certain aspects of the U.K. AML/CTF system have received a positive evaluation.

> The system benefits from an effective network of inter-departmental and inter-agency contact and cooperation both for policy and for operational matters. In addition, the U.K. has regularly reviewed the effectiveness of its AML/CFT systems; results and recommendations of the reviews have been endorsed by ministers and are now being implemented. The U.K. authorities should continue to implement the recommendations of the various AML/CFT reviews (FATF 2007).

SOCA is an innovative setup, but it is too early to see if theory can result in delivery (British expert 2009).

The Netherlands

The Netherlands is a target for financial criminals because it is one of the main financial centers in Europe. Financial criminals use illegal drugs, financial fraud, and other illicit activities to launder money, which constitutes approximately 3 percent of the Dutch GDP (eStandardsForum 2009). A number of recent arrests have also proven the Netherlands to be a breeding ground for terrorists (*Independent* 2005). The Dutch government has been taking steps to reign in terrorist financiers. To achieve this objective, the government has updated legislation and reformed its intelligence agencies.

New legislation, the Act on the Prevention of Money Laundering and Financing Terrorism, came into effect in 2008. Besides replacing the Identification Act and the Disclosure of Unusual Transactions Act, it included provisions of the EU Third Anti-Money Laundering Directive (Directive 2005/60/EC). Business entities are obligated to report suspicious transactions as well as cash transactions over EUR 15,000 under this act. Stricter customer identification requirements are also included in its provisions (eStandardsForum 2009). After September 11, 2001, the scope of reporting requirements was expanded to include terrorist financing in addition to money laundering (Dutch expert 2005). The Act on Terrorist Crimes criminalized terrorist financing in the Netherlands (eStandardsForum 2009).

Business entities have reporting obligations to the Netherlands Financial Intelligence Unit (FIU-NL), which is a hybrid administrative-law enforcement unit. It was established through the merging of the country's former FIU, the Office for the Disclosure of Unusual Transactions (MOT), with the Office of Operational Support of the National Public Prosecutor (BLOM) to form part of the National Police Services Agency (KLPD). Like all FIUs, it receives, analyzes, and disseminates unusual transaction reports (UTRs) and currency transaction reports filed by reporting entities. Through the KLPD, it assumes the function of law enforcement and disseminates its analysis of financial intelligence to the Police Investigation Service (eStandardsForum 2009).

The Dutch began tightening their AML/CTF laws in the 1990s. Until then, the Netherlands financial system was considered to be a "relatively free haven for money laundering and other financial crimes" (Dutch expert 2005). Aruba and the Netherlands Antilles, both part of the Kingdom of the Netherlands, were notorious for being drug trafficking centers. This changed, especially after the events of September 11, 2001, when the Dutch government adopted the National Security and Anti-Terrorism Action Plan, which restructured the supervision of financial markets by delegating supervisory responsibilities among the Dutch National Bank, the chamber that oversees the Dutch pension and insurance sector, and the Authority of Financial Markets (AFN). However, the system is plagued by administrative inefficiency owing to the number of players in the fight against financial crime, their overlapping tasks, and the lack of coordination among them. Given this situation, there seems to be a need to reevaluate what the problem really is, how it should be defined and approached, and whether the government should be involved and in what capacity. Once this is done, financial-crime-fighting agencies can establish a suitable performance management system (Dutch expert 2005).

From this, it is quite clear that the differences in financial-crime-fighting agencies in different jurisdictions are quite profound. This could not be more explicit among those agencies in the European Union and those in the United States. For example, "In the EU, there is relevant legislation just like in the U.S. but there is lack of enforcement unlike in the U.S." (Spanish expert 2008).

North America

The United States of America

Money laundering and terrorist financing are major problems in the United States. Its proximity to the drug-producing countries of South America, along with its size and sophisticated financial systems, make the United States the object of money laundering activity (FATF 1997). Its status as a global powerhouse and its aggressive foreign policy has made it a target for terrorists. In the second round of mutual evaluations, the FATF reported that

> the U.S. anti-money laundering system is very complex; and the large number of law enforcement and regulatory agencies, the huge number of financial institutions, the diversity of federal and state laws, and the absence of comprehensive statistics to inform resource allocation decisions militate against a fully effective and efficient system. However, the U.S. commitment to combating money laundering at all levels of government is outstanding (FATF 1997).

There is some concern that very few financial crime cases are prosecuted. This is attributed to other priorities and limited resources at the prosecutors' disposal (American expert 2008).

The American FIU, the Financial Crime Enforcement Network (FINCEN), was created in 1990, under the U.S. Treasury Department, by Treasury Order Number 105-08 (FINCEN n.d.). Its mission was "to provide a government-wide multi-source financial intelligence and analysis network" (FINCEN 2004). But its scope of responsibility was expanded in 1994 "to include regulatory responsibilities for administering the Bank Secrecy Act" (FINCEN 2004). Hence, FINCEN's function is twofold.

> [It] ... is responsible for expanding the regulatory framework to industries vulnerable to money laundering, terrorist financing, and other crime. Second, FINCEN analyzes and shares the BSA information with U.S. law enforcement at the federal, state, and local levels, and its international counterparts, to help them identify and track the financial aspects of criminal investigations (FINCEN 2004).

However, FINCEN is not the only governmental agency within the U.S. Treasury Department with these responsibilities; it shares a similar mandate with the Office of Foreign Assets Control and the Internal Revenue Service Criminal Investigation Division (FINCEN 2003).

Canada

A report presented by the solicitor general of Canada to Parliament in 1997 noted that "the illicit drug trade in Canada ... generates profits of $10 billion" (Hubbard et al. 2004). Canadian government initiatives to combat financial crime are highlighted in Table 5.3.

At the center of Canada's fight against financial crime is the Financial Transactions and Reports Analysis Centre of Canada (FINTRAC), which was created as an arm's length agency from law enforcement (it has no prosecutorial authority) and other government agencies (Hubbard et al. 2004). Its core function is financial transaction case disclosure.

> When there are reasonable grounds to suspect that the financial transactions would be relevant to an investigation or prosecution of a money laundering or terrorist activity financing offense or threats to the security of Canada, FINTRAC provides the financial intelligence to the appropriate law enforcement, intelligence or other designated agencies (FINTRAC 2004a).

FINTRAC made its first disclosure in 2002 (Canadian expert 2005). It helps ensure that reporting entities are in compliance with the Proceeds of Crime

Table 5.3   A Summary of Canada's Anti-Financial-Crime Regime

Money laundering in Canada is criminalized pursuant to Canada's Criminal Code. Per the 2008 FATF report:

> In Canada, the money laundering offense, which can be found under section 462.31 of the Criminal Code (CC), is part of a broad proceeds-of-crime regime designed to cover all obligations in the 1988 Vienna Convention and the 2000 Palermo Convention to criminalize the concealment or laundering of proceeds of crime and the possession of such proceeds or criminal instrumentalities (p. 39).

In 2000, Canada enacted the Proceeds of Crime (Money Laundering) Act (PCMLA), and soon thereafter the PCMLA was amended in 2001 to become the Proceeds of Crime (Money Laundering) and Terrorist Financing Act (PCMLTFA). The PCMLTFA expanded the list of predicate offenses to encompass all indictable offenses, such as terrorism. Also, the 2001 amendments criminalized (under the Canadian Criminal Code) acts such as knowingly receiving or disseminating funds for terrorism purposes, and the process of freezing and seizing such assets was expedited.

More recently, as pointed out in the 2009 U.S. Department of State (DoS) report, in June 2008, Canada implemented a bill amending the PCMLTFA, thereby aligning the Canadian AML framework closer to international standards. The bill introduces a risk-based approach, mandates new client identification and recordkeeping requirements for real estate agents and brokers, and establishes a national registry of money service businesses.

Canada's FIU, the Financial Transactions and Reports Analysis Centre of Canada (FINTRAC), was established by provisions in the 2000 Proceeds of Crime (Money Laundering) Act as an independent agency responsible for collecting, analyzing, and disclosing financial information and intelligence on suspected money laundering and terrorist financing. It is a member of the Egmont Group.

Other law enforcement agencies tasked with supervising and implementing AML/CTF measures in Canada are the Office of the Superintendent of Financial Institutions (OSFI), which regulates federally chartered financial institutions; the Royal Canadian Mounted Police (RCMP), which operates counterterrorist financing and anti-money-laundering units; the Canada Border Services Agency (CBSA), which monitors unreported currency at airports and border crossings; the Canadian Security Intelligence Service (CSIS), which investigates money laundering and terrorist financing cases threatening Canadian internal security; and the Investment Dealers Association (IDA), now called the Investment Industry Regulatory Organization of Canada or IIROC, which is the national self-regulatory body for the Canadian securities industry.

Source: eStandardsForum. "Netherlands: Anti-Money Laundering/Combating Terrorist Financing," October 2009.

(Money Laundering) and Terrorist Financing (PCMLTF) Act and works actively with international anti-financial-crime bodies to accomplish its overall objective.

There are two characteristics of FINTRAC that distinguish it from other, more established FIUs:

1. FINTRAC's threshold for suspicious transactions being reported is "the reasonable suspicion that a transaction is subject to prosecution" (Canadian expert 2005). While it has no written guidelines to

help its analysts determine whether a transaction is related to money laundering or terrorist financing, it bases its analysis on indicators and typologies issued by other FIUs and the FATF (Office of the Auditor General of Canada 2004).

2. FINTRAC's authority is limited by Section 8 of the Charter of Rights and Freedoms, which states that "everyone has the right to be secure against unreasonable search or seizure" (Electronic Frontier Canada n.d.), and the Privacy Act, which "imposes obligations on some 150 federal government departments and agencies to respect privacy rights by limiting the collection, use and disclosure of personal information" (Office of the Privacy Commissioner of Canada 2004).

FINTRAC has to work around the restrictions imposed by these laws, which limit its ability to implement all of the FATF's 40 recommendations (Canadian expert 2006).

Built around a workforce of approximately 250 employees, FINTRAC is headquartered in Ottawa with three regional offices in Montreal, Toronto, and Vancouver. While staff members located at its Ottawa headquarters are multifunctional, staff members in the other offices play liaison and compliance roles. The director of FINTRAC oversees the operational, management, and administrative functions of the agency (FINTRAC 2003). FINTRAC has an elaborate performance management system that ties resources, activities, outputs, and outcomes (FINTRAC 2006). Although it is a relatively new FIU, "FINTRAC is well on its way" (Canadian expert 2005). It has begun providing feedback to reporting entities on their contribution to specific money laundering and terrorist financing cases (FINTRAC 2004b). It is also in the process of solidifying its relationships with its clients by attempting to enhance the utility, timeliness, and relevance of its reports.

Working with its international partners, adhering to best practices in information sharing, and developing international comparators to counter financial crime globally will help Canada control financial crime and fulfill its obligation to those it is ultimately accountable to—the citizens of Canada (Canadian expert 2005). The same can be written about Australia and the countries described in the following sections.

Asia and the Pacific

Australia

In October 2005, the FATF noted that the amount of money laundering in Australia was estimated between AUD 2 and 3 million. Financial criminals there used financial service and gaming providers to launder money with the assistance of false identities. They moved these funds offshore through international fund transfers and alternative remittance dealers, among other methods (FATF 2005). This is a matter of interest for the Australian Transaction Reports and Analysis Centre (AUSTRAC), the Australian FIU. AUSTRAC is considered to be the most effective FIU in the world, even though this might be because it has a comparatively smaller workload given the relatively small size of the Australian population. In the FATF third mutual evaluation report, AUSTRAC was characterized as an agency with limited resources that lacked the necessary "supervisory skills and training required to conduct on-site inspections and enforcement related activities" (MinterEllison 2005).

The main legislation in Australia related to the collection, analysis, and dissemination of financial intelligence is the Financial Transactions Reporting Act 1988 (FTR Act) and the Anti-Money Laundering and Counter-Terrorism Financing Act 2006 (AML/CTF Act). The FTR Act requires those business entities dealing in cash to report suspicious transactions and cash transactions of AUD $10,000 or more to AUSTRAC. Business entities that fail to report these transactions are assessed penalties (AUSTRAC 2010a). The AML/CTF Act is designed to bring Australia in line with the financial crime-preventive standards set by the FATF. Its provisions include risk management requirements pertaining to recordkeeping and customer identification and verification by reporting entities. It increased the scope of AUSTRAC's functions from regulation to supervision and enforcement over a broader range of business entities such as real estate agents, jewelers, legal professionals, and accountants (AUSTRAC 2010b). AUSTRAC analyzes reported data before proceeding to disseminate it based on typology: tax evasion, welfare fraud, money laundering, and terrorist financing (Australian expert 2006).

There are multiple policy issues surrounding the Australian AML/CTF framework. The macro-policy issues include maintaining autonomy for AUSTRAC (it is now under the attorney-general's portfolio) (Australian expert 2006) and its limited powers to impose criminal sanctions (MinterEllison 2005). Micro-policy issues involve (a) the lack of knowledge on money laundering typologies among reporting entities and their failure to adopt these in their risk-based strategic plans (Australian expert 2006) and (b) the reliability of documents that are permissible in meeting the requirements of the 100-point identification system to open a bank account (FATF 2005). Other policy issues include how to reduce defensive reporting and encourage lateral thinking or thinking along the same lines as terrorists and other criminals to preempt their actions (Australian expert 2006).

India

Anti-India terrorists raise finances through a variety of means. Most of these come from contributions from charitable organizations in Pakistan and the Middle East, transnational criminal groups, and Inter-Services Intelligence, Pakistan's spy agency. Other sources of funding include extortions, ransom payments, drug money, counterfeit currency, and stock market manipulation. Terrorists mainly move money more through the informal banking system to finance their activities. Indian Mujahideen, a militant group in India, and Kashmir-based separatist groups such as Hizbul Mujahideen (HM) and Lashkar-e-Taiba are suspected of using *hawala* transaction as a source to fund their activities (Sulaiman and Kumar 2009).

In order to tackle financial crime, the government of India has passed the following AML/CTF legislation (Saini 2009):

Unlawful Activities (Prevention) Act of 1967: outlaws offenses of terrorism including terrorist financing through fundraising. Its provisions include the seizing of related property, assets, and proceeds.

Prevention of Money Laundering Act (PMLA) of 2002: intended to prevent money laundering by requiring financial institutions to maintain proper records of transactions and furnish them upon request.

Prevention of Money Laundering (Amendment) Act of 2009: incorporates the recommendations of the FATF including those meant to prevent terrorist financing. It obligates a larger number of business entities such as money changers, money transfer service providers, and payment gateways to report suspicious and large transactions (*Times of India* 2008b). Registered nonprofit organizations such as charities, nongovernmental organizations, educational institutions, or societies are required to disclose the source of their funds. Financial crime through stock market fraud and falsifying trade invoices is also forbidden under this law (rediff.com 2009). The local tax authorities are in a push to include tax evasion as an offense under this law (TaxGuru.com 2010).

Other laws that address financial crime in India include the Foreign Exchange Management Act of 1999 (FEMA), the Conservation of Foreign Exchange and Prevention of Smuggling Activities Act of 1974, the Smugglers and Foreign Exchange Manipulators (Forfeiture of Property) Act of 1976, the Narcotics Drug and Psychotropic Substances Act 1985, and the Foreign Contribution (Regulation) Act of 1976.

The union cabinet of India approved of the creation of the Financial Intelligence Unit-India (FIU-India) in 2004 and gave its approval for its signing memoranda of understanding (MOUs) with foreign FIUs for the purpose of exchanging information in 2007 (Press Information Bureau 2007). India assumed observer status at the FATF in 2006 (FATF n.d.b) and is expected to take action in implementing the 40 + 9 recommendations such as making know-your-client (KYC) norms legally binding in order to secure full membership. FATF membership will enhance the level of support India receives in financial crime cases from the international community (AML-CTF 2009). "Membership of FATF would not only allow India to gain easy access to real-time exchange of information on money laundering and terror financing but also help the country raise its diplomatic pitch globally against export of terror from neighboring nations" (rediff.com 2009).

India's central bank, the Reserve Bank of India, plays an integral part in enforcing anti-money-laundering rules in the country. It sends out circulars informing commercial banks about AML/CTF rules and regulations. It has made it mandatory for all banks to report suspicious transactions, cash transactions over 1 million rupees, and those involving forged currency notes to FIU-India. It has also asked banks to install the necessary software to report these (*Times of India* 2008a).

The AML/CTF effort in India is highly politicized. It is not uncommon for the judiciary to be influenced by the executive branch of government and for politicians to be involved in financial criminal activity. Hence, it would be ideal, under these circumstances, for FIU-India to function as an independent authority. FIU-India can tackle financial crime more effectively by focusing more on substance rather than numbers, i.e., on financial criminals and the different methods they use to commit financial crime rather than on financial institutions that commit technical violations. FIU-India recruits from different areas of government including the central bank; however, procedures, equipment, and training alone do not help. Functional autonomy and a more focused mandate could go a long way in increasing the success rate of FIU-India. It should focus on measuring outcomes such as the quality of terrorist financing cases uncovered (Indian expert 2009).

Australia and India are two countries that possibly face the highest risk of international terrorism in the region: India due to its proximity to Pakistan, and Australia due to its proximity to Indonesia. Both, countries are members of the Asia/Pacific Group on Money Laundering (APG), an FATF-style regional organization that assesses compliance of member nations with international AML/CTF standards. It does so by conducting its own mutual evaluations and providing assistance to members to improve their capacities in tackling financial crime (APGML n.d.). However, it deals with a different set of issues than those faced in Latin American and Caribbean countries, which are discussed next.

Latin America and the Caribbean

Latin America

One country that has probably received the most attention in Latin America with regard to financial crime is Colombia. Chapter 2 of this book covered how the major source of funds for financing terrorism here is extortion through kidnapping. Major terrorist groups such as the Revolutionary Armed Forces of Colombia (FARC), the United Self-Defense Forces (AUC), and the National Liberation Army (ELN) were responsible, respectively, for 714, 259, and 875 kidnappings in 2001 alone. They also accounted for approximately 3,500 killings in 2002, mostly because the families of the kidnapped victims were not able to pay these groups ransom money. Drug trafficking is another important source of income for financial criminals in Colombia. According to one source, this narco-money provides FARC with $400 million to $600 million of tax-free income each year and also constitutes 40–70 percent of the AUC's income (Jurith 2003). Colombian authorities actively investigate people who use banks and money changers to send small and frequent remittances from abroad using false identities, hoping to link them to money laundering and terrorist financing operations (BBC Monitoring Americas 2007).

Chapter 1 discussed how the tri-border area of Argentina, Paraguay, and Brazil is a breeding ground for Islamic terrorists. In view of these criminal transgressions, the Organization of American States (OAS) Inter-American Drug Abuse Control Commission (CICAD n.d.) established an Anti-Money Laundering Unit (AMLU) in 1999 to provide AML technical assistance and training to relevant personnel in member countries, and the Experts Group on Money Laundering Control established a legal framework for financial crime prevention. CICAD-AMLU also works with external organizations such as the Inter-American Development Bank (IADB) to not only train financial institution personnel in member countries in financial crime vigilance, but to also help these countries in forming FIUs (CICAD).

The performance of FIUs in Latin American countries is far from encouraging. "The strengths of each FIU are totally dependent on the integrity of the country, the independence of the FIU, security of the information they receive and manage and the absence of corruption influences. This is very difficult in Latin America" (LAC expert 2010). Additionally, there is lack of security of financial information in this area. However, countries in this region have increased reporting requirements and made more stringent anti-money-laundering laws, rules, and regulations. Yet, there have been very few cases that have resulted in prosecution. Besides widespread corruption, this could be a result of lack of training of investigators, lack of security of financial information, threats of violence from drug cartels, lack of strong government support, and no desire to really fight financial crime (LAC expert 2010). A glaring problem to effective counterterrorism operations in this region is the lack of resources. "Resource needs are great, fiscal challenges severe, and available funding insufficient. ... Most countries in the region cannot afford to control their borders, deny terrorists safe haven in ungoverned territories, eliminate money laundering, or restrict terrorists' abilities to operate" (Abbott 2004). Other impediments are the open borders between Latin American countries, friction between the military and law enforcement, and lack of organization within these forces (Abbott 2004).

The Caribbean

The Caribbean faces many of the same issues in tackling financial crime as Latin America. The U.S. Department of State's International Narcotics Control Strategy Report 2009 listed a number of Caribbean states as "jurisdictions of primary concern," "jurisdictions of concern," or "jurisdictions monitored" because (a) they are vulnerable to money laundering and (b) a significant amount of proceeds from financial crime pass through the financial institutions there (BBC Monitoring Americas 2009). Caribbean countries also permit the establishment of offshore financial centers (OFCs) within their borders that contribute to the growth of their economies but also serve as conduits for financial crime. While some countries like the Bahamas and the Cayman Islands have strengthened legislation to address this, the costs of compliance with international standards in this regard are high. These costs cover the hiring of additional audit and supervisory personnel, but they have also diminished the financial advantages of permitting the establishment of OFCs (Suss, Williams, and Mendis 2002). Many Caribbean countries work together on common issues like these through the Caribbean Financial Action Task Force (CFATF), an organization of states and territories that have agreed to implement common measures against money laundering (FATF n.d.c). It has a similar mandate to regional bodies in Africa and the Middle East, which is up for discussion next.

The Middle East and Africa

The Middle East and North Africa (MENA)

Charities are notably the main method of terrorist financing in the Middle East.

> On one hand, countries such as Iran, Saudi Arabia, Kuwait, Sudan, and Pakistan, grant, directly or through official and unofficial foundations and companies, enormous sums of money to most widely range of Islamic

movements, organizations or groups, or to numerous foundations, associations, institutions, charity associations, projects, and institutes all over the world, which often serve as front organizations of groups that engage in terrorism too (Paz 2000).

This allegation was refuted by the Saudi government and the 9/11 Commission, which found no evidence of the involvement of the Saudi government or its officials in the financing of terrorism (Prados 2004).

Financial crime methods other than charities are reportedly used only in rare cases in this region.

Most of the Islamic and Islamist groups do not engage in criminal activities known from non-Islamic terrorist groups in many places over the world, such as robbery of banks and property, extortion and criminal threats, taking hostages for ransom, etc. Few exceptions in this regard were several religious rulings of Sheikhs of terrorist small groups, which permitted robbery of non-Muslims for the finance of the group. Sheikh Asa`d Bayoud al-Tamimi, one of the religious authorities of the Palestinian Islamic Jihad, issued in 1983 a ruling permitting his followers to rob property of Jews. Egyptian Islamists of the Egyptian Islamic Jihad admitted in the investigations that followed the assassination of the late President Anwar al-Sadat on October 1981, that they had robbed jewelry stores owned by Christian Copts in Cairo and Upper Egypt, based upon a religious ruling (Paz 2000).

Countries in the MENA region only began to establish FIUs after the events of September 11, 2001. This followed the global trend where FIUs began to occupy a more prominent role in fighting financial crime (MENA expert 2010). These countries have also taken a number of other steps to tackle financial crime, which are listed in Table 5.4.

The countries also cooperate collectively through the MENAFATF, a regional FATF body that was created in 2004 by 14 countries in the MENA region. The plenary section of the body consists of appointed members in charge of decision making, while the secretariat performs administrative and technical duties on behalf of the body. It is funded by contributions from member countries and a substantial contribution from the host secretariat. Like the FATF, it conducts mutual evaluations of its members to ascertain their compliance with the FATF's standards for financial crime prevention (MENAFATF 2009).

The Rest of Africa

A number of terrorist groups are based in Africa. Al Shabab, a group organized in Somalia, has coordinated attacks in Uganda and has threatened

Table 5.4   Anti-Financial-Crime Initiatives by Middle Eastern Countries in 2005

Saudi Arabia

Demonstrating its commitment to address systemic factors contributing to the flow of funds to terrorists, Saudi Arabia is working to establish a Charities Commission to regulate all charitable donations leaving the kingdom. Saudi Arabia has made important changes to its banking and charity systems to help strangle the funds that support al-Qaeda. Saudi Arabia's new banking regulations place strict controls on accounts held by charities. Saudi Arabia has also ordered an end to the collection of donations at mosques and instructed retail establishments to remove charity collection boxes from their premises. These steps have been extremely challenging for the Saudi government, but they have been ordered because it understands that terrorists are more likely to use funds collected anonymously and without an audit trail than those that move through regular banking channels. On June 19, 2005, a Ministry of Interior spokesman announced that a "special department for tracing illegal financial activities in the Kingdom" (the FIU) will be completed soon. The September 2003 FATF mutual assessment of Saudi Arabia found that the kingdom has taken essential steps—closer bank supervision, tighter banking laws, enhanced oversight— critical to curbing terrorist financing and money laundering. On June 14, 2005, for example, the Council of Ministers adopted a recommendation that private donations to beneficiaries outside the kingdom be channeled only through the National Commission for Relief and Charitable Work Abroad.

Kuwait

The government of Kuwait has formed a working group to draft a new piece of legislation that would specifically criminalize terrorist finance and strengthen Kuwait's anti-money-laundering/terrorist finance (AML/TF) regime. The legislation is intended to address weaknesses in Kuwait's current anti-terrorist finance legal regime (absence of a law specifically criminalizing terrorist finance; prohibition of direct information sharing by the Financial Intelligence Unit (FIU) without prior case-by-case approval of the Public Prosecutor's Office; lack of restrictions on cash couriers).

Bahrain

In November 2004, Bahrain hosted the inaugural meeting of the Middle East and North Africa (MENA) FATF, which will promote the implementation of the FATF Recommendations to combat money laundering and terrorist financing. In April 2005, Bahrain hosted a two-day plenary session of the MENA FATF followed by a two-day anti-money-laundering/counterterrorist financing workshop cohosted by the World Bank and IMF.

United Arab Emirates

The UAE aggressively enforces anti-money-laundering regulations and in 2004 enacted legislation criminalizing terror finance. In April (2005), the UAE hosted the third international conference where ways to prevent use of the *hawala* (informal money transfer) system by terrorist financiers was discussed. Conference attendees included representatives from financial institutions, central banks, law enforcement agencies, FATFs, the IMF, and the World Bank, as well as other international officials involved in regulating money transfer systems. The government registers *hawala* dealers.

Table 5.4   Anti-Financial-Crime Initiatives by Middle Eastern Countries in 2005 (continued)

Oman

Oman has implemented a tight anti-money-laundering regime that monitors unusual transactions. Financial institutions plan to verify customer identities using sophisticated biometrics technology.

Qatar

Qatar has enacted laws to combat terrorist financing and to monitor all domestic and international charity activities.

Source: "Money Laundering and Terrorist Financing in the Middle East and South Africa," E. Anthony Wayne, assistant secretary for economic and business affairs: Testimony before the Senate Committee on Banking, Housing, and Urban Affairs, Washington, D.C., July 13, 2005.

to attack Burundi. While its mission is not aligned with al-Qaeda, it draws inspiration from it (*Globe and Mail* 2010). Al-Qaeda's presence in East Africa from Sudan to Tanzania has grown over the years. While it has tended to avoid Africa's central region characterized by civil unrest, it is known to have links with the South African group, People against Gangsterism and Drugs, which is associated with the radical organization, Qilba. Funds for terrorism are raised locally by selling illicit goods and internationally through cash transfers from Yemen, Saudi Arabia, and Iran. Local financing activities of terrorist groups involve smuggling and illegal arms sales, and moving funds through charities and alternative remittance systems. African governments, such as the National Islamic Front (NIF) in Sudan, have been suspected of funding terror groups around the Horn of Africa, such as the Eritrean Islamic Jihad and the Eritrean Liberation Front. Money laundering and cash couriers play a significant role in terrorist financing in East Africa, but raising funds from extortion through kidnapping and narcotics is minimal (Piombo 2005). This is not the case in other parts of Africa like southern Africa. After 9/11, allegations about terrorists exploiting natural resources to finance their activities were made, but there is no basis to link misuse of alternative remittance systems and charities to terrorist financing (Hubschle 2007). However, terrorist funds from foreign sources are allegedly remitted through embassies of countries like Yemen and Saudi Arabia under the guise of humanitarian aid. There is also uncertainty whether al-Qaeda uses the diamond trade in West Africa to finance its activities like Hezbollah does in Lebanon (Piombo 2005).

   To combat financial crime in the region, seven countries signed an MOU in 1999 to form the Eastern and Southern Africa Anti-Money Laundering Group (ESAAMLG) (FATF n.d.b). Presently, the ESAAMLG has ten members and four potential members. The activities of this body include collecting, compiling, and consolidating ESAAMLG member country AML/CTF laws and regulations in electronic format and conducting a self-assessment questionnaire. These activities are meant to make information exchange easier and to identify and fix weaknesses. Other activities include conducting mutual evaluations, which involves training of mutual evaluators and the identification of technical assistance training needs of member countries, conducting research on money laundering typologies, and raising political awareness on financial crime issues (Eastern and Southern Africa Anti-Money Laundering Group).

Despite these efforts, doubts linger over the political will of governments in the region to do what is necessary in tackling financial crime. FIUs are unable to carry out their purpose because they are not given the needed tools or the authority of their respective governments. There are very few defined performance metrics that would help them establish (a) staffing requirements, (b) what cases they would work on, and (c) how they would gather information properly and build a case for prosecution. In the Middle East and Africa, sociological factors play an equally important role as business processes in tackling financial crime (MENA expert 2010).

This chapter concludes by presenting broad generalizations about how government should measure performance in countering financial crime (Table 5.5). These come from experts interviewed from around the globe.

The lack of consensus is quite clear. What complicates matters even more is that it is difficult to compare the performance of one AML/CTF regime to another, especially with the metrics currently used to measure performance. For example, the number of suspicious transaction reports (STRs) received by Spain's FIU cannot be compared with those received by the FIU in France (Spanish expert 2008). The next two chapters explore how FIU performance can be measured based on function.

Table 5.5   Suggested Performance Improvements in Fighting Financial Crime

- FIUs should gather data on the number and sorts of institutions that report unusual transactions, the number of processed reports and the processing time of unusual cases, the number of suspicious transactions or cases that are reported to investigating authorities, the number of cases with an administrative sanction, the number of cases handed over to prosecutors, the number of cases brought before court, the number of convictions, the total amount of money confiscated, the total amount of money prevented from being misused (by catching money launderers before they have laundered money), the number and type of suspects, and the usage of FIU information in cases. Such information, tracked from the beginning of the cycle (information reported by an entity) to the end (the court's judgment) should be gathered on an annual basis so that performance can be monitored for one year against the other (Dutch expert 2005).

- A lack of convictions could be a sign that anti-financial-crime authorities are doing a good job preventing financial crime. Because the goal here is prevention, it is difficult to measure performance. For example, a fewer number of cases does not necessarily signal that authorities are not doing their job. It could simply mean that authorities have been successful in keeping down the number of cases by deterring financial crime. Another performance measure is the strength of punitive action (Spanish expert 2008).

- Performance measures in the realm of terrorism and terrorist financing are limited. While it is important to create a focus on measurable outcomes, there are limits on performance measures in fighting terror. Financial intelligence involves identifying terrorist cells or cells that are planning a terrorist attack before these attacks take place. But how do you measure the impact of a terrorist plot that has been foiled? Performance measures for terrorist financing should be distinguished from nonfinancial ones. The main outcome is not preventing terrorism, but negating the financial environment for terrorism, which is difficult to measure compared to other measures such as the quantity of intelligence gathered. Because financing terrorism is an essential part of the entire terrorist plot, it is important to look at what financial aspect is misused to commit crime. The ease with which terrorists are raising funds is a vital measure compared to second-tier measures (British expert 2008).

- Intelligence agencies should look at fighting crime in terms of situations, events, and cases: How many situations are being investigated? How many of these have the potential to become events? How many of these develop into cases and what Is the possibility of prosecution, conviction, and sentencing these cases? As far as performance measures are concerned, you cannot set metrics when it comes to human lives (MENA expert 2010).

- One of the best and, perhaps, most obvious measures of success is the percentage of money launderers or terrorist financers caught. Such a system will depend on the approach: (a) repressive, where the focus is on catching and punishing all money launderers and terrorist financiers or (b) preventive, which makes the possibility of laundering money or financing terrorism as difficult as possible (Dutch expert 2005).

- Even if 95% of financial criminals are caught, an act of terrorism can take place. Therefore, putting a figure on success is of no use because, irrespective of the success in stopping financial criminals, a bomb could go off somewhere. Stopping the financing of terrorism is just one part of fighting terrorism that does not stop radicalization. One way to define success is how well the system is working in slowing down or stopping radicalization (British expert 2008).

Table 5.5 Suggested Performance Improvements in Fighting Financial Crime (continued)

- Measuring performance in fighting financial crime requires a degree of sophistication to recognize the value of assets detained, the number of terrorists prosecuted/convicted, the number terrorist acts prevented, etc. There are also long-term outcomes for the work of financial intelligence agencies. For example, if organized crime is prevented, would this impact the health care system (in terms of decreased drug usage, etc.) (British expert 2008)?
- While FIUs generally operate retroactively, investigating financial crime already committed, they produce reports that are key in preventing money laundering and terrorist financing. The success of an AML/CTF system depends, perhaps, even more so on its preventive measures (Dutch expert 2005).

References

Abbott, Philip K. 2004. "Terrorist threat in the tri-border area." *Military Review*, 51.

AML-CTF. 2009. "India may secure entry into FATF BY 2010," June 18. http://aml-cft.blogspot.com/2009/06/india-may-secure-entry-into-fatf-by.html.

APGML. n.d. "About APGML." http://www.apgml.org/about/history.aspx.

Association of Multiple Listing Agents. 2009. "Building development corruption in Marbella?," December 8. http://blog.amlaspain.com/2009/10/13/building-development-corruption-in-marbella/.

AUSTRAC. 2010a. "Anti-Money Laundering and Counter-Terrorism Financing Rules (AML/CTF Rules)," September 16. http://www.austrac.gov.au/aml_ctf_rules.html.

AUSTRAC. 2010b. "Financial Transaction Reports Act 1988," March 3. http://www.austrac.gov.au/ftr_act.html.

BBC Monitoring Americas. 2007. "Colombian authorities probe links between remittances, money laundering," April 13.

BBC Monitoring Americas. 2009. "USA names four Caribbean states in money-laundering report," March 3.

BBC News. 2004. "New 'FBI' unit to tackle UK crime," February 9. http://news.bbc.co.uk/2/hi/uk_news/3471195.stm.

CICAD. n.d. "About anti-money laundering." http://www.cicad.oas.org/Lavado_Activos/eng/about.asp.

Council of Europe. n.d. "What are MONEYVAL's objectives?" http://www.coe.int/t/dghl/monitoring/moneyval/About/MONEYVAL_in_brief_en.asp.

Eastern and Southern Africa Anti-Money Laundering Group (ESAAMLG). n.d. "Activities." http://www.esaamlg.org/work_programme/activities.php.

Egmont Group. n.d. "The Egmont Group of financial intelligence units." http://www.egmontgroup.org/.

Electronic Frontier Canada. n.d. "Canadian Charter of Rights and Freedoms." http://www.efc.ca/pages/law/charter/charter.text.html.

eStandardsForum. 2009. "Netherlands: Anti-money laundering/combating terrorist financing," October. http://www.estandardsforum.org/netherlands/standards/anti-money-laundering-combating-terrorist-financing-standard.

eStandardsForum. www.estandardsforum.org/canada/standards/anti-money-laundering-combating-terrorist-financing-standard.

Europa 1. n.d. "Adoption of anti-money laundering directive will strike a blow against crime and terrorism." http://europa.eu/rapid/pressReleasesAction.do?reference =IP/05/682&format=HTML&aged=0&language=EN&guiLanguage=fr.

Europa 2. 2010. "Money laundering and terrorist financing: The directives." September 10. http://ec.europa.eu/internal_market/company/financial-crime/index _en.htm#study.

FATF. 1997. "Annual Report 1996–97." June. http://www.fincen.gov/faftsum.pdf.

FATF. 2005. "Mutual Evaluations Programme—Australia." October. http://www.fatf-gafi.org/document/32/0,2340,en_32250379_32236982_35128416_1_1_1_1,00. html.

FATF. 2007. "United Kingdom of Great Britain and Northern Ireland: Summary of the third mutual evaluation report—anti-money laundering and combating the financing of terrorism." June 29.

FATF. n.d.a "FATF members and observers." http://www.fatf-gafi.org/document/52/0 ,3343,en_32250379_32236869_34027188_1_1_1_1,00.html.

FATF. n.d.b "Caribbean Financial Action Task Force (CFATF)." http://www.fatf-gafi. org/document/28/0,3343,en_32250379_32236869_34355164_1_1_1_1,00. html.

FATF. n.d.c "Eastern and Southern Africa Anti-Money Laundering Group (ESAAMLG)." http://www.fatf-gafi.org/document/4/0,3343,en_32250379_32236869_ 34355780_1_1_1_1,00.html.

FINCEN. n.d. "About FINCEN/FAQs." http://www.fincen.gov/af_faqs.html.

FINCEN. 2003. "FINCEN Strategic Plan for the fiscal years 2003–2008." http://www. fincen.gov/strategicplan2003_2008.pdf.

FINCEN. 2004. "FINCEN Annual Report 2004." http://www.fincen.gov/fincenannu-alreport2004.pdf.

FINTRAC. 2003. "FINTRAC Performance Report." April 30. http://www.fintrac. gc.ca/publications/DPR/2003/2_e.asp.

FINTRAC. 2004a. "FINTRAC's Annual Report 2004, Overview." November 4. http://www.fintrac.gc.ca/publications/annualreport/2004/1_e.asp.

FINTRAC. 2004b. "Performance report, for the period ending March 2004." November 5. http://www.fintrac.gc.ca/publications/DPR/2004/6_e.asp.

FINTRAC. 2006. "Annual Report 2005." January 24. http://www.fintrac.gc.ca/publi-cations/annualreport/2005/42_e.asp.

Forbes.com. 2009. "ECB wants tweaks in Spanish money-laundering law." http:// www.forbes.com/feeds/afx/2009/09/16/afx6892243.html.

Globe and Mail. 2010. "Al-Shabab's terror without borders," June 9.

GRECO. 2001. "Evaluation report on Spain: First evaluation round." Council of Europe, June 15.

Hubbard, Robert, Daniel Murphy, Fergus O'Donnell, and Peter DeFreitas. 2004. Money laundering and proceeds of crime. Toronto: Irwin Law, xxv, 322–323.

Hubschle, Annette. 2007. "Terrorist financing in Southern Africa: Are we making a mountain out of a molehill?" ISS Paper 132, January.

Independent. 2005. "Dutch terrorism trial opens in confusion as witness stays silent." December 6.

International Monetary Fund. 2007. "Spain: Report on the observance of standards and codes—FATF recommendations for anti-money laundering and combating the financing of terrorism." International Monetary Fund (IMF) Country Report 07/70, February.

Interview with American expert, December 17, 2008.

Interview with Australian expert, May 15, 16, 17, 2006.

Interview with British expert, July 28, 29, 30, 2008.

Interview with Canadian expert, September 6, 8, 2005; October 3, 2005; August 9, 2006.

Interview with Dutch expert, June 13, 14, 2005.

Interview with Dutch expert, June 15, 2005.

Interview with Indian expert, November 20, 2009.

Interview with LAC expert, February 19, 2010.

Interview with MENA expert, February 10, 2010.

Interview with Spanish expert, August 4, 2008; November 27, 2009.

Interview with Spanish expert, October 9, 2008.

Jurith, E. 2003. "Acts of terror, illicit drugs and money laundering." *Journal of Financial Crime* 158.

Know Your Country. 2010. "Spain," June 13. http://www.knowyourcountry.com/spain1111.html.

MENAFATF. 2009. "Fifth Annual Report (2009)." http://www.menafatf.org/images/UploadFiles/MENAFATF_5th_Annual_Rep_Eng.pdf.

MinterEllison. 2005. "News alert—anti-money laundering report card," October 20. http://www.minterellison.com/public/connect/Internet/Home/Legal+Insights/News+Alerts/NA+-+Anti-money+laundering+report+card.

New York Times. 2008. "Spain arrests 14 in plotting attack," January 19.

New York Times. 2009. "Recent ETA arrests raise hopes in Spain of ending violence," October 20.

OECD. 2003. "The Egmont Group of financial intelligence units," August 25. http://www1.oecd.org/fatf/ctry-orgpages/org-egmont_en.htm.

Office of the Auditor General of Canada. 2004. "Implementation of the National Initiative to Combat Money Laundering," November 23. http://www.oag-bvg.gc.ca/domino/reports.nsf/html/20041102ce.html.

Office of the Privacy Commissioner of Canada. 2004. "Privacy legislation in Canada," December 17. http://www.privcom.gc.ca/fs-fi/02_05_d_15_e.asp.

Paz, R. 2000. "Targeting terrorist financing in the Middle East." Paper presented at the International Conference on Countering Terrorism through Enhanced International Cooperation, Courmayeur Mont Blanc, Italy, September 22–24.

Piombo, Jessica. 2005. "Tracing the money: Fighting terror in the horn of Africa." Paper presented at the annual meeting of the International Studies Association, Hilton Hawaiian Village, Honolulu, HI, Mar 5.

Prados, Alfred B. 2004. "Saudi Arabia: Terrorist financing issues." CRS report for Congress 32499. Updated on December 8.

Press Information Bureau. 2007. "Signing of MoU by the Financial Intelligence Unit, India, with foreign financial intelligence units for exchange of information," March 29. http://www.pib.nic.in/release/release.asp?relid=26475&kwd=.

rediff.com. 2009. "Trusts, NGOs under ambit of money-laundering law," November 19. http://business.rediff.com/report/2009/nov/19/trusts-ngos-under-ambit-of-money-laundering-law.htm.

Saini, S. K. 2009. "Problems and prospects of combating terrorist financing in India." *Strategic Analysis.*

SEPBLAC. 2007. "Annual Report 2007."

SEPBLAC. 2009. www.sepblac.es/ingles/acerca_sepblac/comision-comite-secretaria. htm

SEPBLAC. n.d. "About SEPBLAC." http://62.81.224.139/ingles/acerca_sepblac/acer-cade.htm.

SOCA. 2009a. www.soca.gov.uk/about-soca/the-uk-financial-intelligence-unit/legal-basis-for-reporting.

SOCA. 2009b. www.soca.gov.uk/about-soca/the-uk-financial-intelligence-unit/legal-basis-for-reporting.

SOCA. n.d. "What is the Financial Intelligence Unit?" http://www.soca.gov.uk/about-soca/the-uk-financial-intelligence-unit.

Sulaiman, Sadia, and Ankur Kumar. 2009. "Modes and strategies of terrorist financing in South Asia," World-Check Singapore, April 2009.

Suss, Esther C., Oral H. Williams, and Chandima Mendis. 2002. "Caribbean offshore financial centers: Past, present, and possibilities for the future." IMF Working Paper WP/02/88, June 26.

TaxGuru.com. 2010. "CBDT want to book tax evaders under PMLA and looking to jail tax evaders," April 6. http://taxguru.in/income-tax/cbdt-want-to-book-tax-evaders-under-pmla-and-looking-to-jail-tax-evaders.html.

Times of India. 2008a. " RBI tightens anti-money laundering norms," May 23.

Times of India. 2008b. "Govt widens scope of anti-money laundering act," June 6.

Transparency International. 2009. "Combating money laundering and recovering looted gains—raising the UK's game," June 11.

Typically Spanish.com. 2009. "Money laundering reaches 1 billion Euro in Marbella cases," December 8. http://www.typicallyspanish.com/news/publish/article_24249.shtml.

Wayne, E. Anthony. 2005. "Money Laundering and Terrorist Financing In The Middle East And South Africa." Assistant Secretary for Economic and Business Affairs: Testimony before the Senate Committee on Banking, Housing, and Urban Affairs, Washington, DC, July 13.

Financial Intelligence Units
Monitoring Resource and Process Outcomes

6

In 2004, the report of the auditor general on Canada's Implementation of the National Initiative to Combat Money Laundering revealed a number of organizational inconsistencies* within FINTRAC (Financial Transactions and Reports Analysis Centre of Canada). It found that FINTRAC's reporting requirements imposed undue administrative burden and expense on reporting entities. In addition, computer connectivity problems between FINTRAC and the Canada Border Services Agency resulted in a large backlog of unprocessed reports on cross-border transactions. There was also a lack of agreement between FINTRAC and the Canada Revenue Agency as to the criteria for detecting money laundering–related tax evasion and, finally, reluctance on the part of law enforcement to share information with FINTRAC or give much weight to its unsolicited disclosures. Law enforcement found that reports received from banks were more current and useful than those received from FINTRAC. Indeed, the lack of context in FINTRAC's reports prompted the Office of the Auditor General of Canada (2004) to ask, "What led FINTRAC to suspect the presence of money laundering or terrorist financing?"

FINTRAC is not the only organization to experience such problems. Financial Intelligence Units (FIUs) all over the world have been cited for the failure of one or more resources or some aspect of their work processes to forecast outcomes.

Resources

Resources include technology, human labor (hiring, training, performance appraisals), and financial investments. FIUs increase their probability of success by constantly updating technology, hiring those with relevant work experience and training them to keep up with the latest trends in financial crime, and plugging gaps in financial investment.

---

* One government administrator disclosed that this report was prepared during the early stages of FINTRAC's establishment, but modern customer satisfaction surveys show satisfaction with FINTRAC's product (Anonymous, interview by author, Canada, August 9, 2006)

Technology

AUSTRAC, one of the earliest established FIUs, has set the bar for FIUs when it comes to technology (Australian expert 2006). This includes its data mining applications, which have "greatly strengthened [its] ability to analyze data, identify financial networks and locate reporting and compliance information to assist in its regulatory function" (AUSTRAC 2006); ProviderNet and its electronic data delivery system (EDDSWeb system), which allow cash dealers to report electronically; AUSTRAC's Regulatory Risk Assessment System (ARRAS), with which it is able to identify entities and industries at risk and take appropriate action; and its TRAQ Enquiry System (TES) database, through which its partner agencies can access financial transaction reports. AUSTRAC shares its technological prowess with other FIUs through a mentoring program (AUSTRAC). To identify matters of interest, it has in place an automated monitoring system called TargIT (AUSTRAC 2006).

AUSTRAC also uses technology to reach out to its stakeholders. An example of this is the AML (anti-money laundering) eLearning application, which serves as "a tool in providing basic education on the process of money laundering, the financing of terrorism and the role of AUSTRAC in identifying and assisting investigations of these crimes" (AUSTRAC 2006). It has a regulatory educational program for cash dealers that helps high-risk and new dealers to fulfill their reporting obligations under the FTR Act and to report accurately and on time (AUSTRAC 2006). AUSTRAC also gets reporting entities, industry bodies, and partner agencies involved in the decision-making process via consultations through the Provider Advisory Group (PAG) and the Gaming Provider Advisory Group (GPAG). It convenes and participates in various working groups and forums in which relevant personnel from industry and government agencies participate (AUSTRAC 2006).

FINTRAC is one of the most technologically intensive FIUs in the world, which helps it in its role as a central depository for suspicious financial transactions and a point of contact for other agencies, both national and international (Canadian expert 2005). Of the 10–11 million suspicious transaction reports it receives each year, 99 percent are received electronically. However, its database is inaccessible to law enforcement and other agencies, giving it more control over the information it disseminates and helping it abide by Section 8 of the Charter of Rights and Freedoms and by the Privacy Act (Canadian expert 2005).

Other FIUs invest in sophisticated technology to process the large volume of reports they receive, analyze, and disseminate to the relevant police region (Dutch expert 2005). In the Netherlands, the Dutch Ministry of Justice was awarded a grant for the development of FIU.NET, "a decentralized computer network designed to connect (EU) Financial Intelligence Units (FIUs) using modern technology and computers [in order] to (bilaterally) exchange financial intelligence information" (FIU.NET n.d.). UKFIU subscribes to FIU Net* to submit requests for information and also respond to international subject information requests for which it has received positive feedback, especially from U.S. law enforcement. The turnaround time for the latter is about 11 days (FIU.NET n.d.).†

Less-developed FIUs have some catching up to do. If FIUs in the MENA region, for example, want to take their operations to the next level, they would have to develop their technological capacities further. They are presently struggling to cope with the changing technological requirements of the business (MENA expert 2010). More-developed FIUs, while demonstrating the value of technology to FIUs in conducting business, have to make a more concerted effort to tie investment in technology with outcomes.

Manpower

The hiring of personnel by FIUs is probably the most important decision they make. This is due to the technical nature of FIUs' business and the significant role they play in countering financial crime. The constantly changing environment of the business and the new methods adopted by financial criminals to cheat the system emphasizes the importance of effective training for FIU personnel. The following sections describe how FIU personnel are hired, trained, and evaluated and how these can be tied in with outcomes.

Hiring

Among the qualities a financial intelligence analyst must ideally possess are technical knowledge in the areas of money laundering and terrorist financing and "the ability to analyze the reported information not only on a case [by] case basis, but also to determine trends and structure within money laundering [and terrorist financing]" (Dutch expert 2005). Personnel should also have the skill and knowledge to carry out all-source analysis (American expert 2006). They should be set with clear expectations, both for themselves individually and for the groups that they work in (Dutch expert 2005). Besides possessing knowledge of rules and regulations in this area, FIU personnel should ideally be capable of multitasking, maintaining confidentiality, and adhering to safeguards and ethics (Global financial crime expert2 2008).

FIUs have generally kept to these guidelines in their hiring decisions. The Bank of Spain appoints the director of SEPBLAC, whose staff members

---

* An electronic system involving 15 EU countries that allows the exchange of basic identifying information. This is used as a pre-Egmont check that may prompt a full, formal Egmont request if the search results yield a positive hit.
† This was established to promote the use of AWF SUSTRANS, the Europol analytical work file on money laundering in the EU.

include employees of the Bank of Spain, the Ministry of the Economy and Finance, and the law enforcement agencies. Its supervisory inspectors come from a background in government finance, customs, BIDM,* and the Bank of Spain (GRECO 2001). It is important for SEPBLAC staff members to be experienced in these relevant areas to successfully identify suspicious transactions (Spanish expert 2008). FIUs in the MENA region are able to attract capable personnel who are qualified through their experience in law enforcement, investigations, and military intelligence (MENA expert 2010). Half of FINTRAC's staff members come from government, while the other half come from the private sector. "People are hired from sectors that have a reporting obligation to FINTRAC because it looks for specialized skills when recruiting" (Canadian expert 2006). A large percentage of its personnel possess a high level of knowledge about money laundering, as many of them worked for the police force and use their experience to their advantage (Canadian expert 2005). FINCEN has fewer than 200 employees, most of whom are permanent staff with experience in intelligence, the financial industry, and computers. Additionally, it has 40 long-term detailees[†] from 21 regulatory and law enforcement agencies (FINCEN n.d.a). In compliance with the recommendations of the Lander review, the number of permanent staff members at UKFIU has increased over the years to 112 (American expert 2006).

Besides these attributes in their hiring process, there are also some problems in the FIU hiring process. Table 6.1 outlines the deficiencies identified in interviews with experts and in past reviews of FIUs.

A variety of measures could be used to assess the performance of the FIU hiring process. These include the number of job applications received, the reason personnel leave, and where they go after leaving, i.e., whether they go to competitors. The target should be to retain 100 percent of the FIU's high performers (British expert 2008). A mentorship program for newcomers would also be beneficial (Canadian expert 2005).

Training

Training of FIU personnel begins with planning. AUSTRAC engages in workforce planning to ensure that employees develop the skills needed to perform their jobs well (Australian expert 2006). "AUSTRAC has a specialist in workforce planning that does a skill inventory analysis. Staff can avail of a number of courses from technical to management development. A Myers Briggs test is used. A gap analysis is conducted before training employees" (Australian expert 2006). FINCEN has a training office that assesses and strengthens the competencies of its employees (American expert 2005).

---

* Monetary Offences Investigative Squad (BIDM) is a law enforcement unit of the Directorate General for the Police directly reporting to SEPBLAC.
† These personnel work for FINCEN, but their salaries are paid by their home agencies.

Table 6.1 Noted Problems in the FIU Hiring Process

FINCEN lacks leadership, vision, and organization. FINCEN staff is well trained, but middle and senior management is inexperienced (American expert 2006). FINCEN should hire more personnel with a law enforcement background and would be better off contracting out business or hiring former employees as consultants (American expert 2006). Delays at FINCEN are caused by lack of personnel (American expert 2008).

Despite offering employees opportunities for growth and development, AUSTRAC has a hard time retaining personnel, as they have to compete with the private sector, where the best personnel in the field are hired by consulting agencies (Australian expert 2006). Although AUSTRAC personnel are of assistance, they generally seem to have scant experience dealing with reporting sectors (Australian expert 2009).

SOCA hires people mostly from law enforcement but lacks expertise in forensic accounting and financial investigations. Its information-processing capacity in areas such as data mining can also be improved (British expert 2008). SOCA was formed by the merger of four different organizations, and as a result has different identities that constitute its organizational culture. A lot of personnel who have left SOCA were crucial to the organization. SOCA has the legacy of bringing together people from different organizations. The next four to five years will see people leave, and they will hire the right people rather than retrain (British expert 2008). SOCA is understaffed when it comes to analytical personnel (FATF 2007).

FIUs must be staffed by personnel who are beyond corruption influences and who have a sound financial background (i.e., accounting, finance, and banking) and law enforcement background. Most FIUs in Latin America are significantly understaffed (LAC expert 2010).

Employee training at FINTRAC is based on function. Compliance officers can avail themselves of workshops that develop their expertise in policy interpretation, risk assessment, and quality assurance, while financial analysts can advance their knowledge in tracking terrorists online as well as their activities in casinos and tax havens. Interaction with experts in the academic community and with law enforcement agents is encouraged (Treasury Board of Canada Secretariat 2005). The agency trains its employees by providing opportunities to attend workshops and conferences addressing money laundering methodologies, among others, both within and outside the organization (Canadian expert 2007). It also runs security awareness sessions for its employees to help them maintain compliance with the agency's security and privacy policies and practices (FINTRAC 2004). Training costs the agency approximately 4 percent of its budget (Canadian expert 2005).

Specialists within FIUs should be given the opportunity to enhance their skills and knowledge level by enrolling in appropriate courses. For example, policy analysts at FIU-NL can attend courses in compliance. An important component of training is learning on the job. At FIU-NL, technical training is provided whenever necessary using the new intelligence software, Business Objects (Dutch expert 2005).

Among the less-developed FIUs, those in the MENA region have improved the quality of training, but they still have a long way to go (MENA expert 2010). In Latin America, the Office of Technical Assistance (OTA) of the U.S. Treasury Department provides training to FIUs. OTA also provides AML training to bankers, money service businesses, and other private sector agencies in these countries. Training programs include financial investigative techniques, rules of evidence, money laundering methods, and enforcement efforts to identify and prosecute offenders. OTA also supports a bank information reporting process similar to that of the U.S. Bank Secrecy Act (LAC expert 2010). The more-developed FIUs are developing training programs for intelligence officers in their less-developed counterparts. "USTRAC worked with the Egmont Training Working Group to develop training material for use in Egmont's Strategic Analysis Course, which aims to improve the analytical capabilities of other Egmont member countries" (AUSTRAC 2010).

FIUs must adopt a strategic approach to training. "What is important here is what you do in training, how often you do it and how imaginative you are (mode of delivery). Organizations do not spend enough time and resources on training. They don't take money laundering seriously enough" (Australian expert 2006). Performance measures in this area include the time employees have been on the job in relation to competencies acquired on the job and competencies acquired in relation to the requirements of the job (Australian expert 2006), the amount of training FIU personnel receive to raise their skill level and to increase their knowledge to do their jobs effectively (British expert 2008), and the level of investigative techniques. Other suitable performance measures are the amount of training funds allocated and the degree of learning plan development (Canadian expert 2006). Cross-training of personnel among various financial-crime-fighting agencies in the system will also help increase personnel competencies. Opportunities to learn from the private sector and training of personnel in methodologies like trade financing will also benefit FIU personnel (British expert 2008).

Performance Appraisals

At the Dutch FIU, performance appraisals are conducted regularly, one of which is a competencies evaluation by the Ministry of Justice performed twice a year. There is also an annual appraisal conducted by the employee's manager. If an employee fails to perform up to expectations within a period of two competency evaluations and an appraisal, he/she is dismissed (Dutch expert 2005). At FINTRAC, employees are evaluated based on expectations and commitments through two performance appraisals each year (Canadian expert 2005). Performance agreements are established for each employee (Canadian expert 2006). One of the characteristics of FINTRAC's organizational development program is the Rewarding Excellence initiative, which includes "recognition through informal, instant awards as well as organization-wide celebratory events recognizing both individual merit as well as team-based achievements" (FINTRAC 2004). A workforce satisfaction measurement program is in the works (FINTRAC 2008).

FINCEN has implemented an employee performance system (American expert 2005) that is linked to the organization's strategic plan and replaces the old pass-fail employee rating system (FINCEN 2004). It conducts employee satisfaction surveys and follows up on their recommendations (FINCEN n.d.c). At AUSTRAC, personnel are evaluated on a quarterly basis based on their performance agreements. Employees have access to training and development opportunities to meet the requirements of their performance agreements (AUSTRAC 2006). The outcome of mutual evaluations is communicated to staff (Australian expert 2006). Some FIUs have been innovative in this area, like those in the MENA region that have adopted pay-for-performance schemes (MENA expert 2010).

Financial Resources and the Return on Investment

Issues related to organizational investment in the skills needed to tackle financial crime vary from government to government. AUSTRAC, for example, would benefit by increasing investment to help reporting entities achieve higher rates of compliance (Australian expert 2006). In the Netherlands, the biggest impact of budgetary constraint at FIU-NL is probably its expanding agenda with the same number of staff members (Dutch expert 2005). In early 2005, the Dutch government committed more than EUR 400 million over five years to counter terrorism and radicalization. This translated to approximately 600 full-time personnel "being added to the intelligence, security and investigation services involved" (Government of the Netherlands 2005). However, these funds were intended for the National Security Agency (AIVD) and other frontline organizations involved in the fight against terrorism, with little funding allocated to the behind-the-scenes fight against terrorist financing (Dutch expert 2005). The Dutch government would also have benefited from investing more funds to develop expertise in understanding how transgressors operate, how they work within the criminal network, and how they infiltrate the systems of financial and other such institutions (Dutch expert 2005).

In Canada, financial investment is needed for investigations, analysis, and technology at FINTRAC. Investigations are an important part of FINTRAC's business, and additional financial investment here will help produce reports on a more timely basis (Canadian expert 2005). The feeling is that there is too much work for the available workforce and that FINTRAC would be better off upgrading its analytical ability. Other potential areas of investment include creating a reporting structure for newer entities such as jewelers and dealers in precious stones as well as for the numerous money service businesses that are currently unlicensed and unregulated, and upgrading information technology (Canadian expert 2005). Proposals for increased funding are submitted by the Ministry of Finance on FINTRAC's behalf. For certain items, legislation is required to provide funding to FINTRAC (Canadian expert 2005).

In the United States, FINCEN conducts assessments to ascertain the necessity of strengthening management control over its resources (FINCEN n.d.d). "FINCEN has invested heavily in its regulatory function (tasks required in its role as Administrator of the Bank Secrecy Act) and in a new Bank Secrecy Act data management and dissemination system called BSA Direct" (American expert 2005). Additional investment in technology would be helpful (American expert 2006). FINCEN does not compare its performance to that of other FIUs, but measures performance by how well it progresses toward its goals. This includes a number of self-evaluations (American expert 2005), which are listed in Table 6.2.

Investment to enhance FINCEN performance will depend on its future direction. "Planning should focus on its mission: is law enforcement doing enough with FINCEN data? (They don't have adequate resources to do everything.) Should FINCEN be a law enforcement agency or should it be split into two bodies—regulatory and law enforcement?" (American expert 2007). While FIUs are usually established after the relevant anti-financial crime regulation has been adopted, FINCEN was established at around the same time as the regulation it falls under. It has, therefore, had to evolve with the regulation, which has complicated financial planning (American expert 2007).

In Europe, the U.K. government has already increased investment in countering financial crime, with technical expertise being one of the main beneficiaries of increased funding (British expert 2008). In fact, there is more investment in terrorism than in organized crime in the United Kingdom

Table 6.2 Internal/External Reviews Conducted by FINCEN

1 Internal work process reviews that are used as a basis for improving programs and processes.

2. Internal control reviews used to evaluate and, if needed, to strengthen management controls over resources.

3. Internal reviews of technology, case management, and other issues that are used as a basis for making strategic decisions.

4. Customer satisfaction surveys, which are used to identify strengths and opportunities to improve services to external clients, including law enforcement agencies, regulators, and the financial industry.

5. Employee satisfaction surveys, which are used as a basis for making decisions related to human resources activity, employee communications, and other management areas.

6. External evaluations of major program activities, which are contracted for as needed and used in strategic planning.

Source: FINCEN 2006.

(British expert 2008). Nevertheless, there are questions that continue to persist: "Are we slamming the right door? Yes, but can we say we are finished? Changes are needed with changing methods of financing terrorism. Investigations of terrorist groups and their finances can help identify vulnerabilities in financial performance" (British expert 2008). Investment in less known methods of financial crime will certainly help in this regard (Global financial crime expert3 2008). Similarly, Spain is in a phase of continued financial investment. Areas presently in need of funding include those pertaining to strengthening control mechanisms, simplifying its risk-based approach, implementing the *EU Third* Money Laundering *Directive*, reviewing its KYC (know your client) procedures to increase detection of clients with high AML risk, and instituting a parallel system to ensure that all relevant information has been captured (LAC expert 2010). Due to the large number of problem areas, fiscal investment should be dictated by priorities. An emerging priority is money transfers, because tracking these is complicated and is in need of more supervision (Spanish expert 2008). SEPBLAC would also benefit by investing in the general areas of information technology, personnel, financial education, and public awareness of the government's anti-financial-crime program (Spanish expert 2008).

The Latin American and Caribbean region has its own set of priorities. Human resources is on top of the list.

> Panama is strong in that they collect a lot of data from not only financial institutions but also from the more than 2,000 companies in the Colon Free Trade Zone. But they need additional resources to do sound analysis and provide results to investigating authorities or share with other FIUs. In the Caribbean, Haiti did not have adequate facilities to store the financial reporting data their new laws required banks to provide (LAC expert 2010).

There are those that caution about the difficulty in measuring the payoff in committing financial resources in fighting financial crime.

> Trying to measure the success of an FIU in financial performance terms is a recipe for disaster. The FIU is not an income producing entity. That being said, if the country has strong forfeiture laws (most do not) then the FIU can contribute to financial crimes investigations that can lead to the seizure and forfeiture of criminally derived assets from real estate and homes to bank accounts. In those areas, the FIU can generate significant income to the country. Last year, the U.S. law enforcement agencies forfeited nearly $2 billion in criminal assets. Just look at the dollar volume of drug trafficking, corruption and fraud in Latin America and the Caribbean and you can see a strong potential for asset recovery (LAC expert 2010).

This is seconded by another opinion.

> Public policies should be geared toward increasing people's sensitivities in the issues. Invest in enhancing public culture. Performance measurement is complicated. If the numerator is difficult to assess, it doesn't matter what you put in the denominator. It is easy to measure number of jobs created but not this (success in countering financial crime) (Spanish expert 2008).

Table 6.3 contains a list of performance measures that experts suggested can be used to measure the financial performance of FIUs.

To be successful, FIUs must first look within their borders and estimate the nature and size of the problem, because success is measured against the magnitude of the problem. Investment in resources to counter money laundering and terrorist financing should vary with the prevailing degree of the problem and should justify a menace that "touches more people than murder" (Global financial crime expert1 2007). This is a major challenge. Anecdotal evidence suggests that if the government invests in countering one method of financial crime, occurrences of crime through other methods will increase. Criminals are always finding ways to reinvent themselves in their efforts to raise and move money undetected. Therefore, investment in implementing the Financial Action Task Force's (FATF) 40 Recommendations will not stop money laundering but only mitigate it (Australian expert 2006).

Table 6.3   Suggested Performance Measures That Address FIU Financial Performance

Investment in technology and training personnel could see a return on investment in the form of higher conviction rates (MENA expert 2010).

Increase the amount of investment toward nonbanking sectors that have been weakly regulated until recently (Global financial crime expert1 2008).

It is difficult to judge success in the AML/CTF world, as no one quite knows the number of money launderers or the amount of money laundered (American expert 2005).

Financial performance should be measured in terms of improved efficiency and not in terms of case size. Cases differ in size and importance, and it is important to stop crime irrespective of these factors (American expert 2005).

A suitable measure for monitoring an agency's financial performance is the ability of the agency to meet its budget (Australian expert 2006).

The best indicator of an FIU's fiscal performance would be the amount of financial crime these investment efforts help deter (Dutch expert 2005).

Financial performance is based on feedback. The value of investment is an indicator of financial performance, which can be derived through feedback from the agency's stakeholders (Canadian expert 2006).

One can't put a price on enforcing a culture of honesty (Australian expert 2009).

Work Processes

Cumbersome reporting requirements, lack of information sharing and communication, and an absence of suitable accountability mechanisms are some of the shortfalls that hinder FIUs from achieving a higher level of success. This can be improved by strengthening stakeholder relations and tightening work protocols.

Strengthening Stakeholder Relations

The most integral part of an FIU's function is working with reporting entities, law enforcement, and its domestic and international partners in fighting financial crime. Some FIUs operate in a bureaucratic environment, which impedes communication with these entities (American expert 2008). Communication among all parties is essential to making the system work. One way of going about this is for the FIUs to follow up on their reports in terms of finding out how the information they receive and distribute relates to outcomes (American expert 2008).

Reporting Entities

According to a survey conducted by KPMG in 2007, bank costs related to AML/CTF (anti-money laundering/counterterrorist financing) compliance increased over the previous three years by 58 percent. The survey, conducted among 224 banks in 55 countries, showed that American banks experienced a 70 percent increase in these costs. Banks expected their compliance costs to rise by 34 percent over the following three years, an estimate considered optimistic (*Calgary Herald* 2007). In some countries, AML compliance requirements have been a source of frustration among reporting entities who find them time consuming (Dutch expert 2005). One bank, for example, found reporting criteria unclear, especially in areas such as the international cash transfers (Dutch expert 2005). In another case, a money laundering reporting officer (MLRO) provides his country's FIU with a compliance report every year and also reports suspicious matters from time to time on behalf of his organization. However, the organization is never clued about how that information is used once it is reported, and it is also never included in the AML/CTF process past that point (Australian expert 2009). In yet another case, the Financial Services Authority (FSA) in the United Kingdom helps firms identify risks, but also requests that they comply with production orders that they find burdensome (British expert 2008).

While there are problems in the relationship between reporting entities and financial-crime-fighting government agencies, there are also positives. Some FIUs align their compliance requirements with international customer due-diligence requirements, which makes it more convenient for reporting entities (Dutch expert 2005). Some FIUs enthusiastically work with reporting entities to put into practice compliance rules and regulations. These FIUs provide quick responses to queries and always confirm the receipt of information with reporting entities (Spanish expert 2009). Outreach efforts for reporting entities include seminars, workshops, etc. (American expert 2008). FINTRAC has an extensive outreach program that included more than 500 information sessions for reporting entities in the 2003–04 fiscal year and responses to 1,800 queries from reporting entities during this period (FINTRAC 2004). UKFIU organizes conferences for small and medium-sized businesses such as money service businesses (MSBs), accountants, independent financial advisors (IFAs), and solicitors' firms to increase their awareness of the vulnerabilities of their businesses to financial crime and the importance of filing SARs. These conferences are held around the United Kingdom and attract approximately 175 delegates per conference (UKFIU n.d.a). Table 6.4 is an example of SOCA outreach efforts in the United Kingdom.

UKFIU within SOCA facilitates regular dialogue between law enforcement end users and other stakeholders of the SARs regime to ensure that there is constructive communication and input into policy development and into developing and publicizing best practices and guidance. UKFIU also facilitates a quarterly dialogue meeting with representatives from U.K. law enforcement agencies to share knowledge (trends and typologies) and best practices and to encourage working jointly across operational and organizational boundaries. UKFIU provides feedback in the form of a report on the extent to which SARs were used. In certain cases, UKFIU will even provide an individual business with feedback on its reported SARs (UKFIU n.d.b).

Table 6.4   Feedback Provided by SOCA in the United Kingdom

In response to international requirements, FIUs have employed various methods to provide more frequent and meaningful feedback to the private sector through formal and informal information channels. In the United Kingdom, SOCA's more formal, structured means include:

- SOCA meeting with a vetted group of representatives of the reporting sectors, of law enforcement, and of key policy departments to discuss sensitive casework and reporting issues.
- Holding quarterly sector-specific seminars for MLROs and senior management to discuss improving the quality of reporting, how SARs are used to fight crime, and threats to individual sectors.
- Presentations to financial institutions through SOCA's liaison team that provide detail relating to typologies and indicators.
- Information provided in SOCA's annual reports, Web site, and newsletter, which contain statistics, typologies, and other information.

Source: Memorandum by the Fraud Advisory Panel, 2009.

FIUs can improve their relationship with reporting entities in a number of ways. Efficiency in tracing money laundered through new trends can be increased through mutual feedback between reporting entities and FIUs (Australian expert 2006). For example, one of the challenges that FINCEN faces is how to get MSBs to register so that they can be monitored better. An audit by the Treasury Report recommended that "FINCEN needs to develop and track performance indicators to measure how registration is improving BSA compliance by the MSB industry, consider clarifying guidance regarding the dollar threshold for MSB designation, and continue efforts to address data quality issues with the publicly available MSB registration list" (U.S. Department of Treasury 2005). If the FIU were to enhance communication with these cash dealers, it would certainly help (Australian expert 2006). An important source of feedback is those who are first to receive financial transaction information (Canadian expert 2005).

Compliance rates of reporting entities with AML/CTF-reporting requirements could be increased if FIU personnel were less technical and bureaucratic in dealing with reporting entities (Dutch expert 2005). FIUs walk a thin line in this regard, as noncompliance penalties that are too soft or compliance requirements that overimpose on the confidentiality of reporting entities or that result in heavy compliance costs to reporting entities could lower compliance rates (Dutch expert 2005). A satisfaction survey, with multiple-choice and open-answer questions, circulated among reporting entities would provide useful feedback in developing and revising reporting requirements. FIUs can solidify their relationships with reporting entities by reporting back to them the outcome of law enforcements' investigations of cases these entities reported (Dutch expert 2005). Additionally, FIUs could increase their support functions to reporting entities and help them interpret legislation (Dutch expert 2005).

FIUs could also keep track of compliance costs incurred by reporting entities, provide clarity in reporting instructions, and guarantee confidentiality of reported information (Dutch expert 2005). By setting a clear parameter with respect to what FIUs are looking for and providing all relevant information (such as the different financial crime methodologies) to reporting entities, FIUs can help them fulfill their reporting obligations (British expert 2008). FIUs should share knowledge beyond conferences and enhance communication by informing reporting entities how they have contributed in the financial-crime-fighting process (British expert 2008). Where possible, government should refine guidelines to reporting entities to make them more understandable and less burdensome (Global financial crime expert2 2008). An appropriate measure of FIU performance is the level of awareness and comprehension of reporting requirements by these entities (British expert 2008).

Law Enforcement

A good measure of FINCEN's efficiency is its ability to analyze information forwarded to it by reporting entities and produce final reports for authorized law enforcement and regulatory agencies in a timely manner (American expert 2006). Performance can be measured both by the number of leads forwarded by FIUs to law enforcement agencies and by the number of cases for which FIU data is used (American expert 2006). Indeed, if FIU resources are presently directed toward the regulated sectors, then more could be spent on enhancing service to law enforcement (American expert 2006).

FIUs are often criticized for generating reports that lack utility. In Canada,

> Law enforcement and security agencies normally find that the information FINTRAC discloses is too limited to warrant action, given their existing case-loads and scarce resources [and legislation limiting the type of information that can be disclosed]. In short, as the system now works, FINTRAC disclosures do contribute to existing investigations but rarely generate new ones (Auditor General Canada 2004).

Under this state of affairs, law enforcement might understandably be reluctant to allocate scarce resources to fight financial crime, which they might perceive to be an exercise in futility (Auditor General Canada 2004). The end result is that the security net is compromised (Canadian expert 2005). Some FIUs have tried to address this by linking their database systems to law enforcement, thereby providing direct access to the information they need to conduct investigations (Australian expert 2006). A suitable measure of performance here is the percentage of intelligence provided by FIUs that is actually used in investigations (Australian expert 2006).

Another important aspect of FIUs' relationship with law enforcement is organization. When FIUs distribute reports to multiple law enforcement and intelligence agencies, they must ensure that information is well coordinated among these agencies in order to increase the utility of the information. FIUs could address this, for example, if they by-passed sending reports to the headquarters of agencies and distributed them directly among regional offices. This is especially important in the post-9/11 era, which has seen an increase in the number of reports distributed (American expert 2006). They should also keep tabs on how many cases are being forwarded to the police (American expert 2006). Ideally, FIUs must always be responsive to and cooperative with law enforcement and other intelligence agencies and clarify information in reports as needed (American expert 2006). In this case, the appropriate performance measure is the quality of the information FIUs distribute to law enforcement (Dutch expert 2005).

In certain countries, the legal structure impedes FIUs from achieving a higher level of satisfaction for its customers. In Canada, the flow of information from FINTRAC to other agencies and law enforcement is restricted due to the arms-length nature of FINTRAC's relationship with them. The police force can only follow up on investigations with a judicial order in hand. Another problem is that the definition of financial crime differs among law enforcement and FIUs, which causes operational problems. FIUs can help account for these limitations by sharing information in a timely manner, increasing its credibility with law enforcement through the relevance of its disclosures, and streamlining data to them (Canadian expert 2005).

Satisfaction with FIU performance is measured through feedback from law enforcement: "Can people receiving FIUs' product make a contribution? Was it of use? What type of use was it put to? Did it identify activities that were not known?" (Canadian expert 2006). If FIUs are unable to produce a report on a person or entity on which law enforcement needs information, then law enforcement is unhappy (Canadian expert 2005). Of utmost importance are the accuracy, timeliness, extent, and quality of coverage of FIU reports to law enforcement (British expert 2008). To enhance performance in this area, FIUs should look for opportunities to partner with the private sector in the spheres of communication, training, investigations, and feedback, and these efforts must be substantial and not merely rhetorical (British expert 2008).

The bottom line is: Are FIU reports helping law enforcement build a case for prosecution of financial criminals (Dutch expert 2005)? In Spain, the quality of intelligence provided by SEPBLAC to law enforcement and other agencies has fallen short of this deliverable. The major recipients of SEPBLAC's reports, the national police (*Guardia Civil*) and the anticorruption prosecutor, found that reports lack the necessary leads to begin an investigation. Hence, there is a call for the active participation of law enforcement in the analytical process so that SEPBLAC personnel can understand what information will really help law enforcement achieve outcomes (International Monetary Fund 2007). This pragmatic approach should be adopted by all FIUs.

Domestic and International Partners

FIUs work with other domestic agencies, such as industry regulators and bank supervisors, and with international agencies in fighting financial crime. This can be in the form of shared responsibilities or case support. For example, FINTRAC has "26 memoranda of understanding (MOUs) with other countries and with regulatory bodies such as the Office of the Superintendent of Financial Institutions Canada" (Canadian expert 2005). These MOUs have certain advantages: "There is a two-way benefit. People operating within the sectors don't have to see two people show up at their door. It helps FINTRAC in its responsibility, as it has to cover a lot of ground for a small agency" (Canadian expert 2006). In the United States, FINCEN issues case support to

Table 6.5   Reporting Entities and Their Regulatory Supervisors in the United States

1. *Depository Institutions*: The Board of Governors of the Federal Reserve, the Office of the Comptroller of the Currency, the Federal Deposit Insurance Corporation, the Office of Thrift Supervision, and the National Credit Union Administration have been delegated authority to examine the depository institutions they regulate for Bank Secrecy Act compliance.

2. *Securities Broker-Dealers, Mutual Funds, and Futures Commission Merchants/Introducing Brokers*: FINCEN has delegated examination authority to the Securities and Exchange Commission and the Commodity Futures Trading Commission, and relies on their self-regulatory agencies (such as the NASD, the NYSE, and the NFA) to examine these entities for compliance.

3. *Other Financial Institutions*: The Internal Revenue Service (Small Business/Self-Employed Division) has been delegated responsibility for examining all other financial institutions subject to Bank Secrecy Act regulation for compliance, including, for example, depository institutions with no federal regulator, casinos, and Money Service Businesses (MSBs).

Source: U.S. Senate Committee on Banking, Housing, and Urban Affairs.

more than 165 federal, state, and local agencies, issuing approximately 6,500 intelligence reports each year (FINCEN n.d.b). It also delegates authority to a number of its federal regulatory partners to conduct compliance exams. For example, federal regulators of financial reporting entities are assigned responsibility by the type of financial institution, as seen in Table 6.5.

Like FINTRAC and FINCEN, AUSTRAC has been successful in forming partnerships with other agencies. In total, it has established MOUs with 28 partner agencies in Australia (Australian expert 2006). AUSTRAC personnel work onsite with its partner agencies like the Australian Security Intelligence Organization, and personnel from the Australian Crime Commission work at AUSTRAC's Sydney office to enhance cooperation and collaboration (Australian expert 2006). In the United Kingdom, SOCA shares responsibilities of its duties through partnership agreements with regulators such as the FSA, the Gambling Commission, and HM Revenue and Customs. It has MOUs or JWAs (joint working agreements) on SARs with regulators like the Solicitors' Regulatory Authority, the Institute of Certified Bookkeepers, the Association of International Accountants, etc., and is in the process of negotiating with other regulators such as the Office of Fair Trading (UKFIU n.d.b). In Asia, FIU-India has forged partnerships with other agencies to crack down on financial criminals. It has signed an MOU with the Central Bureau of Investigation (CBI), India's intelligence agency, to share information on suspicious transactions and suspected criminal cases, and serves as a link to foreign FIUs on the CBI's behalf (*Times of India* 2010). Unlike in more developed countries, FIUs in the MENA region do not have a high level of authority and input in banking supervision. Therefore, a more robust dialog between FIUs and industry regulators would help in tackling financial crime in that region (American expert 2010).

AUSTRAC has also established a strong bond with the international community. "As an FIU, AUSTRAC is held in high esteem. The requests for AUSTRAC processes and provisions have been numerous" (Australian expert 2006). AUSTRAC completed the Australia-Indonesia Intelligence Unit Cooperation Project through which it helped Indonesia develop its FIU (AUSTRAC 2006). It also has established a strong relationship with other AML networks and FIUs like FINCEN through its 46 MOUs with foreign FIUs and its association with the Egmont Group and the Asia Pacific Group on Money Laundering (Australian expert 2006). Spanish authorities too have engaged in multilateral cooperation and established a close relationship with Gibraltar and other countries associated with money laundering (Spanish expert 2009). In this regard, it is useful for FIUs to adopt performance measures, such as how quickly they respond to information requests from foreign countries.

Despite these positive examples, there are a number of instances that highlight the lack of collaboration between reporting entities, FIUs, law enforcement, and other intelligence agencies. Because police investigations are conducted in strict confidentiality, reporting entities are not always made aware of how to improve the quality of their reporting that might help the authorities improve their success in tackling financial crime. The flow of information is one-way at times (Australian expert 2009). Therefore, an important performance measure here is the quality of the content of FIU communications (SEPBLAC 2007). The level of collaboration (or lack of) among law enforcement, reporting entities, and domestic and foreign financial-crime-fighting authorities is an important indicator of success (Spanish expert 2008).

Better collaboration is advice that is easier to put on paper than in practice. "With regard to industry sectors, FIUs should monitor trends globally, report trends to the reporting community and reflect trends in their own analytical systems in-house. Police, on the other hand, should be reporting new trends to FIUs. It is a two-way street" (Australian expert 2006). Ideally, roles should be well defined among agencies fighting financial crime, and the regulatory structure should be clear so as to prevent any turf wars. There should also be good cooperation between the private and public sectors in terms of the sharing of information, what information to share, and what investigations to undertake. However, there has been concern expressed in some corners that information sharing might compromise investigations (British expert 2008).

In the United Kingdom, UKFIU has followed the recommendations of the "Review of the Suspicious Activity Reports Regime" (the SARs Review) by Sir Stephen Lander and the "U.K. Law Enforcement Agency Use and Management of Suspicious Activity Reports: Towards Determining the Value of the Regime" by Matthew H. Fleming of the Jill Dando Institute at the University College London:

1. Increase communication with reporting entities to improve the quality of their reports and work with regulators to devise a risk-management plan for these entities (UKFIU n.d.c)
2. Increase communication with law enforcement agencies to increase their utility of SARs and the ELMER* database (Fleming 2005)

Finally, a good AML regime must take into account how it impacts ordinary citizens whose contributions to tax revenue help pay for its costs. While the general public may lack interest in AML matters (Australian expert 2006), they are impacted by it. For instance, tighter AML regulations might affect citizens in terms of time and money. For instance, they might find it a nuisance to produce identification just to play at the slot machine at the casino (Australian expert 2006).

Tightening Work Protocols

The organization of FIUs varies from one agency to another. In Canada, for example, FINTRAC falls under Canada's Department of Finance (Canadian expert 2006). FINTRAC personnel at its three regional offices (Western, Central, Eastern) are assigned various sectors within their region where they ensure that reporting entities adhere to compliance guidelines (Canadian expert 2005). UKFIU is divided into a number of teams based on function. These are listed in Table 6.6.

FIUs are specifically structured to carry out their functions. In the United States, for example, the Analysis and Liaison Division is the intelligence arm of FINCEN responsible for collecting financial intelligence and analyzing it to determine links to money laundering, terrorist financing, and other financial crime, which it then forwards to law enforcement and other domestic intelligence agencies. Its products include threat assessments, industry reports, and technical guides to financial transaction mechanisms. The Management Programs Division performs functions such as human resources, financial management, and administrative services, while the Technology Solutions and Services Division provides technical support to FINCEN (FINCEN n.d.). The International Programs Division facilitates information sharing with its foreign counterparts, provides technical advice to them on how to combat

* The database used by SOCA PoC to hold SAR information.

Table 6.6 Organizational Framework of UKFIU

SAR Administration and Control

- Managing the SAR regime and processing Suspicious Activity Reports (SARs) from the reporting sector
- Maintaining control of the supporting IT
- Establishing best practices for ELMER use and ELMER feedback
- Ensuring business continuity
- Responding to CPIA and evidential obligations

Consent

- Collection, collation, and dissemination of consent-derived intelligence, working in partnership with LEA and the reporting sector to ensure best practice
- Developing the use of consent within LEAs and the reporting sector as an intervention tool

Dialogue

- Providing the interface between the UKFIU and the operational stakeholders in the SAR regime, including the reporting sector, regulators, and SARs end users
- Providing individual feedback to stakeholders on SARs reporting standards and activity and feedback from stakeholders to the UKFIU.

Intelligence

- Proactively analyzing SAR-derived intelligence for the purposes of strategic and tactical assessments
- Maintaining an overall view of the U.K. anti-money-laundering picture to provide a context for the exploitation of SARs to meet U.K. and international obligations.

International

- Meeting the international obligations of the UKFIU to the Egmont Group and other FIUs through the provision of financial intelligence upon request, both for U.K. LEAs and for international partners.

Terrorist Finance Team and PEPs*

- Continuing the specialized approach to terrorist finance-related SARs by proactively analyzing SAR-derived intelligence. The team develops relationships with intelligence agencies and the reporting sectors in this discrete area of work.

UKNCO

- The central U.K. office for all matters relating to counterfeit currency and protected coins.

Source: FATF 2007.

* Politically Exposed Persons: It is the activities of a minority of corrupt PEPs that are of concern to reporting institutions and U.K. law enforcement (*Combating Money Laundering and Recovering Looted Gains: Raising the U.K.'s Game*, Transparency International, U.K.).

financial crime, and produces reports on financial crime that involve international matters.

This basic structure is more or less the same for FIUs in all countries, but compliance reporting obligations, information sharing and communications, and the way FIUs are held accountable are different in each country.

Facilitating Compliance Reporting

Much of FIUs' work processes are dictated to by the AML/CTF laws of a country.

> Procedures of FIUs depend on the national laws of each country. The FIUs are formed generally consistent with the FATF and Egmont Group standards, but they can only do what their national laws permit them to do. For example, if the national laws do not permit disclosure of bank information, then the FIU cannot secure bank information nor can it share it with other countries, so it loses credibility (LAC expert 2010).

Laws differ from country to country in determining which private sector entities have reporting obligations to that country's FIU. In Spain, for example, the financial entities that report to SEPBLAC include commercial banks, savings banks, credit cooperatives, and banking branches of foreign entities. These account for about 88 percent of the suspicious transaction reports received by SEPBLAC. Other reporting entities include notaries, casinos, and property development and real estate agencies (SEPBLAC 2007). Besides these entities, authorities and officials who discover unusual or suspicious transactions are also expected to report these to SEPBLAC. Spain's SEPBLAC has seen a steady increase in the number of suspicious transaction reports over the years. In 2007, these reports were up by 23 percent over the previous year. In that same year, the number of reporting entities obligated to report to SEPBLAC under the law grew to exceed 10,000 (SEPBLAC 2007). Despite this growth, the number of prosecutions and convictions for serious cases of money laundering in Spain is reportedly low.

Governments must decide what transactions are to be reported to FIUs. A common problem here is "defensive reporting," whereby entities report more than what is necessary in an effort to conform with compliance regulations and avoid punishment (Australian expert 2006). This raises a question about the quality of data received by FIUs, i.e., "Is it suspicious?" (Australian expert 2006). In the Netherlands, objective and subjective indicators are used to decide whether transactions are "unusual." Objective indicators are a set of criteria according to which entities are obligated to disclose transactions. Subjective indicators are those that would require disclosure subject to the judgment of the entity, i.e., transactions where the institution has reason to believe that they are connected with money laundering or the financing of terrorism (Nederlandse Vereniging van Banken n.d.). The system of indicators used by FIU-NL changes with time as some indicators are deleted and new ones added (MOT 2003). There was a time when the number of objective indicators was reduced while the number of subjective ones was increased, giving reporting entities more liberty to define their own criteria in reporting potential money launderers and terrorist financers (Dutch expert 2005). The changes in these indicators have an impact on the number of unusual transactions reported.

Reporting obligations vary from country to country, but they do share common aspects. Table 6.7 illustrates reporting obligations to AUSTRAC.

The events of 9/11 led to the mandate of a number of FIUs being expanded to include terrorist financing, and this has resulted in a gush of reported information to these FIUs. However, because of operational constraints, FIUs are able to handle only a certain volume (Canadian expert 2005).

Table 6.7   Types of Information Reported to AUSTRAC

AUSTRAC routinely monitors domestic transactions over $10,000 as well as international transactions. There are currently five types of information reported to AUSTRAC:

- *Significant cash transactions reports*: These reports must be submitted by cash dealers/ reporting entities and solicitors for transactions involving A$10,000 cash or more (or the foreign currency equivalent).
- *Suspect transactions reports*: These are lodged by cash dealers/reporting entities when they have reasonable grounds to suspect that a transaction, actual or attempted, may involve the proceeds of crime, the evasion of tax, or other breaches of federal, state, or territory laws.
- *International funds transfer instructions*: These instructions must be reported by cash dealers/reporting entities for monies being telegraphically transferred or wired into or out of Australia. These instructions are reportable for any amount, whether paid by cash or otherwise.
- *Cross-border movements of physical currency (CBM-PCs)/international currency transfer reports*: CBM-PCs are reports about the movement of physical currency into or out of Australia. All movements of A$10,000 or more (or the foreign currency equivalent) must be reported.
- *Cross-border movements–bearer negotiable instruments (CBM-BNIs)*: CBM-BNIs are reports of BNIs being carried into or out of Australia and are not mandatory. A police or customs officer may ask a person to declare whether they have any BNIs in their possession and may then require a report of the BNIs being carried.

Source: Australian Taxation Office, 2009, copyright Commonwealth of Australia, reproduced by permission.

Information-Sharing and Communications

FIUs and financial-crime-fighting agencies realize that information sharing is of utmost importance to the smooth flow of work processes. For instance, AUSTRAC has an information-exchange system with law enforcement.

> Round-table meetings on issues such as financial crime are held periodically with a number of law enforcement agencies in attendance. Documents and conclusions are drafted from these meetings. For example, the future of cyber crime is looked into—what's going to happen in 10 years (Australian expert 2006).

Financial-crime-fighting entities in Spain are also actively engaged in information sharing. Financial service representatives and Spanish authorities, for example, hold forums to update each other on work-related issues and also present any heads-up situations to each other. The Banco de España and the Comisión Nacional del Mercado de Valores (CNMV) are in the process of developing training programs to increase know-how in tackling financial crime. The Spanish authorities are well aware that information sharing and collaboration in tackling financial crime is critical (Spanish expert 2009).

Communications issued by FIUs are just as vital as information sharing. SOCA conducts a threat assessment that includes a financial-risk outlook. This is then passed on to reporting entities. For example, in 2008, firms were asked to look out for mortgage fraud (British expert 2008). FINCEN analyzes new money laundering methods and threats as they arise.

> These analyses are often included in "The SAR Activity Review—Trends, Tips, and Issues," which [it] publishes under the auspices of the Bank Secrecy Act Advisory Group. In the past several years, "The SAR Activity Review—Trends, Tips, and Issues" has included analyses of informal value transfer systems, computer intrusion at banks, food stamp fraud using electronic benefit transfer cards, and use of automated teller machines to avoid Bank Secrecy Act (BSA) reporting requirements (American expert 2005).

UKFIU is part of the European Suspicious Transaction Reporting Project, which promotes AWS SUSTRANS (an analytical work file that keeps track of money laundering for Europol). It has also helped produce a Statement of Intent for the project (Fraud Advisory Panel 2009).

FIU performance can be improved when it comes to information sharing and communications. For example, some FIUs can increase the quality of reporting of activities, statistics, typologies, and trends by meeting FATF standards (FATF 2007). There are also some FIUs that could strive to be more transparent in their external relations, which is presently not the case. For example, SOCA works under a cloud of secrecy, and its business affairs are very internalized. This is probably because a number of its personnel are former spies who prefer shunning publicity. Therefore, the organization is not as transparent or accountable as it should be. By having a more open relationship with the private sector, it would establish greater control over reporting entities. There is also a reluctance on its part to trust people outside law enforcement (British expert 2008). In seeking interviews for this book, some of the FIUs I approached—including the NCIS (United Kingdom), CTIF-CFI (Belgium), and SEPBLAC (Spain)—declined my request and directed me to their respective Web sites instead. In the case of the latter, I was informed that the law prevented personnel from answering my questions.

Developing Accountability Mechanisms

There are a number of building blocks on which FIUs can develop accountability mechanisms that address work processes. For starters, antifinancial crime controls could be preventive rather than detective. There should be appropriate know-your-customer (KYC) protocols to detect the financial crime risk of customers of financial institutions. FIUs should first define control mechanisms, and current protocols should be loosened to make compliance enforcement easier for reporting entities (Spanish expert 2009). In Spain, an attempt was made to improve the business process through Order EHA/2444/2007. According to this, reporting entities must have an external consultant annually evaluate "the existing internal control measures, assess their operational effectiveness and propose, where appropriate, any adjustments or improvements" (Invenia 2007). The motive behind this, besides enhancing risk management of reporting entities, is to increase reporting compliance, which will lead to the reduction of financial crime (SEPBLAC 2007).

Performance measures are the trademark of accountability mechanisms. Besides those measures already discussed—such as the number of reports, i.e., the percentage increase in STRs (Australian expert 2006), the value of information provided to law enforcement (Spanish expert 2008), and the quality of intelligence in reports)Australian expert 2006)—there are still some measures that fall outside the box. These are related to areas that lie beyond the control of FIUs, such as legislation, which brings up the question: "Is the legal framework conducive to helping FIUs fulfill their missions?" (Global financial crime expert2 2008). Table 6.8 contains performance measures that selected FIUs use or could use.

There are complex issues surrounding accountability mechanisms in the broader context of combating financial crime. Because financial investigations are conducted in confidence, there is no real way to determine the success of FIUs.

Table 6.8   Current and Suggested FIU Performance Measures by Country

An appropriate performance measure is how long SOCA takes to respond to consent requests.* SOCA, however, should spend time on gathering intelligence that could potentially result in terrorists being caught. Therefore, it might be best not to have measures (British expert 2008). Another performance measure is the level of utilization of SARs in a given time period (British expert 2008).

FINTRAC has a strong emphasis on performance management. "Output is measured quarterly and annually. It falls on each department to measure success" (Canadian expert 2006). FINTRAC issues an annual Departmental Performance Report. In its performance management plan, FINTRAC ties expected results to strategic outcomes. In the past, FINTRAC received criticism that its performance management plan focused only on operations and not on the impact of its programs. Even the operational measures such as "numbers of reports received, disclosures made, compliance initiatives introduced, contacts made with stakeholders, and memoranda of understanding signed" lacked performance targets. However, FINTRAC is developing an Integrated Performance Management Framework, the implementation of which should provide the backbone for enhanced accountability and disclosure of results (FINTRAC 2004).

Spanish authorities would probably be better served if a comprehensive database was maintained on statistics such as the number of STRs filed for cross-border currency movement and the number of "spontaneous" referrals made by SEPBLAC to non-Spanish authorities (IMF 2007). When it comes to improving performance in countering financial crime, SEPBLAC could use resources efficiently, especially in times of economic downturn, and further develop systems that will help reporting entities increase compliance (Spanish expert 2009).

AUSTRAC is an agency with one output—the reduction of money laundering (Australian expert 2006).

Performance measures adopted by FIU-NL should be based on the entire chain of authority (financial institutions, the FIU, police, justice, special investigating institutions, supervisory bodies, etc.) and include:

Catching ratio (the chance that a money launderer is caught by the chain):

- the number of money launderers that investigating institutions have caught in relation to the estimated population of money launderers
- the amount of money that is caught by investigating institutions in relation to the estimated total amount of money being laundered

Punishing ratio (the chance that a caught money launderer will get punishment from the chain):

- the number of caught money launderers that have received a form of punishment/sanction (this can be an administrative fine or a sentence to jail).

Recidivist ratio

- the number of money launderers that have been caught and punished in earlier cases (indicator of the success of the punishments that are used, as low punishments are not a barrier to committing the crime again) (Dutch expert 2005).

---

* SOCA also allows persons and businesses generally, and not just those in the Regulated Sector, to avail themselves of a defense against money laundering charges by seeking consent of the authorities (via the UKFIU) to conduct a transaction or undertake other activity (a "prohibited act") about which they have concerns (SOCA).

This (lack of transparency) means that FIUs can define success in their own terms and, more importantly, FIUs are the only ones who have the scorecard and keep their own score. This is unsatisfactory. This, in turn, means that FIUs or the attorney general can define success and report on their success scorecard using numbers that can be obtained by a proctologist with a good flashlight. FIUs will always report how successful they are (Australian expert 2009).

The lack of independent oversight of intelligence agency power and authority compromises success.

Methods used to track money launderers and terrorists need only be tweaked slightly to be used to persecute those who are a "political" or "religious" threat or just happen to be related to a terrorist (that is, Dr. Mohammed Haneef being wrongfully arrested and detained because his second cousin tried to blow up an airport in the United Kingdom). No one would know if such a persecution is taking place because there is no independent oversight (Australian expert 2009).

In this concluding segment, I'd like to mention Fareed Zakaria's column in *Newsweek* magazine, where he predicted that the U.S. government's course of action in the fight against terrorism would be to throw money at the problem. Zakaria asserted that there is a pressing need to shore up the country's intelligence capabilities rather than its military strength (Zakaria 2001). He emphasized the importance of gathering information on organizations and people responsible for planning and carrying out terrorist acts such as those that took place on 9/11. He also suggested investing in wiretapping and satellite equipment, but mainly in human intelligence. "We need, for example, to shore up an important weapon in our arsenal—covert operations. They remain the best way to penetrate a terrorist organization, foil a plot or pre-empt an attack on the United States" (Zakaria 2001).

The fight against financial crime faces a similar predicament. When one considers the grand scheme of things, the amount of assets frozen or funds confiscated (or even money recovered) by governments pales in comparison to the volume of money laundered or used to finance terrorism. There is an overwhelming consensus that the success of governments' investment in combating financial crime will ultimately be determined not by their outpouring of human, technological, and financial resources, but by the way these are used, i.e., the outcomes they produce. Governments must go beyond keeping count of SARs received and MOUs with stakeholders and entities that are covered by reporting requirements. Rather, they must link these documents with achieved outcomes to truly measure performance in countering financial crime. Therefore, it might be worthwhile for government to invest in researching new methods of financial crime (such as the use of underground banking and the Internet to launder funds and finance terrorism) while continuing to invest in staff (both in terms of adding new personnel and enhancing skills and knowledge of existing personnel) and the availability and improvement of technology for its financial-crime-fighting personnel (Dutch expert 2005). The bottom line is that FIUs can achieve a higher level of performance by managing resources and tracking processes to monitor the outcomes they produce. This will lead to the ultimate outcome of mitigating financial crime. While most experts agree that financial crime cannot be stopped completely, the problem can be alleviated by methodically producing a higher return on the resources and effort that governments invest in processes to deter financial criminals.

References

Auditor General of Canada. 2004. "Implementation of the national initiative to combat money laundering," November 23. http://www.oag-bvg.gc.ca/domino/repo rts.nsf/html/2004 1102ce.html.

AUSTRAC. 2006. "2004–05 Annual Report," August 31. http://www.austrac.g ov.au/ annualr eport/index.htm.

AUSTRAC. 2010. "Annual Report 2010," October 20. http://www.austr ac.gov.au/ pr_sect ion1_promo.html.

AUSTRAC. n.d. "Operational intelligence." http://www.austr ac.gov.au/operati onal_ intelligence.html.

Australian Taxation Office. 2009. www.ato.gov.au/super/content.aspx?doc=/content/46908.htm&page=22&H22

Calgary Herald. 2007. "Money laundering drives up bank costs," July 10.

FATF. 2007. www.oecd.org/dataoecd/55/29/39064399.pdf

FATF. 2007. "Recommendations for anti-money laundering and combating the financing of terrorism," IMF Country Report 07/70, February.

FATF. 2007. "Summary of the third mutual evaluation report—Anti-money laundering and combating the financing of terrorism: United Kingdom of Great Britain and Northern Ireland," June 29. http://www.fat f-gafi.org/dat aoecd/33/2 0/38917272.pdf.

FINCEN. 2006. www.fincen.gov/news_room/rp/files/strategic_plan_2006.pdf

FINCEN. n.d. "About FINCEN/FAQs." http://www.finc en.gov/af_faqs.html.

FINCEN. n.d. "About Us." http://www.finc e n.gov/aboutus/bio_associate_director_ mp.pdf.

FINCEN. n.d. "FINCEN Strategic Plan for the fiscal years 2003–2008." http://www. fincen.gov/st rategicpla n2003_2008.pdf.

FINCEN. n.d. "FINCEN Strategic Plan for the fiscal years 2006–2008." http://www. fincen.gov/s trategicplan2006_2008.pdf.

FINCEN. 2004 "FINCEN Annual Report 2004." http://www.fincen.gov/fincenannu-alreport2004.pdf.

FINCEN. 2009. "FINCEN Annual Report 2009." http://www.finc en.gov/news_ room/rp/files/Y Ereport/FY2009/ann ualreport.html#OfficeofChief.

FINTRAC. 2004. "Performance Report, for the period ending March 2004," November 5. http://www.fintrac.gc.c a/publications/DPR/2004/6_e.asp.

FINTRAC. 2008. "Report on Plans and Priorities for the years 2005–2006 to 2007–2008," April 30. http://www.fi ntrac.gc.ca/public ations/rpp/2006_2007/1_e.asp.

FIU.NET. n.d. "Welcome to FIU.NET." http://www.fiu.net/.

Fleming, Matthew H. 2005. "UK law enforcement agency use and management of Suspicious Activity Reports: Towards determining the value of the regime," Jill Dando Institute of Crime Science, University College London, June 30.

Fraud Advisory Panel. 2009a. "Inquiry into money laundering and the financing of terrorism." Response to the House of Lords Select Committee on the European Union Sub-Committee F (Home Affairs), February.

Fraud Advisory Panel. 2009b. Memorandum. www.publications.parliament.uk/pa/ld200809/ldselect/ldeucom/132/132we13.htm

Government of the Netherlands. 2005. "Extra budget for combating terrorism," January 24. http://www.government .nl/actueel/n ieuwsarchief/20 05/01January/ 24/0-42-1_42-54369.jsp.

GRECO. 2001. "Evaluation report on Spain: First evaluation round," Council of Europe, June 15.

International Monetary Fund (IMF). 2007. "Spain: Report on the observance of standards and codes FATF Recommendations for anti-money laundering and combating the financing of terrorism."

Interview with American expert, December 16, 2005; January 23, 2006; August 22, 2006; December 17, 2008.

Interview with Australian expert, May 15, 16, 17, 2006; May 7, 2009.

Interview with British expert, July 28, 29, 30, 2008.

Interview with Canadian expert, September 6, 8, 2005; October 3, 2005; August 9, 2006.

Interview with Dutch expert, June 13, 14, 15, 2005.

Interview with global financial crime expert1, March 17, 2007.

Interview with global financial crime expert2, August 1, 2008.

Interview with global financial crime expert3, September 18, 2008.

Interview with Latin American and Caribbean (LAC) expert, February 19, 2010.

Interview with Middle East and North African (MENA) expert, February 10, 2010.

Interview with Spanish expert, August 4, 2008; October 9, 2008; November 27, 2009.

Invenia. 2007. http://www.invenia.es /boe:iberlex :2007.15157.

MOT. 2003. "Administrative processing of reports," *Reports of Unusual Transactions Newsletter*, January.

Nederlandse Vereniging van Banken. n.d. "List of Indicators Unusual Transaction Act (Wet MOT)." http://www.nvb.nl/sc rivo/asset.php?id=12012.

SEPBLAC. 2007. Annual report.

Times of India. 2010. "CBI, Finmin Unit sign MoU on info against economic offenders," April 6.

Treasury Board of Canada Secretariat. 2005. "DPR 2004-2005," October 26. http://www.fintrac.gc. ca/publications/DPR/2 004/6_e.asp.

U.S. Senate Committee on Banking, Housing, and Urban Affairs. n.d. "Statement of William J. Fox." http://banking.senat e. gov/_files/ACF23.pdf.

U.S. Senate Committee on Banking, Housing, and Urban Affairs. www.fincen.gov/news_room/testimony/html/20040603.html

UKFIU. n.d. "SARs Regime Annual Report 2009." http://www.soca.gov.uk/about-soca/the-uk-financial-intelligence-unit/ukfiu-publications.

UKFIU. n.d. "Introduction to SARs." http://www.soca.gov.u k/about-soca/the-uk-fina ncial-intellig ence-unit/ukfiu-publications.

UKFIU. n.d. "Lander Review 2006—Review of the Suspicious Activity Reports (SARs) regime by Sir Stephen Lander." http://www.soca.gov.uk/about-soca/the-uk-financial-intelligence-unit/ukfiu-publications.

U.S. Department of the Treasury's Office of Inspector General. 2005. "Bank Secrecy Act: Major challenges faced by FINCEN in its program to register money service businesses," OIG-05-050, September 27.

Zakaria, Fareed. 2001. "The war on terror goes global," *Newsweek*, September 13.

How to Better the End Outcome of the Fight against Financial Crime

7

This book explores the lack of outcome monitoring in the fight against financial crime by governments all over the world. The type of government agency that it particularly focuses on is the financial intelligence unit (FIU), which is specifically set up to gather and analyze financial intelligence in an effort to address the growing nature of the problem. There is a common perception that while FIUs across the globe have adopted performance measures, they have barely scratched the surface when it comes to monitoring outcomes. In the preliminary research for this study, it was found that the recent rise in terrorist activity has compelled governments to solidify existing initiatives and adopt new ones to counter terrorist financing. These initiatives generally cover all levels of government and transcend sectors. Across borders, there is a pressing need for countries to collaborate and cooperate in intercepting funds of terrorists whose activities, in a number of cases, are transnational. The Wolfsberg Group and Basel Committee are examples of cross-border collaborations to tackle this problem collectively.

While tightening of regulations has been the first plan of action in the playbook of countries affected by terrorism, relatively little action has been taken on the performance-management front. It is profoundly evident from the responses of the anti-financial-crime experts interviewed for this book that organizational effectiveness of intelligence agencies can no longer take a backseat to antiterrorism legislation. In fact, the two must complement each other. In the case of financial crime, for example, much of the success of FIUs is dependent on what private sector entities its governing legislation allows it to monitor and to what extent. In this regard, restrictions imposed by legislation were seen to have negatively affected the outcomes of FIU investigations in more than one country covered in this book.

In agreeing that a number of FIUs are found wanting when it comes to developing and implementing outcome-monitoring systems, experts recommended that all FIUs set substantive targets and monitor progress toward them. There were some who called for the *quality* of intelligence reported to supplant the current system of measuring the *quantity* of intelligence reports processed. There were others who called for collective accountability, that is, a performance-management system that would track financial intelligence from its source of dissemination to those responsible for the indictment and prosecution of financial criminals. There were still others who called for performance comparisons among FIUs.

Interview responses were corroborated by the results of surveys carried out among a bigger sample of anti-financial-crime experts. Other noteworthy comments from survey respondents are also listed in the following sections.

Survey Results

The United States as a Terrorist Target

The U.S. is more of a terrorist target than other countries. However, its financial intelligence agencies do not face a more difficult task countering financial crime nor does their level of performance significantly vary from their non-U.S. counterparts.

America's Fight against Financial Crime

In describing America's vulnerability to terrorism, there are those who feel that America's meddling in the affairs of other nations and evoking sensitivities among ethnic groups in these nations is a major cause of resentment toward the United States. "One of three terrorist attacks worldwide is directed against a U.S. target. And that's not because the United States is a rich capitalist nation. No, terrorists attack the United States primarily for what it does, not what it is" (Eland 1998). Survey respondents confirmed this sentiment.

Survey respondents also felt that success in fighting terrorism can best be achieved through a joint effort with other countries. While the United States has played the lead role in the fight against terrorism and terrorist financing, it has sought and formed alliances with countries globally. This is substantiated in the preface of a 2001 report by the U.S. Department of State, "Patterns of Global Terrorism."

> [T]errorism cast its lethal shadow across the globe—yet the world's resolve to defeat it has never been greater. ... This chilling report details the very clear and present danger that terrorism poses to the world and the efforts that the United States and our partners in the international community are making to defeat it. The cold, hard facts presented here compel the world's continued vigilance and concerted action (U.S. Department of State 2001).

Due to the cross-border activities of terrorists, countering financial crime is a global effort and its difficulty is shared by all.

The Performance of Financial Intelligence Agencies after September 11, 2001

Survey respondents opined that the performance of financial intelligence agencies has improved after the 9/11 attacks, which could be attributed to the introduction of new anti-money-laundering/counterterrorist-financing (AML/CTF) controls. The tightening of the legislative noose after the attacks gave intelligence agencies, in and outside the United States, wide-ranging powers to track down financial criminals. However, general opinion suggests that there is still work to be done as financial criminals find new ways to raise funds for terrorism. Former CIA director, General Michael Hayden, proved this point in an interview when he was asked to describe U.S. antiterrorism efforts: "Certainly, we have put a lot of energy into it. There have been a lot of successes. But as other folks in uniform are fond of saying, the enemy gets a vote, too" (CIA 2007).

Post-9/11 measures, discussed earlier in this book, have possibly resulted in the improvement of financial intelligence agency performance. However, reports indicate that this was not always the case both in the United States and outside it. For example, a bipartisan commission report, "Terrorist Financing," released by the Council on Non-U.S. Relations, accused the Bush government of lacking the political will to compel other governments to combat terrorist financing more stringently (Greenberg 2002). In Canada, FINTRAC investigators "were reportedly surprised to discover that the cash tied to terrorism had risen to 10 percent of the total from less than 5 percent the previous year. ... Despite the large and apparently increasing scale of terrorist fund-raising in Canada, the government has yet to file a charge" (Collacott 2006).

Survey respondents also noted the difference in financial intelligence agency performance in countering traditional and nontraditional methods of financial crime. This could be attributed to regulation. Loopholes in AML/CTF regulations governing financial institutions around the world were addressed almost immediately after the 9/11 attacks. Financial crime that is considered nontraditional was generally only addressed when governments studied the problem in greater detail and realized the extent to which financial criminals resorted to nonbanking conduits to raise and move funds. Survey respondents attributed this to governments' lack of vision. By increasing the level of regulation in vulnerable sectors or freezing the assets of suspected persons or entities, the government is merely pushing terrorists to find alternative means of financing their activities.

Process and Resource Outcomes Are Vital to Financial Intelligence Agency Performance

The previous chapter dwelt on how FIU processes and resources can be tied to outcomes. Responses to the surveys confirmed the importance of doing so. Based on this, recommendations are made for FIU performance improvement. They are organized according to the four perspectives of the Balanced Scorecard.

Business Process

- The operations of the FIU should tie in with its mission, objectives, and goals. Consequently, the FIU should possess the technological capability to achieve these. Study participants opined that terrorists are constantly finding new ways to finance their activities. Advancement in technology could help counter some of these. Technological strength can also enable an FIU to process, analyze, and disseminate a larger volume of suspicious transaction reports (STRs), thereby making it more efficient. Data-mining technologies can also help the FIU meet its regulatory obligations. For example, an FIU can use programs such as GIS to track and register businesses such as money service businesses, which might otherwise be difficult to do.

- Silos or bottlenecks existing within the FIU or the broader chain of authority should be dealt with effectively (Schott 2002, 86–87). If, for instance, the FIU decision-making process were to include employees to the greatest extent possible, it would eliminate feelings of isolationism. Also, experts stated that coordination among government agencies is a major impediment to fighting financial crime. The elimination of bottlenecks in the coordination process will result in greater efficiency in countering financial crime.

- Some recipients expressed dissatisfaction over reports forwarded to them by FIUs. Therefore, the FIU should add value to the information it receives in order to fulfill its role and meet the expectations of entities that follow it in the chain of authority (Schott 2002, 86). An FIU that adopts a more integrated approach in its operations, that is, operates in unison with other players in the fight against financial crime such as reporting entities, law enforcement, and prosecution can alleviate the risk of a broken-up approach to fighting financial crime.

- An FIU must work to institute an effective mechanism that facilitates information sharing and the avoidance of overlapping of duties among crime-fighting agencies. The creation of a central czar that oversees financial crime prevention and controls operations can help facilitate this (American expert 2006).

- In the same vein, well-drawn-out memoranda of understanding (MOUs) between the FIU and reporting entities can enhance the quality of compliance inspections conducted by the FIU. This also increases the likelihood of regulated sectors meeting reporting requirements and reduces the possibility of them engaging in defensive reporting. This addresses some of the major concerns expressed by reporting entities to FIUs.

- Some FIUs address the improvement of operations by hiring advisory consultants (Australian expert 2006). It was suggested that an FIU could go about this by hiring former employees as consultants (American expert 2006).
- An FIU can improve accountability through internal reviews and external evaluations. This will enable it to take corrective action to improve performance. While some FIUs already undergo these evaluations, others would certainly benefit from them.
- Relevant performance metrics suggested by experts include the number of internal and external reviews/evaluations of the FIU, the rate of technological advancement made by the FIU, the number of times the FIU shares information, and the accuracy, timeliness, and relevance of analyses conducted by the FIU.

Customer Satisfaction

- As experts indicated, it is essential for an FIU to forge relationships with its public service counterparts to economize and, at the same time, maximize the scope of efforts to counter financial crime. For example, partnerships with regulatory agencies can help avoid reporting redundancy, that is, reporting to more than one agency.
- Reporting entities expressed a number of concerns in relation to compliance with FIU reporting requirements. Compliance on the part of reporting entities is key to the FIU performing its function; in turn, the FIU must keep in check administrative burdens or costs on reporting entities in order to encourage compliance. The FIU can also improve its relationships with reporting entities by providing clear guidelines or indicators as to what constitutes a suspicious transaction, thereby reducing complexity in the reporting process. FIU training of reporting entities in how to achieve compliance will stem the flow of reported information that is not required from these entities to the FIU.
- A structure and a reliable instrument for feedback from the reporting entity to the FIU and back, and from the FIU to law enforcement and back on case details, can result in more effective communication among financial-crime-fighting partners. This was a point made by a number of experts, especially by those associated with reporting entities, who stated that they do not know whether reported information helps solve cases. Outreach programs, whether on an FIU's physical space or via technology, can also help win the confidence and cooperation of the FIU's customers. An FIU can also create goodwill by including its customers in the decision-making process through their participation in various advisory groups.

- Cooperation extends beyond national borders, and an FIU can help other newly established, less developed FIUs catch up with the most advanced among them by sharing operational and technical know-how. Experts indicated that this is a widely prevalent practice.
- Relevant performance metrics, according to experts, include the degree of compliance against costs imposed by the FIU on reporting entities; the number of support functions provided by the FIU to reporting agencies, partner agencies, and law enforcement; the ratio of resources allocated by the FIU in serving regulated sectors to resources allocated in serving law enforcement; and the FIU's contribution to an investigation, that is, the percentage of information provided by the FIU that is used in investigations.

Human Resources

- The private sector is an important source with respect to the hiring of FIU personnel. Many of the tasks performed by an FIU involve dealings with private sector entities such as banks, casinos, insurance companies, jewelers, etc. It will benefit the FIU to hire those experienced in these businesses. Those with experience in law enforcement and other intelligence agencies are also valuable assets to the agency. Intelligence analysis and technological expertise are also key to the FIU meeting performance targets. On the other hand, an FIU must find ways to attract the best and the brightest and avoid losing personnel to the private sector by offering competitive salaries and benefits that match the private sector. FIU loss of employees to the private sector and the inability of the FIU to complete with higher private sector salaries are some of the problems experienced when it comes to retention of personnel.
- Experts also cautioned against underestimating the importance of workforce planning. Through skills inventory and gap analysis, an FIU can design training programs for its employees. Additionally, the FIU must ensure that personnel are (a) well trained in the technical areas of the business so that they understand trends in money laundering and terrorist financing and the constantly changing money laundering and terrorist financing methods and (b) able to properly analyze information received from reporting entities. Cross-functional training, both through courses and on-the-job orientation, will help achieve this. Part of the training program should also include compliance with the FIU's rulebook on security and privacy.
- Experts indicated that there is a strong sense of awareness of the importance of staff member training, especially due to the highly technical nature of FIU functions. From an organizational

development perspective, attendance of FIU personnel at workshops and conferences related to AML/CTF is integral. Through these and other avenues for interacting with the outside community, like academicians and law enforcement, employees have the opportunity to gain different perspectives on how to counter financial crime and hone a broad set of skills to provide solutions to problems. Because FIU work is computer-intensive in nature, the technical skills of personnel should constantly be upgraded. New FIU employees can certainly benefit from a mentorship program. It is also necessary for FIUs to ensure that their budgets for training keep up with the requirements of the job and are not affected by government cutbacks.

- In the context of performance appraisals, FIU personnel can be made to understand what is expected of them in relation to the priorities of the FIU. They should also be allowed to provide input during the appraisal process in what is known as participatory performance appraisal (Roberts 2003). Employee performance should be linked to the FIU's strategic plan. Regular performance evaluations and appraisals of personnel, at which their strengths and competencies are assessed, help achieve this. A rewards-based system recognizing individual as well as group contributions to the performance of the FIU can sustain motivation and instill a sense of empowerment among personnel. Experts encouraged FIUs to be innovative in this area. In addition, newer methods of performance appraisals should be explored, such as multisource or 360-degree appraisals where performance assessments are obtained from different sources, including the various stakeholders with whom FIU personnel interact (DeNisi and Kluger 2000).
- Experts suggested adopting relevant performance metrics, including the percentage of the FIU's budget allocated for training, the extent of learning-plan development undertaken by the FIU for its personnel, time worked at the job in relation to competencies acquired on the job, and competencies acquired by FIU personnel in relation to the requirements of the job.

Financial Investment
- The FIU must "strive to produce what it must produce in a manner proportionate to the resources devoted to it" (Gottselig and Underwood 2004). A focus on outcomes, in addition to the right amount and areas of investment, will guide it in achieving this. Some experts felt that the current focus on outputs is unproductive. Others were of the opinion that too much is being invested in antiterrorism security measures and not enough in terrorist financing.

- Experts advocated FIU investment in human resources to enhance functions such as compliance inspections of reporting entities, investigations that will end up being more timely and accurate, and analyses that help investigations.
- Additionally, experts were strongly in favor of the need for investment in technology to reinforce and bolster reporting of strategic activity reports (SARs), fulfill regulatory requirements, and track and manage vital information.
- Experts identified the need for internal financial performance metrics, including the ability of the FIU to meet its budget, improved efficiency in proportion to investment, and the amount of investment in human and technological resources in relation to the amount of financial crime deterred. They also suggested external financial performance metrics such as feedback from the FIU's stakeholders to gauge value for investment, the dollar value of dirty money interdicted per employee, and the number of prosecutions and convictions per dollar expenditure.

It should be noted here that FIU performance is dependent on the performance of other entities within the chain of authority as well. So performance metrics would work for the FIU only to the extent its partners in fighting financial crime incorporate them into their functions.

Metrics Used to Track Performance Must Be Definitive

The utility of performance measures by financial intelligence agencies is the core concept of this book. A key ingredient of outcome-driven performance management is the metrics used to measure the impact of governments' efforts in fighting financial crime. Among the key metrics mentioned by the experts interviewed were the number of financial criminals interdicted in proportion to the total number of financial criminals, the amount of dirty money interdicted in proportion to the total amount of dirty money, the number of financial criminals convicted, and the number of repeat offenders. These should be monitored over a period of time, so that FIUs and their financial-crime-fighting partners can make necessary adjustments in planning and implementation. However, this comes with the caveat that the exact amount of dirty money is unknown, leaving the success percentage of the financial-crime-fighting regime a matter of conjecture.

When asked to rate the utility or appropriateness of selected performance measures, survey respondents confirmed expectations that FIU performance in fighting financial crime would be enhanced with a strong emphasis on outcome measures. The following is a list of respondents' ranking order of selected measures from highest to lowest:

1. The value of intelligence that leads to interdiction and prevention of financial crime
2. The accuracy and timeliness of suspicious transaction reports
3. The number of financial criminals convicted
4. The number of support functions provided to reporting agencies, partner agencies, and law enforcement
5. The number of repeat offenders
6. The amount of laundered money interdicted in relation to the estimated total amount of laundered money
7. The number and dollar value of suspicious transactions identified annually
8. The total number of financial criminals interdicted in relation to the estimated number of financial criminals
9. The number of employees that complete training
10. Percentage of payroll devoted to training
11. The dollar value of suspicious transactions identified annually in relation to the total amount of the budget
12. The dollar value of dirty money interdicted per employee

In the private sector, financial performance measures enjoy top billing, but this is just the opposite when it comes to the public sector, as evidenced by experts' low ratings of the suitability of financial measures for FIU adoption. Here, the focus is on cost efficiency rather than cost.

Survey respondents were clearly in favor of FIUs moving beyond widget counting to more useful measures of performance—those that measure results. Of the performance measures suggested by them, there are those that can be broken down further:

- The number of SARs that are actually investigated and prosecuted (successfully or unsuccessfully); total SAR positives in relation to SARs received monthly; the dollar value of dirty money interdicted per state; and SARs classified on the basis of financial sector, geographic zone, kind of economic activity, etc.
- The quality of feedback to financial institutions, the turnaround time of the FIU in responding to private sector entities on their reporting of suspicious cases; circulation of black-listed criminals' names among reporting entities; sharing of information about new crimes with reporting entities
- The number of high-quality cases cleared; the number of interdictions that identify and negatively impact major financial crime organizations
- Measured objectives relating to the number of arrests made from information provided by the FIU to the appropriate enforcement

agency; convictions/prosecutions per currency unit expenditure as a result of FIU data or analysis
- Peer-to-peer comparisons among reporting entities within an industry about suspicious activity reporting; level of coordination between law enforcement and regulators; level of communication between reporting entities and regulators about expectations/concerns/trends
- Measured objectives relating to budgeted training costs; number of training programs provided and number of employees trained annually
- The share of criminal proceeds that the police are allowed to keep (gain sharing)

There are those who call for a tighter focus in the measurement of success in apprehending financial criminals. This includes moving beyond using the dollar amount of a seizure as an indicator of performance to more concrete measures such as the seniority of the interdicted person or persons within the terrorist organization. Those caught are generally lower down in the chain of command of the terrorist group and have limited contribution in masterminding terrorist attacks (Donohue 2008, 405). To elaborate further, "The Achilles heel of terrorism financiers is not at the fundraising end, but at those key chokepoints critical to laundering and transferring funds." It is impossible to "dry the swamp" of funds available for illicit purposes, but by targeting key nodes in the financing network, we can constrict the operating environment to the point that terrorists will not be able to get funds where and when they need them. The number of overall designations (like the Office of Foreign Assets and Control's Specially Designated Nationals List in the United States) is also misleading. It is not uncommon for a potential designation target to remain unnamed due to diplomatic or intelligence issues, policy considerations, or ongoing investigations. What we are left with are trends and anecdotes—most of them classified—that point to success. For example, officials report that, in one case, a terrorist cell abandoned a plot because of a dearth of cash; groups like al-Qaeda and Hamas have also, at times, been pressed for funds" (Levitt 2007).

FIUs are only at the elementary stage when it comes to measuring outcomes. Consider AUSTRAC as an example. The Australian government determines priorities for AUSTRAC and ties these to outputs and outcomes. There is essentially one outcome: to reduce financial crime. AUSTRAC develops a business plan and sets targets to achieve this outcome. One of its targets is to increase the significance of investigations to which it contributes. "AUSTRAC's law enforcement, social justice and revenue partner agencies indicated that AUSTRAC information contributed significantly to 689 investigations conducted during the year (compared to 717 investigations in 2008–09)" (AUSTRAC 2010). The Australian government decides whether to adopt a broader range of outcome measures (Australian expert 2006). In the

United Kingdom, the following is among the performance indicators proposed for adoption by the Financial Services Society (FSA): "To what extent do particular FSA powers and actions have leverage in terms of 'reducing the extent to which it is possible for a business carried on by a regulated person to be used for a purpose connected with financial crime,' from the perspectives of those most intimately involved?" (FSA 2009). Outcome monitoring is more of a way to track the performance of FIUs against a set of benchmarks rather than help get rid of the problem.

Current Challenges Facing FIUs

Overcoming Administrative Impediments

FIUs are at a stage where much progress has been made over the years and with changing times and events. Yet, there is also room for improvement:

- There is a disconnect in the way FIUs operate. The supervision of financial institutions is conducted by supervisors, while the responsibility of enforcement is with the FIU. FIUs could raise their level of success in fighting financial crime by playing a role in supervision (Global financial crime expert3 2008).
- Reporting entities lack the know-how to determine if a transaction is related to financial crime. Therefore, FIUs receive numerous reports due to defensive reporting that result in false positives (i.e., reports of transactions that are not suspicious). This impedes better financial intelligence that could lead to more successful investigations. Most investigations are initiated by law enforcement, and FIUs never disclose if investigations have been initiated by SARs (Global financial crime expert3 2008).
- Lack of resources to perform vital functions such as trend analysis is a common problem among FIUs. Investment in infrastructure is always beneficial, but some FIUs have focused too much on technological resources and not enough on human resources (Global financial crime expert1 2007).
- FIU success is a product of political will. Because FIUs are not typically part of a country's national strategy, they lack the power to make an impact in the fight against financial crime. FIUs play an important role in the fight against financial crime just as much as the FBI and IRS, and one of its vital functions is to share information with them (Global financial crime expert1 2007). Information sharing is impeded due to a lack of political commitment (Global financial crime expert3 2008).

- Problems encountered by FIUs take time to fix and, thus, require a long-term commitment. As is often the case, FIUs are too quick to take credit for success and do not take the time to think through solutions to these problems. In order to solve problems, FIUs must work within the system and within the context of who they are serving, whether it be prosecution, law enforcement, or another entity (Global financial crime expert1 2007).
- High staff member turnover at FIUs due to more attractive salaries in the private sector continues to be a concern, as is the rising average age of FIU staff members. FIUs have relied on outsourcing to get around the problem of losing their institutional memory (Global financial crime expert1 2007).
- FIUs are impeded by the lack of an autonomous budget and constraints on their independence to carry out investigations. In some countries, no action is taken against politicians who could possibly be associated with financial crime (Global financial crime expert2 2008).

Increasing Communication

AML/CTF networks consist of a number of components: financial and other entities that report suspicious transactions; the FIUs that process, analyze, and disseminate this information; intelligence agencies and law enforcement, who charge criminals using information disseminated to them; and prosecutors who attempt to prove charges and convict these criminals. Communication among these entities, in the form of feedback, is an essential element of success in countering financial crime, even when restrictions are imposed on such communication.

In the European Union (EU), FIUs have a defined framework set by a European Council decision that enables them to exchange information among themselves. The problem is in providing smart feedback to reporting entities such as banks, which are required under EU law to file STRs or their equivalent. In that respect, the banking industry often claims that it would be useful for FIUs to improve and refine the reporting system so that they could receive actual feedback on the "leads"/suspicions that they have communicated to the FIUs. However, FIUs are usually prevented in doing so due to confidentiality and security reasons (European Union expert 2009).

A study by the Financial Action Task Force (FATF) concluded that FIU feedback to reporting entities has an impact on its own performance level in identifying and reporting suspicious transactions. It recommended feedback in the form of statistics, current techniques, methods, and trends and that case studies be provided to reporting entities. This could be accomplished in various ways: written feedback, meetings, and video or electronic information

Table 7.1   Netherlands—Best Practice: Automatic Matching of STRs with Police Registers

In the Netherlands, suspiciously reported transactions (unusual transactions) to the FIU are matched automatically every night with the different police databases. These matches take place on the basis of an individual "Name/Code number" under which all suspected criminals are being registered. This database, called VROS-system, consists of three different type of registrations:

1. All criminal intelligence subjects are registered.
2. All persons involved in criminal police investigations are registered.
3. All known offenders are registered.

The Name/Code key is also used in the registration of unusual or suspicious transactions. In case of hits with the police databases, these STRs are automatically sent to the law enforcement agencies (LEAs) in the country. No analysis, screening, or updating takes place. This way, each police organization in the Netherlands (26 in total) has immediate access to the suspicious transactions. The unusual reported transactions are investigated first by the FIU personnel in order to find grounds to disseminate them to the police forces.

Table 7.2   Netherlands—Best Practice: Police Requests for Information

If an LEA wants to receive information from an FIU, there is a specific procedure for this, and in some cases the LEA will have to give some details (feedback) of the investigation for which they need the financial information.

Table 7.3   Netherlands—Best Practice: Priority Systems for Dissemination of Reported Transactions to LEA

The database of the FIU-NL contains some 750,000 reported transactions. Suspicious and unusual transactions are registered in this database. Every night, SQL (structured query language) questions are run over the database to determine the priority of cases to be dealt with. The selection is mainly on text queries but also on currency, country, etc. Every morning a list of high-priority cases is delivered to the FIU investigators.

Best Practices

systems (FATF n.d.). A study was sanctioned by the European Commission to explore best practices in feedback between FIUs and both reporting entities and law enforcement. Tables 7.1–7.11 describe and provide recommendation for these practices in the EU countries covered in this study.

There are a number of organizational management models recommended to enhance coordination in combating financial crime. Some propose the use of network management to coordinate the number of actors involved not only for this, but for other major governmental programs and policy initiatives. Under network management, coordination can be improved and goals met through a sort of regulatory or contractual structure or partnership where goals are listed, each agency's role in achieving them is defined, and requirements for meeting targets are specified (Waugh et al. 2002).

Table 7.4   Netherlands—Best Practice: Financial Weather Reports

Financial "weather reports" are published for law enforcement authorities in the member state. They include analyses of reported transactions for different (police) regions in the Netherlands. The reports try to alert the regional police forces to act upon interesting information for their particular region or specific tasks (e.g., human trafficking).

Table 7.5   United Kingdom—Best Practice: Accessibility of STR Databases

Some 200,000 reports of suspicious activities (SARs) are forwarded to SOCA, the Serious and Organized Crime Agency that incorporates the financial investigation units (FIUs) in the United Kingdom. The SARs are sent directly to law enforcement units by SOCA, selected on Post Office box number. The FIU database is accessible to the approximately 3,500 accredited financial investigators of the local FIUs in the United Kingdom. In addition, the police intelligence officers also have direct access to the reported SARs. This dramatically reduces the time lag for dealing with the SARs and gives great possibilities for feedback between LEAs and FIUs as well as LEAs and reporting entities (REs).

Table 7.6   United Kingdom—Best Practice: Automatic Feedback

The ELMER system (the FIU registration system) generates a so-called feedback form to be filled in by the financial investigators who are investigating the report. This form feeds back information to the FIU on how SARs are being used in police investigations, etc. Statistics can be acquired on the use of SARs and the results of investigations.

Best Practices

Determining Direction for the Future

The SARs regime is a heavy pull on any government's purse strings. In the United States, for example, it is estimated that fighting financial crime accounts for roughly 2 to 3 percent of total regulatory and enforcement expenditures. In the fiscal year 2003, the U.S. government spent what is estimated to be $1.5 billion on its AML regime, which constituted 0.014 percent of nominal GDP for that year. The estimated amount that banks spent on compliance activities in 2003 was also $1.5 billion, while the total spent by the entire private sector was estimated at $3 billion. It is estimated that $1 billion of this cost was transferred to the public. If the ultimate goal of this exercise is the number of convictions and the amount of laundered money interdicted, then the benefits do not seem to justify the costs. "About 2,000 people are convicted of money-laundering offenses (primary or otherwise) each year in the U.S. Only 20 percent of those convicted are reportedly involved with laundering more than $1 million (at the time of being caught)" (Reuter and Truman 2008, 97–102). The results are similar for other countries. In the United Kingdom, for example, only 6 percent of SARs disseminated by the country's FIU produced an outcome (i.e., prosecution, confiscation, cash seizure, etc.) (Reuter and Truman 2008, 97–102). This certainly calls for changes

Table 7.7 United Kingdom—Best Practice: Feedback Every Half Year from LEA to FIU

RESTRICTED WHEN COMPLETE

TWICE YEARLY FEEDBACK QUESTIONNAIRE FOR THE POLICE FORCES OF ENGLAND, WALES AND NORTHERN IRELAND

The questionnaire should be returned by email to:

fiudialogue@soca.x.gsi.gov.uk

If you experience any problems in returning this document or if you have any queries please contact the Dialogue Team on 0207 238 3804 or by email to the above address.

PERIOD TO BE COVERED: ………….. TO …………. (Inclusive)

TO BE RETURNED NO LATER THAN (Insert appropriate dates)

The boxes supplied for further comments can be expanded as required; there is no limit to the amount of text/detail that can be entered.

If a question requires an answer from another department/section within your organization, please ensure that you obtain the answer and include it in the questionnaire that is returned.

Section 1 – Current Activity Statistics

Section 2 – Current Activity

Section 3 – Exploitation of the SARS Regime

Section 4 – General Remarks on the SARs Regime

Here is an opportunity for you to provide a short narrative on your views on the SAR Regime as a whole. This could encompass issues such as how court orders, etc., are dealt with, SAR quality, could improvements be made, etc.

Table 7.8 United Kingdom—Best Practice: The Vetted Group of Compliance Officers

A group of vetted compliance officers is created in order to be able to discuss some of the more confidential AML topics. Meetings take place regularly, and the group is informed about new trends, typologies, and other recent confidential AML information. The group of compliance officers comprises compliance officers from different reporting institutions and is chaired by the FIU. The group of vetted or accredited compliance officers should be able to be compared to the accredited financial investigators and could be given some admittance to the ELMER database in order to improve and adapt their client profiles on the reported transactions.

Table 7.9 United Kingdom—Best Practice: FIU (Financial Intelligence Unit), ARA (Asset Recovery Agency), and SOCA (Serious and Organized Crime Agency) in One Organization

Around April 2008 ARA, the Asset Recovery Agency, will be included in the SOCA organization so that all three major topics involved in combating organized crime are located in one vicinity. Coordination, cooperation, and feedback will be improved.

Best Practices

Table 7.10   United Kingdom—Best Practice: Dialog Team

The Dialogue Team is the outward-facing section of the UKFIU responsible for relationship management with all stakeholders in the UK AML Regime. It has specific responsibility for continued delivery of the recommendations of the Lander Review, and its functions can be considered under the headings of "Research, Analysis, and Development," "Communications," and "Coordination of Delivery."

Research, Analysis, and Development

Twice Yearly Feedback Questionnaire—Every six months a questionnaire is sent to all end users of suspicious activity reports (SARs), asking for statistics and feedback on their use of SARs.

Case Studies—Collation of examples of cases where good use has been made of SARs for development into typologies for feedback to reporters and end users themselves.

Best Practice—Collation of best practice for feedback in order to improve performance. Reports to major financial institutions providing feedback on the SARs they have submitted.

Analysis—of all incoming communication material regarding SARs and tasks identified. Maintaining profiles on regulators and end users of SARs.

Communications

Correspondence—Answering external correspondence, e.g., letters, e-mail, etc.

Press—Providing articles for publication in relevant trade or law enforcement magazines.

SAR Annual Report—Provision of statistics and material for the SAR Annual Report.

Core Messages—Development of key communication messages for delivery by UKFIU.

Internet/Money.web—Provision of communication material for publication on external Web site and Money.web, which is the Web-based portal utilized by end users.

Intranet—Provision of material on internal intranet (n.b., SOCA enforcement and other departments are also end users of SARs).

Communication Material—Leaflets, presentations, podcasts, forums, etc.

Guidance—Provision of guidance material for end users and awareness documentation for the reporting sector.

Coordination of Delivery

Diary of Events—Maintenance of a diary of forthcoming events, e.g., conferences, meetings, etc.

Coordination of Speakers—Provide speakers/representatives for external events, e.g., conferences, law enforcement meetings, etc.

Conferences and Seminars—Arranging sector-specific seminars or larger scale conferences to highlight issues within the UK AML regime.

Meetings—Arrangement of specific meetings between key stakeholders.

One-on-One Visits—Coordination of specific visits to end users, reporters, and regulators. These visits can have a variety of purposes, which may include relationship management, communication, feedback on quality or problem issues, collation of case profiles/best practice, etc.

Regulators Forum—Provide administrative function for quarterly meeting of regulators designed to promote a joined-up approach. This activity is underpinned by joint working agreements.

Table 7.10 United Kingdom—Best Practice: Dialog Team (continued)

Vetted Group—Provide secretariat function for quarterly meeting of reporters. The members of this group are security and vetted and are included in the dissemination of confidential intelligence.

New Business—Negotiating access to SARs by end users underpinned by partnership agreements and information-sharing agreements.

SAR Training—Coordination of training for end users of SARs.

Best Practices

to be made. Responses to the following questions could provide answers for creating and enhancing cost efficiency in tackling financial crime.

Should the Private Sector Play a More Active Role in Fighting Financial Crime?

The private sector is playing a more active role in fighting financial crime, albeit for different reasons than governments. They seek to mitigate reputational risk. A number of financial institutions have set up their own FIUs. They generally have (a) a transactions monitoring unit that goes through new cases, analyzes transactions manually in looking for alerts (transactions that cross thresholds set by the financial institution), and decides whether to file a SAR, (b) an investigations unit that works with the institution's money laundering reporting officers or law enforcement to get to the bottom of a case, and (c) a risk services unit that is responsible for quality control. Surveillance involves a periodic trend analysis of transactions initiated by suspect clients. Open-source research is conducted to establish a profile for these clients, and the validity of their transactions is checked against their respective profiles.

Like government FIUs, private sector FIUs hire those from a mix of backgrounds such as law enforcement, fraud prevention, and bank operations (Private sector FIU expert1). They also hire forensic accounting experts, data miners and analysts, and those with business and legal backgrounds (Private sector FIU expert3). They establish career paths for personnel and encourage professional development by financing their enrollment in AML certification courses; inviting guest speakers; providing them with updates on legal issues, new products, and new spins on old methodologies; and encouraging them to attend seminars and conferences. In some cases, personnel are required to attend a minimum number of in-house training sessions, while managers must attend an out-of-state conference (Private sector FIU expert1).

Similar to government FIUs, private sector FIUs have a set of measures that help them fulfill their obligations to regulators, the organization, the shareholders, and customers. These measures are run through a scorecard and address the health of the institution, its business value, and its ability to mitigate risk and identify high-risk customers. To improve the possibility of success in countering

Table 7.11   Spain—Best Practice: Feedback on Quality of STRs

In Spain, the FIU started to provide general feedback on the quality of the reports received in 2002. The FIU staff annually evaluates the quality of STRs by giving some points for each of the six main fields of information to be provided:

1. Identification
2. Knowledge of the customer
3. Operations
4. Signs, indications
5. Management
6. Documents

Internally, the Spanish FIU assigns individual scores to each report and then calculates an overall score for each of the reporting entities (REs), defined as the average of all the scores given to each STR for that specific RE. No more than this overall score is sent to each individual RE. No individual general feedback on quality is sent to all REs, as the quality of major banks cannot be compared with small ones, and the overall scores have to remain confidential to avoid discouraging or offending an RE. The overall score is classified into several categories: very good, good, regular, not good.

We believe it is essential to provide minimum feedback on the quality of the STRs to help REs to improve their methods for fighting against AML and to know much better whether the assumptions considered are in line with the expectations from the FIU. We understand that the FIU cannot provide an individual report feedback related to the quality of each STR submitted, as this would require substantial input and resources from the FIU.

However, feedback on quality should be provided for each STR submitted by the RE based on an overall score taking into account the previously mentioned criteria. This quality assessment scores could be submitted at least every six months or, at a minimum, once a year. The following quality assessment could be provided:

Entity: _____

Evaluation period: _____

Average quality: _____

STR Number	STR Name	Date	Quality Assessment Identification	Knowledge	Operations	Indicative Signs	Management	Documents	Quality Score

Average Score

Source: Study on "Best practices in vertical relations between the Financial Intelligence Unit and (1) law enforcement services; and (2) Money Laundering and Terrorist Financing Reporting entities with a view to indicating effective models for feedback on follow-up to and effectiveness of suspicious transaction reports." A study commissioned by the European Commission (http://ec.europa.eu/home-affairs/doc_centre/crime/docs/study_fiu_and_terrorism_financing_en.pdf).

financial crime, private sector FIUs conduct risk assessments including residual and product-risk assessments. In most cases, plans are implemented through a project-management framework and through formal execution plans. Part of the planning process is to account for emerging trends in financial crime such as human trafficking. Accountability is established through one-on-one meetings with money laundering reporting officers and an annual update to the board of directors (Private sector FIU expert3). In certain cases, management reviews a daily productivity report. Subpoenas received from law enforcement are given priority (Private sector FIU expert1), and high-risk cases are forwarded directly to law enforcement and not through the government FIU (Private sector FIU expert3). Private sector reporting entities look to periodically upgrade their technological and analytical capacity to enhance their performance. Personnel are also expected to abide by strict performance guidelines: They are required to process cases in a timely manner and maintain a certain level of accuracy according to established standards. Timeliness is important because the government FIU sets a certain number of days by which private sector organizations have to file SARs. Accuracy is important because any error on the SAR form could mislead law enforcement. Hence, quality control performance metrics are vital (Private sector FIU expert1).

By establishing their own FIUs, the private sector could certainly limit the number and quality of SARs flowing to the government FIU. Moreover, they could quite possibly track financial criminals before the government FIU alerts law enforcement and other intelligence agencies to take action. Timing plays a crucial role in criminal investigations.

Why Not Mandate All Private Sector Reporting Entities to Create Their Own FIUs?

It might not be feasible for all private sector reporting entities to have their own FIUs, and it would be irrational to make them all do so.

Whether private sector reporting entities should form their own FIUs should depend on volume of activity, geographical reach, organizational structure, class of trade, etc. I do not think you should enforce by law the creation of an FIU. Reporting entities are required to have a risk-based compliance program to do a number of things. One of these is to identify and report suspicious activity. However, I would avoid a reporting entity having multiple FIUs. The key to an FIU is centralizing the risk in one place so you see everything. The laws are generally written to require a reporting entity to produce whatever the country wants them to produce—in this case SARs. Generally, they do not write regulations telling us how to do things—just the output they want. Another body [the government FIU] would be looking at things more holistically and hopefully find stuff that their [private sector reporting entities] surveillance missed (Private sector FIU expert2).

If Private Sector Reporting Entities Form Their FIUs, Is There a Need for Government FIUs?

Although private sector entities might have their own FIUs, these cannot replace government FIUs. Financial criminals use multiple methods and institutions to raise and transfer funds. The government FIU acts as a coordinator and a point of reference for cases that "cross boundaries." Therefore, FIUs should exist irrespective of the number of cases that end up being prosecuted. The role of government FIUs is crucial in preventing economies from collapsing as a result of financial crime (Private sector FIU expert3).

If Private Sector Reporting Entities in Developed Countries Form FIUs, Can Those in Developing Countries Follow Suit?

Because the establishment of FIUs within private sector reporting entities in developed economies is gathering momentum, those in less developed economies might follow suit. "Most developing countries do not have as sophisticated an AML regime as developed countries. The first step would be to get the reporting entities in underdeveloped areas to rise to the level of sophistication with their program so they could support an FIU process" (Private sector FIU expert2). It is difficult to generalize, and this notion cannot be applied to all FIUs in developing countries, as some are more advanced than others.

How Can Governments Improve the Quality of SARs Flowing to FIUs so That the Process Is More Effective?

SARs were thought to serve a useful purpose because stopping financial crime through regulation or freezing assets obstructs the main purpose of AML/CTF, which is to "trace the funds to interrupt an operation or to find people linked to terrorist networks" (Donohue 2008, 346). This unfortunately has not happened. "SARs did not, nor should they have, nor would they now, discover any of the financial activity in which the September 11 hijackers engaged" (Donohue 2008, 349). The FATF's original scope of responsibility included money laundering until the attacks of September 11, when its responsibility was expanded to include terrorist financing. There is a general sense of disagreement with this. "The inclusion of terrorist funding in the AML regime is far from gathering consensus, even among FATF experts who, even before 9/11, expressed disagreement on this linkage" (Scherrer 2006). Unfortunately, there are very few alternatives to the SARs regime: "A better system of incentives to reduce false positives while not increasing false negatives should be devised" (Gordon 2008). A possible alternative is to get rid of SARs (or STRs) completely. The private sector would play only a limited role by forwarding all client profiling data and financial transactions to the FIU. FIUs could use general criteria in deciding whether to investigate a transaction such as the relative level of suspicion of the transaction. The

FIU could also use statistical methods such as regression analysis in deciding which transactions to investigate. These methods are used by tax administration officials to determine the probability of tax evasion in deciding who to audit. (Global financial crime expert3 2008).

A Final Word

Solutions to enhance performance in combating financial crime can certainly be achieved through better coordination and collaboration on measuring performance based on outcomes. Under the current system, there is miscommunication between the private sector, law enforcement, and government. Private sector organizations see industry regulators as the problem. There is a strong perception that a vast amount is spent on KYC (know your client), risk assessment, and the compliance regime that does not produce results. There is way too much emphasis on crossing the t's and dotting the i's. There is too much focus on compliance for the sake of compliance without much thought of the ultimate goal. Regulators always play by the rule book, but financial criminals don't have rule books. Regulators are also criticized for not being able to understand the environment that is conducive to running investigations. For example, banks are reprimanded for not monitoring intrabank transfers. These transactions are numerous and clog the SAR system, that is, they create chatter. The regulators, who insist that SARs on these transfers must be filed, seem to want more SARs. The question is, "Are these good SARs?" This should be established by the government FIU and not the government regulator. Banks are more concerned with low-incidence, high-risk transactions (Private sector FIU expert1).

Besides problems with FIUs, regulators also do not seem to communicate with law enforcement. To address these issues, a dialogue should be initiated between regulators, law enforcement, and the private sector. This could be done by forming fusion centers, which have been created in the United States and the United Kingdom (Joint Terrorism Analysis Centre) to counter terrorism (see Chapter 1). Here, those fighting financial crime should be given a clear purpose and incentives such as splitting up proceeds of the outcomes they produce. These fusion centers should be divided regionally, as different methods of financial crime are specific to particular regions of a country. For example, in California, which has a large migrant population, the use of cash is more prevalent than the use of financial institutions, and therefore the risk of cash-based financial crime is higher (Private sector FIU expert1).

The scene from the television series *24*, scripted at the beginning of Chapter 1, takes a twist. Faroush becomes vigilant when he realizes that the authorities are on to him. He moves out of his hotel room in an attempt to escape. Sergeant Amis of NYPD informs CTU that he is moving in on Faroush, ignoring the pleas of CTU to hold off until its personnel arrive at the scene. With the help of an accomplice, Faroush escapes by outwitting NYPD, who are not as well prepared to handle the situation as CTU. Lack of cooperation and definition of roles in such a scenario led to a highly volatile criminal slipping from the gasp of authorities. In reality, we see this happening all too often—even when it comes to countering terrorist financing. A terrorist financer that evades authorities might end up being responsible for the destruction of life and property on a large scale all over the world. Expert opinion, in this regard, is quite clear: It is easy to measure what is convenient, but it is not easy to measure that which leads to success. Within this realm, financial intelligence agencies must adhere to the three tenets of success discussed at the end of Chapter 1: balancing action with civil liberties, cross-training personnel to enhance coordination, and providing incentives for cooperation and disincentives for failure. Without monitoring and measuring progress against those outcomes that count, the fight against financial crime will produce only marginal results, as presently is the case.

References

AUSTRAC. 2010. "Annual Report 2010."

CIA. 2007. "Transcript of General Hayden's interview with WTOP." Press release, June 1. https://www.cia.gov/news-information/press-releases-statements/press-release-archive-2007/transcript-of-general-haydens-interview-with-wtop.html/.

Collacott, Martin. 2006. "Canada's inadequate response to terrorism: The need for policy reform," The Fraser Institute (February).

DeNisi, Angelo, and Avaraham N. Kluger. 2000. "Feedback effectiveness: Can 360-degree appraisals be improved?" *Academy of Management Executive* 14, 1: 135.

Donohue, Laura K. 2008. *The cost of counter-terrorism: Power, politics and liberty.* Cambridge University Press.

Eland, Ivan. 1998. "The U.S. government is endangering," Cato Institute, September 25.

European Commission. 2008. "Best practices in vertical relations between the Financial Intelligence Unit and (1) law enforcement services and (2) Money Laundering and Terrorist Financing Reporting entities with a view to indicating effective models for feedback on follow-up to and effectiveness of suspicious transaction reports." http://ec.europa.eu/home-affairs/doc_centre/crime/docs/study_fiu_and_terrorism_financing_en.pdf

FATF. n.d. "Providing feedback to reporting financial institutions and other persons: Best practice guidelines." http://www.fatf-gafi.org/dataoecd/32/46/34046950.pdf.

Financial Services Authority. 2009. "FSA scale and impact of financial crime project," August.

Gordon, Richard. 2008. "Trysts or terrorists: Financial institutions and the search for bad guys," *Wake Forest Law Review.*

Gottselig, Glenn, and Sarah Underwood. 2004. *Financial Intelligence Units: An overview*. Washington, DC: International Monetary Fund, World Bank Group, 87.

Greenberg, Maurice. 2002. "Terrorist financing," Council on Non-U.S. Relations, October.

Interview with American expert, August 22, 2006.

Interview with Australian expert, May 15, 17, 2006.

Interview with European Union expert, January 7, 2009.

Interview with global financial crime expert1, March 17, 2007.

Interview with global financial crime expert2, August 1, 2008.

Interview with global financial crime expert3, September 18, 2008.

Interview with private sector financial crime expert1, July 19, 2010.

Interview with private sector financial crime expert2, July 30, 2010.

Interview with private sector financial crime expert3, October 18, 2010.

Levitt, Matthew. 2007. "Follow the money: Challenges and opportunities in the campaign to combat terrorism financing," The Washington Institute, *PolicyWatch* 1207, March 6.

Reuter, P., and Edwin M. Truman. 2008. *Chasing dirty money*. Institute for International Economics.

Roberts, Gary E. 2003. "Employee performance appraisal system participation: A technique that works." *Public Personnel Management* 32, 1: 89.

Scherrer, A. 2006. www.g7.utoronto.ca/scholar/scherrer.pdf

Schott, Paul Allan. 2002. "Reference guide to anti-money laundering and combating the financing of terrorism: A manual for countries to establish and improve their institutional framework," The World Bank: VII-9.

U.S. Department of State. 2001. "Patterns of Global Terrorism." http://www.state.gov/s/ct/rls/pgtrpt/.

Waugh, William Lee, et al., 2002. "Organizing the war on terrorism," *Public Administration Review* Special Issue (September): 145–153.

Index